JOHN GIBSON LOCKHART

JOHN GIBSON LOCKHART
From a portrait by H. W. Pickersgill, R.A., 1830

John Gibson Lockhart

BY
MARION LOCHHEAD

*

JOHN MURRAY
50 ALBEMARLE STREET, LONDON

DEDICATED TO
THE GOOD MEMORY OF
SIR WALTER MAXWELL SCOTT
OF ABBOTSFORD
AND TO HIS DAUGHTERS
PATRICIA AND JEAN

FIRST EDITION . . . 1954

Made and Printed in Great Britain by Butler & Tanner Ltd., Frome and London
and Published by John Murray (Publishers) Ltd.

CONTENTS

CONTENTS

ILLUSTRATIONS

PREFACE
DISCOVERING J. G. L.

JOHN GIBSON LOCKHART has, for long, been known chiefly
if not entirely as " Scott's Lockhart ", with an occasional
turn of the phrase to " Lockhart's Scott ", having the
great biography in mind. The two names are as closely
intertwined as Johnson's and Boswell's. Both Johnson and
Scott, great in their own genius and personality, living in
their work and in other men's memories, have been invested,
by the genius of their biographers, with a secondary, re-
created life like that of two immortals in fiction or drama.
They belong, respectively, to Boswell and to Lockhart.

Lockhart is Scott's Lockhart because his greatest book is
about Scott, and this has so overshadowed all his other work
that for many people he seems not to exist apart from his
hero. He appears almost like the bird in the parable,
quoted by the Venerable Bede, of the life of man : the bird
that flits across a lighted hall, flying in from the darkness
outside, disappearing again into that darkness. But could
Lockhart have lived only in that flight of genius across
the bright room of Scott's life ? A major work of literature, especially in a form demanding so much discipline,
selection, re-creation as biography, cannot come suddenly
into being.

Lockhart must have lived in his own right, achieved
more than this, his undoubted masterpiece ; lived intellectually and emotionally. He must be a person. Could
he be a personality ? The fact that his personality is, in
the *Life*, unobtrusive, is a proof of his artistry, not of his
nullity. He survived Scott by twenty-two years, in which
he did not vanish from social or literary life. The discovery
of Lockhart himself has the lure of detection ; and there
have been many documents in the case, clues to follow,
gossip to overhear. In himself Lockhart appeared enigmatic, and therefore all the more attractive.

There was no vagueness about his background or circumstances. He was of known parentage and birthplace, the

latter being no more than three miles from the present writer's former home. He was born in the manse (or parsonage) of Cambusnethan, in the valley of Clyde in Lanarkshire, a member of one of the oldest families in the county, and besides his descendants at Abbotsford, he had collaterals at Milton Lockhart, a mile or two along Clydeside. He was one of Lanarkshire's greatest sons ; he was real, he was himself, with his own background and place in the world. But for a while nothing more about him was discovered.

The discovery of the real Lockhart probably began, though at first it was only the glimmer of a glimpse, through friendship with that fine and kindly scholar, the late Dr. Alexander Mitchell, who spoke of his intention of writing a *Life* of Lockhart. Dr. Mitchell was at home in the period, and he had been captivated by the strange personality. He visited Milton Lockhart and found stimulus there. He had, in the National Library of Scotland, three sources of knowledge about his hero : the Abbotsford Letters, those of Scott, of Lockhart himself, of his wife Sophia and her sister Anne Scott, her brothers Walter and Charles, and friends of the family ; the Blackwood Letters relating to the early years of *Blackwood's Magazine* and Lockhart's dealings with the first William Blackwood ; and, in photostat, the huge collection of Lockhart's letters to John Wilson Croker, his chief contributor to *The Quarterly Review*, to whom he wrote more fully, frequently and confidentially than to any other friend.

For the last days of his life Dr. Mitchell stood upon a peak in Darien. That was in the dark days of the war ; and he was still paying, in bodily weakness, for his own valiant service in the war of 1914–18. His payment was exacted in full, when he fell suddenly dead, one day, in Edinburgh. Much learning died with him ; much kindness and courtesy have lived in the memory of his friends.

The interest quickened in one mind sank under the pressure of other work. Lockhart and his period were not immediately alluring. But the other work, a study of social history, formed the habit of research ; its enclosed sketches of personalities suggested the fascination of a full-length

Life. Lockhart came out of the shadows, presenting himself as a possible, an attractive, an irresistible sitter.

The sources were abundant. Besides those in manuscript there was Andrew Lang's *Life of Lockhart* : long, voluble, with some brilliant passages ; essential to any study of the subject, but somewhat difficult reading—it is like rambling talk from which the listener tries to disentangle the relevant facts in sequence. There were contemporary or near-contemporary references to be gathered from the Lives of Lockhart's friends and colleagues : John Wilson (" Christopher North "), James Hogg (The Ettrick Shepherd), Croker ; from the chronicles of the two distinguished publishing houses with which he was associated, Blackwood's and John Murray's ; from the Letters and Journal of Sir Walter Scott. There were his own works, not only the *Life of Scott* but the little-known essays, novels, poems. For sign-posts at the beginning of this road of discovery there were the note-books of Dr. Mitchell which had been acquired by the National Library.

For further help on the way there was the kindness of Lockhart's kin. His great-grandson, Sir Walter Maxwell Scott, offered, for copying, those letters still treasured at Abbotsford, including the few exchanged between Lockhart and Sophia during their engagement. Among these papers was found a written list of " Mr. Lockhart's " contributions to *The Quarterly Review* which was of great help in studying his professional work. Part of this *Life* was prepared at Abbotsford itself, in the study next to the chapel, added to the house by Lockhart's son-in-law, in an atmosphere alive with memories that were as vivid, almost, as personal encounters.

The warm interest and encouragement of Sir Walter and his daughters has been of incalculable stimulus, and has been matched by that of Lockhart's namesakes and grand-nephews, grandsons of his brother Laurence : Stephen Lockhart, Esq., the head of the family, Major J. G. Lockhart, himself a distinguished biographer, Dr. Laurence Lockhart who lent the manuscript Family History, and the Rev. D. D. A. Lockhart who kindly and patiently read bundles of untidy typescript, and offered that rare thing—

constructive criticism. A fellow-admirer of J. G. L., a scholar most learned in his period, Mr. W. M. Parker provided many valuable suggestions with the encouragement of frequent discussion.

For Lockhart's strictly professional life there were the Murray Letters at 50 Albemarle Street ; read and copied in the rooms that so often held his presence, that saw Scott and Byron meet, and many a good symposium of Georgian wit ; where John Murray the Fourth, grandson of Lockhart's first " chief ", was christened. To Sir John Murray, K.C.V.O.—John the Fifth—Lockhart's present biographer is indebted for a hospitality that has helped to break down the barriers of time.

The Lockhart motto : *Heart in Fetterlock*, gave its own stimulus ; a hint of the complexity of Lockhart's personality.

The author is much indebted to Miss Adeline Hamilton for her expert typing and proof-reading ; to the staff of the National Library of Scotland for unfailing help ; and to those editors who published articles on Lockhart in *The Quarterly Review* ; *The Scotsman* ; *The Edinburgh Evening News* ; *The Dispatch* ; *The Bulletin*.

PART 1

THE YEARS OF PRIDE

Chapter 1

LOCKHART AND THE WORLD HE ENTERED

THERE is, by way of complication—and also of stimulus to the discovery of Lockhart, the still persistent tradition that he was detestable—" the floating dislike " that Saintsbury noted (and did not share) ; a dislike so profound that Stevenson, born four years before Lockhart's death, could write to Saintsbury that Lockhart was a cad : write in a tone of personal anger as one suffering under direct insult or grievance.

He is still remembered, even by those who have read nothing of his critical work, as the author of that savage review of Keats in *Blackwood's*. In his life there is no youthful dissipation to conceal, condone or expose according to the fancy of the biographer. One reason why he has never caught the half-shocked imagination of later generations, as Boswell has, is that he lacks the appeal of bawdry. The sins of his early years are those of pride, which are, to the average man, less exciting than the sins of the flesh. Lockhart lived cleanly. He was of a most constant loyalty ; he had integrity. These virtues were in him as a young man as well as in his waning years. But he was, in those first, flashing years of his literary career, reckless in his use of his talents ; his pen wounded. One has to accept, and not try to condone his faults : the attack on Keats (it may not have been entirely his ; Wilson may have added to it, for it is difficult, almost impossible, to say exactly how much each separately of the *Blackwood* cronies contributed to the reviews and articles ; but to assume the worst, let it be wholly Lockhart's) ; the vituperation against Leigh Hunt ; the insolence of the letter to Dr. Playfair. These left a

I

stain. And Scott, wise and charitable, loving Lockhart for the true and good man he was at heart, knew it and deplored it and used all his influence to draw him aside from that path of pride.

But even at that time the loving and lovable Lockhart existed. He was, from childhood, intensely affectionate. His grief for the death of a younger brother and sister was so intense as to bring upon him a serious illness. He was all his life a devoted son and brother, a good friend. Then the lover in him came to full, undying life when he met Scott and Scott's daughter, Sophia. The depths of tenderness in him were touched. Lockhart in a marriage like Byron's, or even in a *mariage de convenance*, would have been marred and embittered. Sophia's gentleness, the feminine counterpart of her father's magnanimity, and that father's great warmth of faith and charity made, if not a new man of Lockhart (for he would never have lacked nobility) certainly the man he was meant to be.

His oldest friend, Jonathan Christie, who might have found cause in the tragedy of the duel (told hereafter) to break the friendship, remained devoted to him ; and after his death was to write : " The love of children was stronger in Lockhart than I have ever known it in any other man—it was womanly love. It was an early characteristic of his and he never lost it. . . . I never saw so happy a father as he was, while dancing his first-born child in his arms."

To be born towards the end of a golden age is to come into a goodly heritage. John Gibson Lockhart can hardly be placed among the Scots of the eighteenth century ; for he was born only six years before that century's end : on the 14th [1] of June, 1794, in the Manse of Cambusnethan. But his father's generation belonged to that golden age, as did the middle-aged and elderly men whom he met in his youth ; and his own judgements and standards were influenced by theirs.

His young manhood belongs to the Regency ; his maturity to the age of elegance that lies between the Napoleonic wars and the Victorian era ; and he saw seventeen years of

[1] 14th June according to the entry in the Presbytery's Record of Births : 12th June by the Parish Register.

2

Victoria's reign. His life spanned the change from the old world to the new ; the former, though shaken at Culloden, endured for more than half a century afterwards in Scotland, because of the racial sense of tradition, the individuality of the Scot, the vitality of memory, the conservative force of rural life. This conservatism was fostered by the wars, when peril bred insularity. But with the industrial revolution and the political reforms of the 1830's, and the rise (from both these events) of the middle classes, especially in the towns, the world changed in this island. The little cities, the country towns and the villages dwindled ; large cities like London and Glasgow grew to monstrosity ; new towns arose and developed enormously, filled with mills and factories. Mining villages swarmed over southern Scotland and northern England and there were soon large tracts of " black country ". The aristocratic eighteenth century yielded to the bourgeois nineteenth, the country and the county gradually gave place to the town.

In his lifetime his own country changed ; Scotland of the poets and ballad-singers, of the lost cause of the Stuarts and heroic loyalty, Scotland of the gentry and the peasants was nearly lost in the Scotland of the industrialists and manufacturers, the engineers and inventors, tradesmen and merchants.

In literature there was a peaceful revolution (or sometimes not so peaceful, sometimes acrimonious) as the formal elegance of the Augustans was disturbed by the Romantics ; Pope was deposed, Keats and Shelley were—first scorned and denounced, then honoured. The novel as a form was developed beyond all expectations ; in two main lines, however, both begun at the turn of the century : the romantic, historical saga of action superbly achieved by Scott, and the domestic comedy that was Jane Austen's masterpiece. Fielding's epic activity, Richardson's sensibility and observation influenced different types of novel— however far short the result might fall of the prototypes and examples.

For Lockhart himself, the great classics of the eighteenth century made the background and source of culture in his boyhood and youth ; they formed his standards. As reader and critic he considered, in the second half of his life, many of the Victorian masterpieces.

It is difficult to place him mentally and spiritually in a period. He is not of the eighteenth century, and he is assuredly not a typical Victorian. Perhaps part of his fascination lies in his belonging to the intermediate period. He never lost the distinction given by the golden age. Even his fault of pride in youth, that was modified and mellowed, but never quite destroyed by later wisdom and suffering, had the splendour of the aristocratic age about it.

His immediate geographical or regional world, that of his birth and boyhood, was like the wider background one of change and contrasts. Lanarkshire is one of the divided counties of Scotland. Within its compass lie two contrasting regions : that of the pastoral valley and uplands, the orchard country of the same freshness and charm to-day as invested them in Lockhart's boyhood ; and the black country of mining villages and industrial towns, that has developed in the past century and a half. The estate which his elder brother William bought, which Scott visited and which was a second home for Lockhart and his children, lies on the border between the two regions. Milton Lockhart stands on the Clyde and looks towards Lanarkshire's hill, Tinto ; it is neighboured by villages of comely names : Dalserf, Rosebank, Crossford ; and by the orchard-country that in May is a delicate glory of blossom, or " flourish " to use the pretty Scots word. From Garrion Bridge—where the coach used to stop for visitors to Milton Lockhart— one may go either towards the country and river-side, or towards the grim towns. Clyde runs clear and there is trout-fishing. Lockhart wrote, in middle life, to Wilson, with a nostalgic memory of those early scenes :

" I used to have a real friendship for the water of Clyde and some half-dozen of its tributary Calders and Nethans, familiar from infancy, and most of all for certain burns with deep, rocky beds, and cold, invisible cascades."

Lockhart's father, the Rev. Dr. John Lockhart, a cadet of the ancient family of Birkhill and Wicketshaw, held the family living of Cambusnethan. Until the second half of the nineteenth century, the Established Presbyterian Church

4

of Scotland continued, like the Church of England, the system of patronage ; and the patron-laird of Cambusnethan was a kinsman : Lockhart of Castlehill.

Dr. Lockhart contributed, like other parish ministers, an account of the place to the first *Statistical Account of Scotland :* " The haughs on the Clyde are extensive and beautiful. A considerable part of them forms a lawn in front of the mansion-house of Cambusnethan, the other part is regularly enclosed and well cultivated. On the bank which rises over the haugh ground there are extensive orchards, behind these coppice-woods or regular plantations afford a complete shelter from the east winds."

There was other treasure in the earth. " There is abundance of excellent coal, capable of being wrought with great ease." It was sold at 1s. 6d. for 8 cwt. " The colliers have, in general, half the coal put out as wages. Many of the colliers employed here took themselves to their disagreeable labour at an advanced period of life, and they abundantly compensate for their want of regular training by their sobriety and diligence."

In 1791 the population was 1,684 ; the great majority of these—1,070 by Dr. Lockhart's reckoning—belonged to the Established Church ; the remaining 614 to one of the Presbyterian sects that had broken away from the parent stock. " The value of the living, exclusive of manse and glebe, amounts to nearly £130 sterling "—which in 1791 was a very tolerable stipend.

Dr. Lockhart thought well of his parishioners—morally and intellectually : " The inhabitants of this parish have given a good specimen of their character and taste in the institution of two libraries, supported by annual subscription, and containing a judicious selection of books, entertaining, historical, moral and religious." It is a nice set of distinctions.

Dr. Lockhart was presented in 1796 to the College Kirk of Blackfriars in Glasgow ; so that young John's first experience of rural Lanarkshire was brief and his boyhood was spent in that small but rapidly growing and flourishing city. He was a delicate child and for some time after an illness was tutored at home by his father, who must in the years to come have taken to himself no small or unmerited credit for the foundations thus laid.

Andrew Lang describes Dr. Lockhart as a strict and narrow cleric of the old school, and quotes Lockhart's comment to Sophia, that if her father were the greater poet his was the greater proser. He may have been heavy in pulpit discourse, but congregations in those days were much-enduring, in fact they liked to endure long harangues, and would have thought poorly of a minister who gave them a mere half-hour of exposition. He must, however, have had an instinct for narrative and human drama. It was he who told his son the true story that was made the theme of *Adam Blair* ; and his description of his parish in *The Statistical Account* is sufficiently lucid and succinct to be read with interest. Lockhart was the most filial of sons ; he might beg Sophia in one letter not to tell the Doctor of his having spent Sunday in a manner not likely to be approved (in amusing theatrical company) but his letters, his memories of childhood indirectly expressed in his novel *Reginald Dalton*, all his references to his father show a true affection. This is reflected in his description of Reginald's quiet but happy boyhood.

Reginald was with his father " almost all the hours of the day, either as pupil or as plaything. . . . The solitary man neither had, nor wished to have any better companion than his only child. His intellect stooped, but it was not ashamed—perhaps it was scarcely conscious—of stooping ; when they read together, for the first time, *Robinson Crusoe*, *The Seven Wise Masters*, *The Pilgrim's Progress* or any such manual, the delighted interest the father took in every incident, was such that the boy scarcely suspected him of having previously perused the book any more than himself."

Mutatis mutandis, this may be a fairly accurate picture of one period of Lockhart's childhood. (He was not motherless like Reginald, nor was he an only child—far from it ; he was embedded in a large family of brothers, of whom he was second ; and had one sister, Violet, to whom he was devoted.) There is much about the Lockhart home life to remind us of Jane Austen's youth, and of the setting of

6

some of her novels : she would have appreciated the strong bond of family affection in this Scots manse.

The foundation, lasting and solid, of the boy's studies and his reading and all the rich culture he was to acquire, was that of Latin and Greek. Dr. Lockhart was a sound scholar, and taught his son well. His love of books may be reflected in Reginald's father :

" His father's library was well selected, and contained not only an excellent collection of theology and classics, but a considerable store of the best French and English authors."

The Church of Scotland bred scholarly clergy. There had been throughout the previous century two main types : one the narrow and fanatic zealot, though this class tended more and more towards dissent ; the other the urbane, learned, sometimes worldly divines like " Jupiter " Carlyle, Principal Robertson and the delightful Dr. Somerville of Jedburgh. In the nineteenth century there was a tendency towards a middle path, and there were many parish ministers who were neither zealots nor over-worldly : men of breeding and education, devoted to their duties, earnest and sincere ; very sure of themselves and their authority and of the dignity of their Church ; but not without tolerance. Secular learning was valued. Dr. Lockhart, from what we know of him, would seem to have been of this type.

In circumstances, he was prosperous. His first wife brought with her an estate and mansion outside Glasgow, Germiston. The family lived there part of their time. It would seem that the household was comfortable and that Mrs. Lockhart and her daughter had time for visits and for pastimes not possible in a poor and busy manse. Dr. Lockhart was, as Mrs. Oliphant says, a " squarson ". The type was to be found in the Church of Scotland, at that period, as well as the Church of England, though the Scots squarson was probably less addicted to field sports than his neighbour.

Dr. Lockhart was twice married. By his first wife, Elizabeth Dinwiddie of Germiston he had one son, William. By his second—another Elizabeth—he was, as the schoolboy said of Bach, " a numerous parent ". The second Mrs.

Lockhart was the daughter of the Rev. John Gibson, minister of St. Cuthbert's, Edinburgh, and from him, in the old Scots fashion, of giving the second son in the family the name of his maternal grandfather, our John Gibson Lockhart was named. Through his mother, Mrs. Lockhart was descended from the Erskines of Cardross and from the Pringles of Torwoodlie, that ancient Border house, that was to be neighboured by Scott at Abbotsford, and also from a certain godly Covenanter, Mr. James Nimmo, whose *Narrative* makes curious reading. Whether Lockhart valued this particular strain in his blood is a matter for considerable doubt. But he could boast of a long pedigree on both sides of his parentage : the Lockharts were deeply rooted in the soil of Lanarkshire ; as old and gentle (in the old Scots sense of that term) as the lordly Douglases and Hamiltons. They were linked by marriage with the equally ancient families of Inglis and of Somerville ; while on the other side, Erskine and Pringle brought no less honourable connections. Lockhart was gently born and bred, and he knew it ; he was proud of it in his innermost mind as he was proud of his intellect and scholarship. Time and sorrow and salutary harshness of life mellowed what might have been a deadly sin in him. But he could not lose pride in his heritage of race and descent ; and few Scots can find such pride unforgivable.

Chapter 2

LOCKHART'S YOUTH :
GLASGOW AND OXFORD

GLASGOW UNIVERSITY stood, in Lockhart's day, in the place where it had been built, after its founding by a Bull of Pope Nicholas in 1451. The High Street was still the heart of the city, with the Cathedral and the College as near neighbours—established both of them to maintain and show forth sound faith and learning : the one expounding Glasgow's motto : " Let Glasgow flourish by the preaching of the Word " ; the other remembering the words of the Incarnate Word : " Via, Veritas, Vita "— The Way, the Truth, and the Life. The College, though its Faculty of Divinity might denounce Catholic theology and teach strict Presbyterian doctrine, was still largely mediaeval in discipline and curriculum : the Master's degree still demanding Humanity (as the Scots still worthily term Latin), Greek, Logic and Metaphysics, Moral Philosophy and Mathematics. Until recently, all lectures had been delivered in Latin. Like a mediaeval University also, it welcomed the poor students : lads from the parish schools came to town with a few books and a few guineas and a poke of meal to see them through the session, as well as the sons of the country gentry, of the professional men and of the well-to-do merchants.

It was common at that time for boys to matriculate at an age when they would now enter a High or Secondary School ; the " bejants " were, most of them, aged from 11 to 14. Lockhart was a very young student, but not abnormally so, when he came up, in 1805, at the age of eleven, put on the scarlet gown, and sat on a bench in the Humanity Class Room. Richardson was Professor ; his colleague of the Greek Chair was Young.

Lockhart was popular with his fellow-students. A " comic " is always appreciated in Scotland, and his wit was apparent even in first youth ; he was, besides, for all

9

his shyness and reserve, an affectionate creature, eager for friendship, ready to give generously in return. He had been well prepared by his father and could, without difficulty, take a leading place in his classes. College life was in no way hard upon him ; yet these Glasgow days appear to have left little impression and warmth of memory, compared with his remembrance of Oxford. This may have been because Oxford was a new and exciting home for him ; a new world, discovered by himself. At Glasgow, he was still living at home, merely attending classes. The very familiarity of the scene destroyed enchantment.

He was, however, happy and successful enough ; he worked and played and made friends ; won prizes, the best being a prize of friendship. One of his contemporaries, Rainy (later Professor), told the story, years afterwards, to G. R. Gleig, who told it again in his brief, admirable biography of Lockhart in *The Quarterly Review*. The prizes in the Junior Latin class were awarded by the vote of the students themselves, who were trusted to assess the achievement of their most brilliant fellows. Lockhart was placed second ; his disappointment at not being ranked first was so obvious, and his popularity so great that his sympathetic class-mates clubbed funds to buy him a special prize-volume which, by an amiable caprice on the part of Fate, happened to be a copy of *The Lay of the Last Minstrel*. Scott, the poet, was in the full flower of his fame then. This was presented publicly to Lockhart, by the Professor, on the last day of the session.

He may not have cherished his memories of Glasgow as he did those of Oxford, but he none the less recalled with gratitude the learning he had won there and the scholars who had taught him. His Glasgow College is best seen through the eyes of his first created character, Dr. Peter Morris, whom he presented to the public in three volumes of Letters : *Peter's Letters*, in 1819. Dr. Morris on his tour of Scotland came to Glasgow, and wrote to a friend of all he saw :

" The University consists, as in Edinburgh, of a single college, but it is a much more venerable and wealthy foundation, and the Professors . . . are lodged, all together, in a very handsome oblong court (like the close of some of our Cathedrals) immediately beside the quadrangles."

Lockhart—through Dr. Morris—described the scene in the Greek class-room and paid tribute to Professor Young —a scholar known far beyond the bounds of Scotland, and a teacher well-loved and remembered : the class was opened with roll-call, read by one of the students, and punctuated by comments and questions from the Professor in " a sharp, cutting voice " and in the Latin tongue : as " *Quid agas tu, in isto angulo pedibus strepitans et garriens ?* "—The Glasgow student's versatility of foot-work is of centuries' fame ! Young's lecture and commentary on the Greek texts inspired the listener with enthusiasm. " He is, without exception, the best reader I ever heard of Greek, and I have heard very few readers of English that I could for a moment compare with him. . . . Assuredly if the young men educated here do not become fervent Grecians it is not for want either of precept or example in their Professor."

Dr. Morris approved also of Professor Jardine—whose class in Logic and Rhetoric Lockhart attended at the age of thirteen. Part of the lecture-hour was spent in questioning the students upon the previous day's lecture ; this tutorial method was uncommon in Glasgow, and commended itself to the Doctor ; and no doubt prepared Lockhart for Oxford ways.

Lockhart's career at Glasgow ended in glory. He sat the Blackstone examination, and won the medal in Greek, having " professed " a formidable list of books and shown an intimate knowledge of them in translation and comment. The " Blackstone " is one of the traditionary, ceremonial examinations, in which the candidate sits in a chair with a slab of black marble—the black stone—inset in the seat, and announces or professes the texts in which he suffers himself to be examined. The professor puts him through a severe test, and to win the gold medal in either Latin or Greek is to be proved a very sound classicist. Lockhart was further awarded a Snell Exhibition to Balliol, always the Scots College of Oxford since its foundation by the Lady Devorgilla of Galloway. In the autumn of 1808 at an age (fourteen) when a boy of our day might be going from his preparatory to his public school, young John went off over the border towards new and enchanted lands, to that ancient University that was to give him learning and more than learning—" laughter and the love of friends ", and be a kindly mother to him, well loved and lovingly remembered all his life.

That he kept some kindly memories of Glasgow has been made apparent in *Peter's Letters* ; that Glasgow had a pride in him was proved, many years later, when in 1831 he was nominated as Lord Rector by the Tory students. This office is one bestowed by the students themselves ; by vote, the electors voting in their " nations " or regional groups. With some exceptions, the tradition has been political. The Whigs chose Cockburn. Glasgow was predominantly Whiggish and Lockhart was most emphatically a Tory. Cockburn was elected by a majority of votes ; but the honour and pleasure of having been nominated by his own party were sweet to Lockhart.

As Glasgow is remembered in *Peter's Letters* so Oxford is reflected in the novel : *Reginald Dalton,* which is probably the first Oxford novel to be written ; it precedes *Pendennis* and Newman's *Loss and Gain* and the engaging *Mr. Verdant Green* of Cuthbert Bede.

Reginald at Oxford is not Lockhart himself, but Reginald on his way south saw what Lockhart had seen and loved and remembered :

" The boundless spread of beauty and of grandeur— for even hedges and hedgerows are woven by distance into the semblance of one vast wood—the apparent ease— the wealth—the splendour—the limitless magnificence—the minute elaborate comfort—the picturesque villages—the busy towns—the embosomed spires—the stately halls— the ancestral groves—everything, the assemblage of which stamps ' England herself alone '." There is almost a hint of poetry and magic about the long description of his journey. Lockhart, it must be remembered, saw it first as a boy, a learned boy but one childish in worldly experience, coming from the austerity of the Scottish scene.

Lockhart—and Reginald—came up to the unreformed Oxford where it had not yet entered into the heart of man

12

to conceive anything so heretical as a degree without Greek ; when there were solid layers of privilege and snobbery, and the " gentlemen commoners " could fleet the time carelessly and expensively if not quite profitably ; when for the dons and fellows college was a secular monastery with all the monastic shelter from the world and no uncomfortable rules of piety.   Dinner in hall, as seen by Reginald, is described by the waggish and impudent Lockhart, not without zest.

" The solemn bell . . . the echoing vestibule . . . the hall itself with its high lancet windows of stained glass and the brown obscurity of its oaken roof, the yawning chimneys with their blazing logs—the long, narrow tables—the elevated dais . . . the haughty line of seniors . . . the Latin grace chanted at one end of the hall and then re-chanted from the other—the deep silence maintained during the repast—the bearded and mitred visages frowning from every wall—there was something so antique, so venerable, and withal so novel in the whole scene that . . . our youth felt enough of curiosity, and withal, of a certain kind of awe to prevent him for once from being able to handle his knife and fork quite *à la Roxburgher*.   These feelings, of course, were not partaken by the rest of the company, least of all by the senior and more elevated portion of it."   The High Table feasted grandly.   " Red faces grew redder and redder as the welcome toil proceeded, short, fat necks were seen swelling in every vein, and ears half hid by luxuriant periwigs could not conceal their voluptuous twinklings."

Oxford was still a stronghold of the Church of England. Whether Lockhart was now at all drawn towards Angli-canism is uncertain.   Years later, in 1845, he wrote : " In Balliol in my day, there was very regular religious instruc-tion.   We had lectures on Greek Testament, Articles, etc. on Sunday, and the tutor always made the lecture both critical and doctrinal.   There were also lectures on divinity in chapel at certain times of the year.   And nothing was, then as now, more rigidly looked to at the University examinations " —than a decent knowledge of theology and Christian evidences.   In the same letter he noted the wholesome decline of the " Gentleman Commoner system " and the ending of " the foolish liberality of old tuft-hunting statutes."

His own youthful reception of these lectures and instructions was not quite so favourable as was his recollection. He wrote to his mother :

" Mr. Jenkyns lectures to us a little on Sunday forenoons but I am sorry to say milk-and-water are the articles which chiefly compose his instructions, though I am sure he is really a good man." He also thought poorly of the sermons in St. Mary's (he was too early for Newman, the Chrysostom of his day), but he approved of the lectures on the Creed given in chapel.

Another letter home shows him as being little attracted by the Scots Episcopalians he met at Balliol ; most of his fellow-Scots were members of that ancient Church. He found them " a great deal more bigoted than any Englishman I have yet met with ". He was not yet aware, as he afterwards became, of the history of the gallant and suffering Episcopal Church in Scotland ; of the temper bred in her sons, defensive and uncompromising. One of these Scots was to become his life-long friend and to write of him a memoir that is a masterpiece of brief biography. He was George Robert Gleig, son of the Bishop of Brechin. Lockhart was still a son of the manse, with generations of sturdy Presbyterians behind him, but he learned something of the Anglican way at Oxford ; Scott's influence taught him more ; Sophia's perhaps most of all. Gleig, as their friendship grew, may very well have been his guide to those truths that are often conveniently ignored in Scottish history and ecclesiastical discussion.

Whatever Gleig's influence in that way he and others gave to Lockhart and received from him the inestimable riches of friendship ; that was begun lightheartedly, no doubt, with jests and follies as well as with the comradeship of work and mental adventure ; but that endured steadfastly through the years when those golden Oxford days were a memory. Only two of the group were lost to him : one, Alexander Scott, by early death ; the other, William Hamilton, by an estrangement caused, as Lockhart long afterwards told Croker, by " foolish politics ". Others in the group were Jonathan Christie, perhaps the closest friend of all, and John Williams the Welshman, naturally known as Taffy.

Hamilton was the most brilliant; older than Lockhart by six years, he left Glasgow University about the time that Lockhart was entering it. He survived Lockhart by two years. Religion as well as politics may have sundered them; Hamilton was agnostic and rationalist, Lockhart a devout Churchman of deep though reticent faith. But the two men were in many ways complementary to each other; both brilliant, both men of principle. That they should have suffered themselves to be parted is sad beyond the sadness of any spoiled friendship, because some quality in each was thwarted without the influence of the other.

Gleig, two years younger than Lockhart, had a boyhood very like his; kept at home by ill health, he was educated in great measure by his father the Bishop. Like Lockhart and Hamilton he went to Glasgow University, and like them gained a Snell to take him to Oxford. In his case the purpose of the founder of that Exhibition was more nearly fulfilled; for the Snell was originally intended to help in the education of clergy for the Scots Episcopal Church. Gleig took Holy Orders, though he did not serve in the Scots Church. Before ordination, however, he saw military service a little to Lockhart's envy; there is a story that he (J. G. L.) suggested taking Orders and going out as a Chaplain with Wellington's army to the Peninsula. This idea was suppressed and may never have been a vital one. Gleig served in the Peninsular Campaign, and wrote a vivid account of it in *The Subaltern*.

John Williams, like Gleig, took Holy Orders—in the Welsh Church; as Vicar of Lampeter he received private pupils, one of whom, through Lockhart's introduction, was Charles Scott, Sir Walter's younger son. Scott called him " a heaven-born teacher " and young Charles flourished under his care. As a result, Scott worked zealously on his behalf when the new Edinburgh Academy was founded, and secured for him the appointment of Rector in 1824. It was he who read the burial service over Scott's grave at Dryburgh. After resigning from the rectorship in 1847 he returned to Wales.

As for Christie, the *fidus Achates* he seems to stand, in every portrait of Lockhart, with him, a little behind him, but very close ; in less vivid colours, but not dim. He was always there : *dimidium cordis*. His home was in Bristol, and some of Lockhart's earliest letters were written to him there—after Christie had gone down and after Lockhart had returned to Scotland. In the incident of the duel with John Scott (one of the dark spots on Lockhart's youthful reputation) he alone emerges with complete honour—although on him was laid the guilt of manslaughter. That this tragedy should have left unmarred his friendship with Lockhart shows a magnanimity in Christie beyond common generosity.

There was Milman too, afterwards Dean of St. Paul's and one of Lockhart's *Quarterly* contributors. The Church predominated in his friendships in those Oxford days, and it is not surprising that his interest in Church matters was, in later life, so profound.

Such then was the group whose life together was an intensity both of work and of play. Lockhart described it in one of Dr. Peter Morris's letters, to one on the edge of the intimate circle, the Rev. David Williams, elder brother of " Taffy " :

" What a life was ours in that thoughtless prime of our days ! We spent all the mornings after lecture in utter lounging—eating ice at Jubb's—flirting with Miss Butler—bathing in the Cherwell, and so forth. And then, after dinner, we used to have our fruit and wine carried into the garden (I mean at Trinity) and there we sat, three or four of us, sipping away under the dark refreshing shade of these old beeches' bowers. Evensong was no sooner over than we would down to the Isis and man one, or sometimes two of Mother Hall's boats and so run races against each other or some of our friends to Iffley or Sandford. . . . I would give half I am worth to live one week of it again."

His terms, however, must have been filled with laborious days and lamp-lit nights as well as with the frolics he recalled. Had he done no more than read for Greats with such assiduity as to take a First, his record would be admirable enough. But he read besides, for sheer intellectual amusement, a great deal of English literature, especially

16

the Elizabethans, much French, and at least some of the Italian classics.

"I don't know what good genius whispered in my ear to begin Italian but I am sure I owe to him every enjoyment of the last six weeks," he wrote to Christie, after the latter had gone down. "I have read two thirds of Tasso and a few cantos of the Inferno, and, besides, several sonnets of Petrarch. I am sure if you will just commence, you will swear that you never read poetry so bewitching."

From Italian he went on to Spanish and Portuguese, not much of the last because of lack of books. He wrote to his mother that he had acquired some knowledge of these tongues during the Long Vacation of 1812 (which he would appear to have spent at Oxford, or at least away from home, in reading) ; and had also read all the books he professed for examination. There are glimpses of his Oxford life in those early letters, and other glimpses, by reflection in *Peter's Letters* and in *Reginald Dalton*. There is, moreover, the recollection of his friends : chiefly of Christie who supplied Gleig with much fine material for his memoir.

Gleig himself could recall him as a very boyish figure who may well have appeared ingenuous, solemn and provincial to the other men—but not for long. The comic devil in him was soon apparent. Christie wrote of his "exuberant animal spirits which found vent in constant flashes of merriment in season and out of season, brightened and pointed with wit and satire at once droll and torment-ing. . . . He was at once a favourite and formidable ; his tongue and pen were able and ready, and both employed for merriment and keen satire." His pencil was equally ready, for he was an "incessant caricaturist", with a passion for this form of mockery so strong that, Christie declared : "I was surprised when in after life he repressed it at once and for ever."

For Lockhart this exuberance of satirical laughter, this constant temptation to mockery, was as strong and dangerous as any physical lust ; and in youth he yielded to it, too often and too easily. His struggle to subdue it in maturity, as the years brought wisdom and developed his real, innate kindness, and as Sophia's gentle influence worked on his

17

spirit, was as fierce a combat as any against the pride of the flesh.

There was indeed a devil in him—not the cold, satirical demon attributed to him by his enemies, but a wild, mocking devil that rode and mastered him for a time. He was truly possessed. In every other way he was ruled by principles of morality, by honour and generosity ; he had integrity, even nobility. But this one passion he could not, or would not, in his youth subdue.

His first exuberance in those undergraduate days was probably harmless enough—though of an impudence ! The famous example is of his announcing that he had begun to learn Hebrew, and his handing in a Hebrew exercise to his delighted tutor. That guileless don loudly praised his pupil, and showed the exercise to a genuine Hebrew scholar ; who at once destroyed the donnish illusions by pointing out that the exercise was in plain English, only transliterated into the Hebrew alphabet, and further that it was a lampoon on the tutor himself.

Lockhart never became a recluse ; he was the best of company. Christie remembered his talk as lively, piquant and very much to the point ; " but he never sought more than his share ". Even at the height of his mental pride and recklessness Lockhart did not try to dominate others, or to assert himself and this grace was recalled, years later, in the obituary written of him in *The Quarterly*. He had good manners, though shyness and reserve sometimes, among those who hardly knew him, gave an impression of aloofness. He was sociable, even affectionate. If he could not wholeheartedly quote the Terentian : " Homo sum, nil humani a me alienum puto," yet he was interested in other men's views and ways of life. And if he had a predilection for criticising these views and trying to adjust those ways—he was in that a true Scot ; for most Scots in their heart regret not having been created first, in order to help and advise their Creator in His further achievements.

Aware, perhaps, of his own besetting sin of pride he was alert to pride and vanity in others. Christie admitted this : " If his best friend or his nearest relation had been mortified in his self-love by anything touching his vanity, it is not to be denied that Lockhart was not the man to heal the wound. If resorted to for sympathy he would probably make it smart afresh by a thousand unpleasing gibes." He was merciless to the pretentious.

There was the other side. Christie added that in any real distress : " Lockhart was of all men he to whom you might most safely resort for sympathy and consolation." And Christie spoke of his tenderness, especially of that profound, gentle, almost womanly love of children that was so marked in him. That true and tender Lockhart was not easily known, especially in youth. His shyness made him put up barriers, not only of reserve, but of mockery ; and many saw only those barriers.

Did Lockhart, when he wrote that strange and terrible tale : *Matthew Wald*—of a man with much good in him, gradually possessed by hatred and jealousy—look into his own heart and see the demon that had nearly mastered him ? He may have said humbly and remorsefully—and with thankfulness : " There, but for the grace of God, go I."

Every aspect of him, of his complex character, his enigmatic personality, began to appear in those Oxford days : golden days that left more than fairy gold in his possession ; left him with treasures of learning and with riches of friendship and remembered laughter.

Chapter 3

THE YOUNG LOCKHART

I. RETURN TO GLASGOW : 1813–1815

COLLEGE years can be a golden age for those who are at once scholarly and companionable, adventurous and swift of mind—as Lockhart was. Oxford to him meant enchantment. But the golden age is often followed by one of brass or copper ; and such may have appeared to him the phase of Glasgow life to which he returned in 1813. He came down covered with glory and laden with treasure, both of learning and of friendship. But the next year or two were almost stagnant. He was not sure of himself or his destiny. He was never completely happy or at home in Glasgow, though happy in his family life, and by no means idle, as regards reading, or unobservant—as *Peter's Letters* were soon to prove.

Andrew Lang has suggested that he would have done better to go to London—like William Hamilton—and read, perhaps, for the English bar ; it would have introduced him to the wide world of letters, at that period a very exciting one. Byron was at the height of his fame, Coleridge was bringing enchantment back to earth, Wordsworth was— in a most virtuous way—shocking contemporary thought and taste by his new theory of poetry, Southey was industri- ously producing verse. The young Lockhart might have met the young Keats and Shelley. He would have dis- covered a wider world than Oxford ; and might have been saved from the provincialism, the intellectual arrogance and aloofness that marred his young manhood.

Glasgow was far from being stagnant in itself ; but it was not the place for Lockhart. The give-and-take of college intercourse, the mutual rub and polish of wit were lacking. Lockhart may have been admired and praised by Glasgow society, by his parents' friends and the young people he met ; he may have been criticised adversely for reserve of manner which is never commendable in Glasgow.

But he needed at that moment neither such praise nor such depreciation ; he needed equal intercourse, exchange of views, literary gossip, casual and friendly criticism.

His first winter in Glasgow Lockhart spent reading a good deal, writing long letters to Christie, talking of writing other matter, smoking, in fact the " enchanted cigarettes " of books planned but not achieved. He had thought of a novel : not one of the four novels he did actually write within the next few years, but one—in the style of Galt— on Scottish life and manners. The hero was called John Todd. Christie also was planning a novel, with a hero much more impressively named Thirlestone Leslie :

" I don't think the novel I have in hand will at all jumble with yours," Lockhart wrote. " I mean it chiefly as a receptacle of an immense quantity of anecdotes and observations concerning the state of the Scotch, chiefly the clergy and elders. It is to me wonderful how the Scotch character has been neglected."

Lacking the gift of second-sight, he could not foresee how variously and superbly it *was* to be portrayed—by Scott whom he had yet to meet and whose greatest work was to come. It is amusing if not profitable to speculate on what that lost novel might have been ; even in his best work of fiction, *Adam Blair*, Lockhart is not a great novelist. He probably lacked, at this stage, both the necessary creative force and the magnanimity to achieve living portraits. He might have set too much down in malice. Scottish literature may have lost something in that still-born infant of the imagination ; but the Lockhart family and intimate circle probably gained (though unawares) in peace of mind. He was writing too close to his subject and characters and the portraits might have been too recognisable.

But even a spoiled novel or other work has its uses for the writer and he had begun his apprenticeship. Possibly some of the " lost " characters found their way into *Peter's Letters*. He was, too, reading solidly and widely if discursively ; and he kept his critical faculties alert. He read *Waverley* with enjoyment, and declared that it must have been written by two authors in collaboration : " It seems a young friend of Walter Scott's sketched the story and outlined everything. Walter Scott inserted the humour and brushed it all up. . . . Most of my novel was written before I read *Waverley*, but I fear the rush upon Scotland consequent upon that popular work is such that mine is likely to be crushed among the row. I intend letting it sleep a year or two, and making use of it as a drawable for some more extensive thing."

From the first he recognised Wordsworth's genius; it was a deep and lasting admiration—though in his last years, reading some of the poet's late and unworthy verse he could touch him with a caustic pen. In the winter of 1813-14 he wrote to Christie, about Wordsworth: "He strikes me as having more about him of that sober, mild, sunset kind of gentleness, which is so dear to me from the recollections of Euripides and the tender parts of the Odyssey, than any English poet ever possessed save Shakespeare, the possessor of all."

Byron, too, he admired: "*Lara* I look on as a wonderful production . . . I think it shows more depth of insight into human nature to invent such a terrible band of ideas . . . than ever poet surpassed. I delight in all the great poets of our day, and am willing to put Wordsworth and Byron at the top."

Most of his Glasgow impressions went into *Peter's Letters*; apart from the college-portraits they tend to be satirical. But having relieved himself of some spleen, he could truly value the genuine sort of Glasgow citizen, with his energy, his generosity, his desire for elegance and culture. This was the period of Glasgow's expansion; when her wealthy merchants and shipowners were buying or building country mansions, acquiring lands and estates, founding county families. Lockhart could appreciate this vitality, this magnificence and magnanimity; but even at its best, Glasgow was not his setting.

He went to Edinburgh in 1815 to read law and so begin what his family, and probably himself thought would be his career, as an advocate or barrister. Edinburgh was attractive to him; much might happen there; it might become his permanent home, once he was settled in his profession. Much did happen; including two events that shaped his future. He began to write for *Blackwood's Magazine*. He met Sir Walter Scott ; met his daughter Sophia ; fell in love with her and married her. Because of the tears in human things it cannot be said that they lived happily ever after ; but it can be truly said that he found in her his heart's love and the blessing of his life. Until he went to Edinburgh, his history had been prologue and preparation ; the main drama or chronicle now began.

II. EDINBURGH : 1815–1818

The Edinburgh of Lockhart's youth was beginning to wear its modern aspect. The New Town on the northern slopes towards Fife had been begun some fifty or more years earlier, in the 1760's : with the draining of the Nor' Loch, the laying of the foundations of the North Bridge, the planning and beginning of Princes Street, George Street and Queen Street, of St. Andrew's Square, and of the queenly and incomparable Charlotte Square. As the second half of the eighteenth century drew towards completion, more and more was added to the grace of the New Town, in comely buildings and in pleasant spaces : The Royal Botanic Garden was laid out, and Register House was built, to the design of Adam. The classical buildings of the University rose on the South Bridge, in the Old Town, forming as it were a prelude to the classical composition of the New. New streets led from Princes Street northwards ; the town became more and more a place of formal yet friendly houses, with the lovely doorways and fan-lights, the gracious proportions that still give serenity to the city's outward look. Edinburgh of the Middle Ages, of the Stuart Kings and the unforgettable Stuart Queen, was like a ballad. The New Town was prose—the most polished and balanced and exquisite of prose ; yet somehow the two became one organic whole.

Lockhart knew both the old and the new town in his everyday life. As a fledgling lawyer and young advocate or barrister, he walked the floor of Parliament House that no longer saw the assembly of the Scots Parliament, but was still the headquarters of the Law. The New Signet Library was building : then and now one of the most gracious buildings in a town of noble architecture. On the other side of Parliament Square stood the High Kirk of St. Giles with its memories of mediaeval Catholic worship, of " ding-doun the Papists " denunciations by John Knox and his followers, of the brief restoration of Episcopacy, and of the return of the Genevan faith and discipline.

Lockhart's other activity—which was to become his true vocation and career—his writing and journalism took him down the Mound to Princes Street to the office-cum-book-shop-cum-club of William Blackwood, where the famous magazine was published. He had lodgings in George Street, and later, lived in King Street where he wrote his first letters to Sophia, and where he brought her as his wife.

Lockhart became a citizen of Edinburgh at a period, when, though the Golden Age might be ended, the splendour and after-glow were still warm and radiant in her atmosphere ; the city knew and cherished her heritage. Having achieved so much urbanity, she was not prepared to sink into provincialism. The theatre, which is perhaps the least provincial or parochial of the arts, and certainly the least puritan, was at last, after a stormy history, safely established ; visibly established in the building of The Theatre Royal, ready to welcome Kemble.

Perhaps he fell a little in love with Edinburgh, as assuredly he had done with Oxford. He found out much of her secret, and in *Peter's Letters* told something of his discovery : conveyed the fascination of the mingled urbanity and sternness that is still part of the city's spell.

" Edinburgh ", wrote Dr. Peter Morris, " could never be merely a city . . . Here, the proudest of palaces must be content to catch the shadow of mountains and the grandest of fortresses to appear like the dwellings of pigmies perched on the very bulwarks of creation. . . . The very buildings of the Old Town, the tall ' lands ' of the High Street—seen through the lowering mist which almost perpetually envelopes them . . . are not easily to be distinguished from the yet larger and bolder forms of cliff and ravine among which their foundations have been pitched."

The brave lost Cause of the Forty-Five was an old song now, though a haunting one. There was still Jacobite feeling, which was far more than a sentimental anti-quarianism. But for the most part, the former passions were diverted into politics ; the feud now was between Whig and Tory ; and a lively feud it was, then and for years to come.

Possibly in private and in the secrets of his heart, a Tory or a Whig might admit that an opposing Whig or Tory was a good man, a loyal citizen, a sound judge of claret and of letters. But in public, in all writing and oratory, and often in private too, prejudice and politics guided or mis-guided men's opinions and pronouncements. Prejudices, however, are rarely found in the moribund, and this city of feuds was alive : with wit and learning, with some passion and not a little poetry ; with a vivid sense of tradition and alert interest in the present ; with the pride of intellect and of life ; and, in some measure, with the fear of God which is always a quickening influence.

Edinburgh had been, since Allan Ramsay's day, a city of book-shops ; and, as jewellers and goldsmiths store and display wealth and splendour, so booksellers gather and spread learning in its most genial forms. The book-shops of that day were informal clubs. Books were bought and read and discussed, gossip—legal, literary and social, was ex-changed and there were also those minor but valuable vehicles of thought and culture, the magazine and periodical. *The Spectator* had, long ago, set the fashion in London ; in recent years two similar periodicals had been begun in Edinburgh—*The Mirror* and *The Lounger*, by that gifted and agreeable person Henry Mackenzie. His novels are un-bearably tearful, but in his minor work (as he probably considered it) he is pleasantly readable, and in his remini-scences delightful ; in personality he was amiable, amusing and civilised. His influence was considerable. Like Scott he carried into this new century the tradition of the Golden Age. He was indeed a living link with the Forty-Five, having been born in that year, on the day of the Prince's landing in Scotland.

Henry Mackenzie founded *The Mirror* in 1779 ; and though its life was short, only five years, its influence survived. It was sold from one of the principal book-shops —that of Creech ; its contributors were chiefly Mackenzie himself and his young fellow-lawyers. *The Lounger* had an even briefer portion of life, from 1785 to 1787 ; but like its elder brother this attractive infant was long remembered in the household of Scottish letters.

The growth of the reading habit, the development of lending libraries which circulated not only literature but also talk about books, a certain increase of leisure and security in general life were gradually making a larger public for a magazine more vigorous if less bland than Mackenzie's delicate progeny. Such a publication was produced by the Edinburgh Whigs, in *The Edinburgh Review*, with Francis Jeffrey as editor. Some years later the Whigs also achieved a daily newspaper, *The Scotsman*, in 1817. The Tories, however, were not long in gaining upon their opponents.

A clever and ambitious young man, William Blackwood, who had been apprenticed to an Edinburgh bookseller, and later, gone to Glasgow for further experience, returned to Edinburgh in 1804, to open a book-shop on South Bridge. He prospered in business, married and set up house, and founded not merely a family but something like a dynasty of publishers. His success and importance increased when John Murray, the already famous London Scot who had preceded Blackwood in founding such a dynasty, appointed him his agent in Scotland for the young but flourishing *Quarterly Review*, and for the publications of the house of Murray. Before long, Blackwood moved his business to 17 Princes Street ; opening what was to be at once book-shop, publishing office and literary club. He had the good fortune to publish two of Susan Ferrier's novels : *Marriage* and *Inheritance* ; and he might—with the exercise of tact— have secured Scott's *Tales of My Landlord*. What might have followed such a lucky event is matter, now, for mere conjecture ; but it is permissible to suppose that had Scott then " thirled " himself to Blackwood and parted company with Constable and the Ballantynes, the disaster of his failure might have been escaped, the tragedy of Abbotsford

26

averted. Unfortunately, young Mr. Blackwood permitted himself to criticise one of the tales, *The Black Dwarf*, with the sweet reasonableness and kindly condescension of which youth alone is capable ; he offered advice as to its improvement. Scott went into one of his rare and royal rages, which every author must envy him. He talked wrathfully of " Blackwood's impudent letter," and wrote : " I belong to the Black Hussars of literature who neither give nor receive criticism." The proposed alliance came to nothing.

Blackwood had many ideas ; one of them was to found a Tory magazine, to counter-balance the Whiggish review and to be a Scots cousin to the *Quarterly* in London. In 1817 he produced the first number of *The Edinburgh Monthly Magazine*, entrusting it to the editorship of two men, Cleghorn and Pringle, whose literary reputation was not in the least doubtful. Their capacity for dullness approached genius. The new magazine was unreadable. The publisher soon realised how barren was the soil, and set about finding more fertile land. He had not far to go.

Talent, good Tory talent was not lacking among the young men in Edinburgh. There were some who were by no means so absorbed by their profession as to have to resist the allure of this new and exciting form of writing, with its swift appeal to the public, that was offered by a periodical. Journalism was a new venture, attractive by its very novelty, its excitement, the element of risk. Among those young intellectuals was Lockhart, with his brilliant academic record, his well-known connections and background, his accepted if not over-successful position as an advocate. Lockhart, though he writes what has been called " advocate's prose "—presenting his arguments, his plots in his novels, his case for or against an author, as a pleader might in court, was never, as he himself was the first to admit, eloquent at the bar. It is doubtful if he would have risen to the eminence of the bench had he continued in his profession ; and it is certain that at this time, he was earning little, and that he had time on his hands which he was glad to use for literature, and sometimes for literary mischief.

He had, either at Oxford or in the almost static period

that followed at home in Glasgow, learned German ; for he was never mentally inert, and he acquired languages easily and happily. This knowledge was an unusual accomplishment in the first quarter of the century ; the interest in German literature and philosophy and way of life was still to come, two decades or more hence. The splendour of German poetry of the eighteenth century was hardly known in Britain. Lockhart's attainment brought him a speedy and agreeable reward in the shape of a tour of Germany, paid by Blackwood as a form of advance royalties on a work of translation which Lockhart was to produce after his return. The work chosen was Schlegel's *Lectures on the History of Literature*. This was not without its influence on the development of Lockhart as critic ; still more important, perhaps, was the opportunity given him for discovering men and cities. Of book-learning he had a generous share ; but now he began to know the world. To his solid education, his genuine scholarship, his sound culture, he added that cosmopolitan touch that gave him distinction.

He enjoyed his travels and discoveries ; and most of all enjoyed his particular " Shelley plain " or " *Virgilium tantum vidi* ". *His* Virgil (or Shelley if you prefer) was Goethe, whom he visited at Weimar in 1817. The scene was afterwards described in one of *Peter's Letters*.

Among Lockhart's more commendable contributions to *Blackwood's Magazine* (as it was re-named) were his articles on German literature, his series on Greek Tragedy which gave full play to his academic learning, and his *Sketches of Foreign Scenes and Manners*, a pleasant by-product of his tour. These *Sketches* began to appear in June 1817. Lockhart had a keen eye for both scenery and manners ; especially for any oddities of foreign life. He wrote deftly and incisively. The articles were signed X. Y. Z. and by way of further disguise (already the game of " spoof " or mystification had begun) the writer referred to himself as tutor to a young man making his first tour abroad ; and contrived to write in a somewhat elderly manner, as a young wit might well choose and delight to do. He was soon an essential part of *Maga* as it was known to its contributors.

Chapter 4

BLACKWOOD'S MAGAZINE: THE TRIUMVIRATE—LOCKHART, WILSON, HOGG. 1817-1820

I

LOCKHART was not the only clever and not over-employed young advocate to be found walking the floor of Parliament House. With him was often found his friend and senior, John Wilson ; like him a graduate of Glasgow and of Oxford. The two were at this time " verra brithers " ; and they found a congenial fellow, though one of very different background, in James Hogg, the Ettrick Shepherd. They formed a triumvirate in *Maga* ; lived much of their intellectual life together and shared adventures, many of them regrettable, which does not mean that Lockhart was led into dissolute ways. The scandals so often expected and so often enjoyed in the lives of great men do not occur in Lockhart's, but none the less, in these years from 1817 to the early 1820's, he did commit many faults and follies through pride of intellect, and through an exuberance of that undergraduate impudence which sometimes recurred, even in his maturity, and which, at this time, was a dominant element in his character.

Mrs. Oliphant who wrote the *Annals of the House of Blackwood* with all her own agreeable flow of description and warmth of style, called Wilson " a genial giant but not a mild one ", and his geniality did not go deep. He was of a type unfortunately not rare in Scottish character : on surface, sentimental, emotional, prone to tears if that should seem agreeable or expedient, but underneath, and not far under, hard and cruel, proud with a devastating vanity and self-love. Physically he was handsome in what is usually called the Nordic style ; tall and broad, fair and florid in colouring, with a certain glow and swagger about him that some found attractive. Lockhart was a complete contrast : slim in build, elegant, almost classical in feature, as dark as a Spaniard. (Scott used to call him " the Hidalgo ", and the nickname suited him well.) Mrs. Oliphant has described the two, coming down the Mound from Parliament Square to Princes Street, walking arm in arm, wearing the elegant dress of the Regency man, tail coat in dark but not drab colours, high collar and stock and shirt frills, Hessian boots with tassels, swinging a cane. Such a costume set off a good figure and straight carriage and doubtless many a woman thought them a pair of bonny men. Mrs. Oliphant has compared the contrasting kinds of virulence the pair emitted :

" Lockhart pensive and serious, almost melancholy in the fiery fever of satire and ridicule that possessed him, launching the javelin with a certain pleasure in the mischief as well as the most perfect self-abandonment to the impulse of the moment : Wilson with Homeric roars of laughter, and a recklessness still less under control, not caring whom he attacked, nor with what bitterness." There enters also, Hogg : " bustling in all flushed . . . heated with a new idea in which the rustic daffing of the countryside gave a rougher face to the keener shafts of the gentlemen."

It was Lockhart's fate, throughout his career, both in youth and in maturity, to be in close touch with a person who reflected, magnified and sometimes distorted his own tendency to intellectual arrogance. In his second phase, the person was John Wilson Croker, one of his chief contributors to *The Quarterly Review*, and through all difficulties and differences, one of his most intimate friends. By that time, Lockhart had mellowed ; he was mature and strong enough not only to resist Croker's dominance but to try to influence that extremely rigid and acrid personality.

He could not, in his youth, resist Wilson with his tremendous vitality of mind and body, his virility that might be termed brutality, his exuberance and florid charm that could blind people to his coarseness of texture. Wilson was the older, by nine years ; a seniority which has importance, between the twenties and the thirties. He was born in 1785, son of a wealthy gauze manufacturer of Paisley ; on his mother's side he came of gentle blood and a long pedigree. From Glasgow University he had proceeded to

Oxford, to Magdalen, as a gentleman commoner, where he distinguished himself as an athlete, and won almost equal credit in scholarship. He took a First in Schools, and he won the Newdigate, with a poem on Greek and Roman architecture.

From Oxford he went down to Elleray on Lake Windermere where he spent some years in country pursuits, in the many sports that delighted him, and in writing essays and descriptive prose and much poetry. His *Isle of Palms* was published in 1812. He had been unhappy in his first love ; the attachment came to nothing, through his mother's opposition. But his second love was fulfilled in a happy marriage, in 1811 ; and like Lockhart he was to enjoy domestic serenity, ended too early—again like Lockhart's, by the death of his wife, in 1837.

The idyllic life at Elleray ended abruptly through a financial disaster which Wilson bore manfully enough. He came to Edinburgh, to share for a time his mother's home ; and proceeded to qualify for the bar. He made little of that profession however ; literature was his choice of vocation, and the door was opened, widely and hospitably, by *Blackwood's Magazine*.

James Hogg was the oldest of the triumvirate ; born in 1770 and thus a grown man—and long since a bread-winner —when Lockhart was born. He was of that type which is so honourable in Scottish tradition—the poor " lad o'pairts" —the herd-laddie who finds time for reading and learning, and sometimes for creative thought and for poetry. In his own calling, as a shepherd, Hogg proved most capable ; he was able to take full charge of a flock when he was sixteen. His master, for ten years from 1790 to 1800, was Mr. Laidlaw of Blackhouse, Yarrow, father of Scott's faithful and beloved Will Laidlaw. The Laidlaw household was a good place for a lad of eager and hungry mind ; there were books, and there was talk of books and of poetry and traditions, and Hogg's genius began to stir. In 1800 he went to live with his parents at Ettrick. His mother was a remarkable woman ; much of his genius came from her. She had a rich store, handed down by oral tradition, of the Border ballads and legends, and gave some of her treasures to Scott, who met mother and son on his tour of the Borders in quest of such matter. Hogg himself began writing original poems in the manner of the traditional ballads.

In farming he was unfortunate ; and came to place more and more hopes on literature. He wrote copiously, and sometimes with genius. There can be no question about that. Hogg *was* a genius ; he has the quality of pure magic ; he can enchant us—as the ballads enchant—with the murmur and rumour of faery ; there is, in *Kilmeny* and in the best of his poetry, that stillness of beauty, that unearthly luminance that is the rarest and most inexplicable part of genius.

He was far from being an obscure or neglected genius. Blackwood published his *Queen's Wake* ; Murray published him in London, and treated him with great kindness ; and some prosperity came to him in his other way of life too. The Duke of Buccleuch, fulfilling a benign desire of his Duchess, presented Hogg with the farm of Eltrive in Yarrow. Hogg married and settled down to a life of letters and farming combined ; and played with gusto the part of homely, rustic genius, taking care that the last aspect was never overlooked by any observer.

He wrote many remarkable tales in prose : *The Brownie of Bodsneck* among them ; and above all that strange and lurid document *The Confessions of a Justified Sinner*, than which there is no more vivid expression of the Calvinistic mind. He contributed exuberantly to *Blackwood's* ; he may have had a share in the " Noctes Ambrosianae ", though these belong more to Wilson. A man of genius, of courage and of character, he was also one of the supreme nuisances of his time. His conceit and vanity were beyond measure, and with that almost ethereal delicacy of imagination he united a coarseness of mind (due largely to vanity) that he made no attempt to refine, but rather developed. He nearly exhausted the wellnigh inexhaustible patience and charity of Scott, and far outdistanced the limits, admittedly not wide, of Lady Scott's tolerance. He is at once fascinating and repelling ; even at the distance of a century and more he can be infuriating. Many people thought well of him, and with reason ; but no man ever lived who thought better of himself.

Wilson was fortunate in his first biographer who was his own daughter—Mary Gordon. She wrote with filial piety rather than with judgement, and was ready to remove all possible faults from her father's shoulders and lay them upon Lockhart.

" Very rarely does it happen," she wrote, " that the same individual possesses an equal proportion of mental and bodily activity, of intellect and imagination . . . It was this combination of gifts that made Wilson singular among the men of his time, and the preservation of their harmony was proof that, amid the various influences tending to overthrow the balance, a healthy moral nature reigned supreme." (Filial piety is indeed a beautiful quality and very mellowing to the organ of vision, besides fertilising the imagination.) " . . . Enough for his vindication that in a long and laborious literary life he wielded a wholesome and powerful influence in the world of letters."

Mrs. Gordon admitted, however, the savagery (though she did not use that word) of many of the *Blackwood* reviews ; pleading, with justice, the ferocity of contemporary politics, and the inherent malice of human nature :—" Most people, however virtuous, have a kind of malicious pleasure in seeing others sacrificed, if the process be artistically gone about, and the *Blackwood* tomahawks were undeniable adepts in the art." But she maintained that the publisher knew the limits of public taste in this matter, and permitted only " a reasonable modicum of abuse ". There are, undoubtedly, varying standards of what is reasonable, but " modicum " seems a meiosis. One fact she has made clear (which is as well for the reputation of both Wilson and Lockhart) is that William Blackwood was " the only real editor " of the *Magazine*,—and therefore must share responsibility for what appeared therein.

Her description of Lockhart is vivid if unsympathetic. Naturally—if not commendably—she disliked him. Jealousy and resentment were mingled with her filial piety.

" Mr. Lockhart's pale, clear complexion had something of a Spanish character in it that accorded well with the sombre, or rather melancholy expression of his countenance, his thin lips compressed beneath a smile of habitual sarcasm, promised no genial response to the warmer emotions of the heart. His compact, finely formed head indicated an acute and refined intellect. Cold, haughty, supercilious in manner he seldom won love, and not infrequently caused his friends to distrust it in him, for they sometimes found the warmth of their own feelings thrown back upon them in presence of this cold indifference."

Compare with that, the description by Mrs. Oliphant who saw through the darkness of malice and satire that surrounded the young Lockhart, to the clear light of his true self, his youthful follies and who regarded him across the years with an almost maternal wisdom and tenderness :

" All energy and darting wit on one side, all kindness and tender domestic feeling on the other, fastidious, keen, refined, yet quite capable of picking up the coarsest missile and flinging it with a sudden impulse hotter and swifter than anything the ruddy Berserker was capable of. Men like Wilson are to be found everywhere in Scotland, if seldom with his endowment of genius. Men like Lockhart are very rare anywhere." Elsewhere she writes of " This reticent, sensitive, attractive yet dangerous youth " ; and she has wisely diagnosed Lockhart's malice as an almost pathological condition : " His satire was mischievous, virulent, not so much from hate as from nature. It was as if he had a physical necessity for discharging that point of venom which he emitted suddenly, without warning, without passion or excitement," sometimes, it would appear, putting in " his sting . . . with the mere intention of giving point to his sentences ".

The trio sketched each other ; and one of the most famous descriptions of Lockhart is that written by Wilson (as Mrs. Gordon states) but put into the mouth of Hogg in one of the " Noctes " :

" Lockhart . . . wi' a pale face and a black toozy head, but an e'e like an eagle's, and a sort o' lauch about the screwed-up mouth o' him that fules ca'd no' canny, for they couldna thole the meanin' o't, and either sat dumbfoundered, or pretended to be engaged to sooper and slunk out o' the room."

J. G. L. in turn (writing as Dr. Peter Morris) thus portrayed Wilson :

"A very robust athletic man,—broad across the back,—firm set upon his limbs—and having altogether very much of that sort of air which is inseparable from the consciousness of great bodily energies . . . In complexion he is the best specimen I have ever seen of the genuine or ideal Goth. His hair is of the true Sicambrian yellow ; his eyes are of the lightest, and at the same time of the clearest blue . . . His forehead is finely but strangely shaped ; the region of pure fancy and of pure wit being both developed in a very striking manner—which is but seldom the case in any one individual." (Dr. Morris and his friends chose, at this time, to toy with the " science " of phrenology.)

Hogg's decidedly rustic appearance was described by the Doctor with a detail that is unlikely to have pleased the sitter : his face and hands brown from exposure, his hair with " a coarse stringiness about it . . . ' hanging ' in playful whips and cords about his ears in a style of the most perfect innocence imaginable. His mouth, when he smiles, nearly cuts the totality of his face in twain "—his forehead " towering with a true poetic grandeur ".

Hogg was destined to be both the clown and the " stooge " of the group ; and did not always enjoy the casting of parts.

II

With its change of editor—to Blackwood himself, and of name, *Blackwood's Magazine* changed its nature even more violently. The change, in fact, almost brought about fighting in the streets of Edinburgh. In one wild leap it became, from the dullest of publications, the best or the worst periodical (according to the reader's opinion and political prejudice) ever produced in the capital. The contribution that chiefly caused that revolution was *The Chaldee MS*.

" It is not too much to say that in its way it moved the world . . . Edinburgh rose to it like one man, delighted, amused, offended, furious." Thus Mrs. Oliphant has described the effect of this renaissance. To say that it moved the world is a large claim ; but the world was smaller then, especially the literary world. *Maga* and *The Chaldee MS.* between them certainly moved the world of Edinburgh and of literary Scotland ; and some tremors were felt in London too.

The *Magazine* might thereafter be condemned for many faults ; but one word could not be used against it and that was " dull ". It could not be damned with faint praise, nor could it be praised with faint damns, for the latter when uttered, were invariably strong, and well-deserved. Even now, the passion of old rivalries and controversies long since spent and forgotten, it can startle us in these early numbers ; and especially in the notorious " Chaldee ". Every age has its own way of being frank, its own kind of violence of expression, and we are milder in criticism than they were in the first quarter of the nineteenth century. Some of the early *Blackwood* articles would give points to certain politicians in their public utterances. And though we could hardly be called a devout generation there are still many who find parodies of Holy Writ to be in poor taste and lacking in humour.

The Chaldee MS. may have, as Mrs. Oliphant believes, been Hogg's conception, elaborated by the other two ; there is also a story of an after-dinner session of the trio and others, when with much wine and more laughter the fantastic satire was composed. They were all, but Hogg chiefly, familiar with Hebraic style and imagery from their youthful reading and hearing of the Bible.

In the issue of *Blackwood's* of October 1817, then, *The Chaldee MS.* appeared ; presented, in the usual way of mystication, as a recently discovered treasure of scholarship :

It began with the dream-convention :

" And I saw in my dream and behold one like the messenger of a king came toward me from the East, and he took me up and carried me into the midst of the great city that

looketh toward the north and toward the east, and ruleth
over every people and kindred and tongue that handle
the pen of the writer . . . And I looked, and behold a
man in plain apparel stood in the door of his house, and
I saw his name and the number of his name ; his name
was as it had been the colour of ebony, and his number
was the number of a maiden when the days of her virginity
have expired." To this man—Mr. Blackwood at his shop,
17 Princes Street—entered his first editors, Pringle and
Cleghorn : " And behold two beasts came from the lands
of the borders of the south . . . Their faces also were
like the faces of men . . . And they said unto him :
Give us of thy wealth that we may eat and live, and thou
shalt enjoy the fruits of our labours. . . . And they
proffered unto him a Book : and they said unto him :
Take thou this and give us a piece of money that our souls
may live. And we will put words into the Book that shall
astonish the children of thy people, and it shall be a light
unto thy feet and a lamp unto thy path ; it shall also bring
bread to thy household and a portion to thy maidens."
To this the " man in plain apparel " assented, and the two
beasts departed : " And I heard a great noise as if it had
been the noise of many chariots and of horsemen horsing
upon their horses "—which is a reference (to some minds
brutal) to the fact that both Pringle and Cleghorn were
lame and went upon crutches.

They failed in their bargain, the man was " astonied
and waxed wroth " and demanded : " How shall I answer
those to whom I am engaged ? And they said : What is
that to us ? See thou to that." (Before this last parody
comment falters.) Then Ebony was made to appeal to
all the Tory literati of Edinburgh, whom the Chaldee
introduces under the lightest cloak of allusion, in mock-
scriptural disguise which contemporary knowledge and
gossip must easily have penetrated. .First came a reference
to Blackwood's rival, Constable ; " A man crafty in counsel
and cunning in all manner of workmanship." Then Ebony
appealed to " the great magician who dwelleth in the old
fortress hard by the river Jordan which is by the Border "—
in plain (and recognisable) language, to Scott of Abbotsford

—who answered cannily : " Lo, my heart wisheth thy good, and let the thing prosper which is in thy hands to do. But thou seest that my hands are full of working, and my labour is great . . . Moreover, thine adversary also is of my familiars . . . Yet be thou silent, per-adventure I will help thee some little."

There followed the roll-call of contributors ; the trium-virate among them :

" The first that came was after the likeness of the beautiful leopard from the valley of the Palm Trees." (An allusion to Wilson's long poem : *The Isle of Palms*, of which he thought highly.) " There came also from a far country the Scorpion which delighteth to sting the faces of men." Thus Lockhart was stamped, by a strange perversity of self-denigration with the name that still clings to him. There came also, " the great wild boar from the forest of Lebanon "—Hogg the Ettrick Shepherd ; with many other strange beasts.

The human figures are described with some decorum : Henry Mackenzie being an " aged man . . . in whose hand there was a mirror wherein passed to and fro the images of ancient days ". But there was no decorum in dealing with the " man crafty in counsel " and his gang.

The catalogue of Constable's men was of a scurrility that could be expected. It ended with a reference to the female readers and admirers of *The Edinburgh Review* : " Many women who knew not their right hand from their left." There must have been a *fama clamosa* at many of the Edin-burgh tea-tables throughout that October. The Scots-women of the period were not addicted to the prunes and prisms of conversation and comment.

The end is tumult ; the rivals having met " The city was moved, and my spirit failed within me, and I was sore afraid . . . And I fled into an inner chamber to hide myself, and I heard a great tumult but I wist not what it was."

Scott wrote to William Blackwood in November 1817 : " The article . . . possesses a great deal of satiric humour, but the prudence of publishing it may be seriously ques-tioned. Edinburgh is rather too narrow for satire so markedly personal, and there are certainly several individuals who, from their character and situation, have reason to resent having been so roughly treated. And I must add that, disapproving of the whole in point of prudence, I am not greatly pleased with the mode in which one or two of my particular friends have been mentioned." He did not at all resent " the good-humoured pleasantry " of the description of himself, but he put his finger on the weakness of the manuscript ; it is too local and particular. The great satires—those of Pope and Dryden and Swift, go beyond personalities ; that which they mock, however bitterly, is the vice of mankind, not the fault of one man at one period only. The Chaldee is spiteful and irresponsible, rather than satiric.

Lockhart's biographer, at this period, is tempted to escape with Jane Austen's famous apology : " Let other pens dwell on guilt and misery." But to present the whole man, in his recklessness as well as in his gentleness, " the guilt and misery " of his early, foolish writing must be shown. He seems, at times, to have written in a frenzy of pride and mockery. For his review of Keats, even if, as is possible, Wilson also had a hand in it, there is great difficulty in pardoning him ; indeed it would be impossible to forgive him, did not his own remorse and his own suffering in later life help to cleanse him. Even the attack on Leigh Hunt, which began the famous series on The Cockney School, though it deals with a man and with work of little repute, is still revolting. Hunt was not worth such a mauling.

The immediate occasion was the publication of Hunt's poem : *Rimini* ; a work better forgotten and now celebrated merely as a *casus belli*. The title of the article and its successors, " On the Cockney School of Poetry ", gave Lockhart as much pride as the creation of any work of art could have done. He claimed, as it were, the copyright :

" While the whole critical world is occupied with balancing the merits . . . of the Lake School, it is strange that no one seems to think it at all necessary to say a single word about another new school of poetry which . . . has not as yet, I believe, received any name ; but if I may be permitted to have the honour of christening it, it may

39

henceforth be referred to by the designation of The Cockney School. The chief doctor and professor is Mr. Leigh Hunt, a man, certainly, of some talent, of extravagant pretensions, . . . and withal of exquisitely bad taste . . . He is a man of little education. He knows absolutely nothing of Greek, little of Latin, and his knowledge of Italian literature is confined to a few of the most popular of Petrarch's sonnets, and an imperfect acquaintance with Ariosto." Leigh Hunt's lamentable ignorance, and the reviewer's admirable knowledge of French, Spanish and German literature are exposed in detail ; then comes the onslaught on *Rimini* itself, delivered with such violence that the reader to-day is disposed to echo the man who saw a giraffe for the first time, and said : " I don't believe it " ; for it seems incredible that a man of breeding, culture and principle (and Lockhart possessed all these) should have so debased himself even in demolishing an example of literary squalor :

" One feels the same disgust at the idea of opening *Rimini* that impresses itself upon the mind of a man of fashion when he is invited to enter for a second time the gilded drawing-room of a little mincing, boarding-school mistress who would fain have an At Home in her house. Everything is pretence, affectation, finery and gaudiness. The beaux are attorney's apprentices . . . fiddlers, harp-teachers and clerks of genius ; the belles are faded fan-twinkling spinsters, prurient, vulgar misses from school, and enormous citizens' wives. The company are entertained with lukewarm negus and the sounds of a paltry piano-forte." As a picture of the most tedious type of society, this might have been permissible, if unamiable, in a satirical novel : as criticism of a poem it is hardly relevant.

Lockhart's culmination of contempt can be condoned only by his sincerity ; he was, no doubt, truly shocked by Leigh Hunt's choice of subject and by its treatment :

" His poetry is that of a man who has kept company with kept-mistresses. He talks indelicately like a tea-sipping milliner-girl. Some excuse for him there might have been had he been hurried away by imagination of passion. But with him indecency is a disease, and he speaks unclean things from perfect inanition. The very concubine of so impure a wretch as Leigh Hunt would be to be pitied, but alas! for the wife of such a husband. For him there is no charm in simple seduction ; and he gloats over it only when accompanied by adultery and incest."

The readers of that age were fairly strong in stomach, and, if a mixture of metaphors is permitted, the critics often wrote with a pen dipped in vitriol and wielded like a paint-brush. Part of the reason for the vitriol in this case is given in the conclusion : *Rimini* had been commended in *The Edinburgh Review*—and by Hazlitt who, being on the wrong side in politics, was therefore infamous. Jeffrey and he are together denounced for their tolerance ; a tolerance that has driven *Blackwood's* to " the resolution of laying before our readers a series of essays on The Cockney School—of which here terminates the first ".

Thereupon, doubtless, many readers sat back in happy anticipation. They were not disappointed. The attack on Leigh Hunt was renewed in two further articles with no loss of virulence. Then, in August 1818 there appeared one of the most notorious criticisms ever published : the review of Keats' *Endymion*.

It is impossible wholly to absolve Lockhart from this guilt though it may have been shared ; many of the articles in *Maga* were written by more than one hand ; so, Wilson may have lent his pen to this. But even so, none that had any part in this writing can be held guiltless. Keats him-self held Lockhart entirely guilty : " If I die you must ruin Lockhart," he said to Reynolds. Years after this, when Scott and his daughter Anne were in Rome—in the last, sad phase of Scott's life, they met Keats' faithful friend, Severn, the artist. He showed them many of his sketches, including one of Keats, and spoke of his dead comrade lovingly and with pride in his genius. He saw Anne flush and turn aside her head, while Scott said, falteringly : " Yes, yes, the world finds out these things for itself at last." Severn felt in them a sense of vicarious remorse—for Lockhart.

The review begins with a crack of the whip at all poetasters and at the folly of the age, named by the reviewer Metromania :

" The just celebrity of Robert Burns and Miss Baillie has had the melancholy effect of turning the heads of we know not how many farm-servants and unmarried ladies ; our very footmen compose tragedies, and there is scarcely a superannuated governess in the island that does not leave a roll of lyrics behind her in her band-box." Then comes the particular attack :

" To witness the disease of any human understanding, however feeble, is distressing, but the spectacle of an able mind reduced to a state of insanity is ten times more afflicting." (" ' I weep for you,' the Walrus said. ' I deeply sympathise ! ' ") " It is with such sorrow as this we have contemplated the case of Mr. John Keats. This young man appears to have received from Nature talents of an excellent, perhaps even of a superior order—talents which devoted to the purposes of any useful profession must have rendered him a respectable if not an eminent citizen . . . But all has been undone by a sudden attack of the malady to which we have already alluded. Whether Mr. John has been sent home with a diuretic or composing draught to some patient far gone in the poetic mania we have not heard. This much is certain, that he has caught the infection and caught it thoroughly. The phrenzy of the *Poems* was bad enough in its way ; but it did not alarm us half as seriously as the calm, settled, imperturbable drivelling idiocy of *Endymion*."

Lockhart, like many older men of letters, resented the depreciation of Pope by the new Romantic School : " To deny his [Pope's] genius is just about as absurd as to dispute that of Wordsworth or believe in that of Hunt . . . It is most pitiably ridiculous to hear men, of whom their country will always have reason to be proud, reviled by uneducated and flimsy striplings, who are not capable of understanding either their merits or those of any other men of power—fanciful dreaming tea-drinkers who, without logic enough to analyse a single idea, or imagination enough to form one original image, or learning enough to distinguish between the written language of Englishmen and the spoken jargon of Cockneys, presume to talk with contempt of some of the most exquisite spirits the world ever produced, merely because they did not happen to exert their faculties in laborious, affected descriptions of flowers seen in window-pots, or cascades heard at Vauxhall."

This rebuke was not undeserved, and is fair comment, though it might have been expressed with less ferocity. But the analysis that follows of *Endymion*, with copious quotations, is scathing, and ends in virulence :

" Mr. Hunt is a small poet, but he is a clever man.   Mr. Keats is a still smaller poet, and he is only a boy of pretty abilities which he has done everything in his power to spoil . . .   We venture to make one small prophecy, that his bookseller will not a second time venture £50 upon anything he can write.   It is a better and a wiser thing to be a starved apothecary than a starved poet.   So back to the shop, Mr. John Keats, back to ' plasters, pills and oint-ment-boxes ' . . .   But for Heaven's sake, young Sangrado, be a little more sparing of extenuatives and soporifics in your practice than you have been in your poetry."

The Scorpion stung, with poison in the sting and with unholy delight, the face of a dying poet.   It must be remem-bered, in Lockhart's defence, that he did not know of Keats' illness.   Had he known more of the fragile creature who was coughing his lungs into dissolution, who was look-ing his last on all things lovely, crowding his sensations of beauty into a day he knew would be brief, it is likely that he would have written with some mercy if not with justice.

The *Letter* to Dr. Chalmers also appeared in this year of disgrace, 1818 ; in the May issue of *Blackwood's*.   Dr. Chalmers, one of the most esteemed clerics of his day (and some twenty-five years hence to be one of the founders of the Free Kirk), had joined the contributors to *The Edin-burgh Review*—which, to the other side, appeared the act of a renegade.   Again it must be said in Lockhart's defence that he regarded the *Review* as an infidel or at best, agnostic publication, and was truly shocked by finding a clergyman among its contributors. The *Letter* opens with some pompous and patronising compliments, a little absurd as coming from a young man to one fourteen years his senior :

" You are assuredly a great man.   Your mind is cast in an original mould . . .   You have no admirer more sincere than myself . . . [but] I think you cannot possibly be the worse of being told that in my apprehension and that of many who admire and love you as I do, you have lately fallen into a great and dangerous error . . . Your conscience has already spoken . . . You are sensible that the world has reason to wonder at your conduct in becoming a contributor to *The Edinburgh Review*."

The rest of the article is an unmitigated sermon. Lockhart might be an indifferent pleader in Court of Session, but he would seem, on occasion, to have inherited from his father a gift for exhortation and denunciation that would have edified the godly, had he (in the Scots Presbyterian phrase) " entered the ministry ". Chalmers was solemnly warned against joining " certain scoffing priests and envious renegadoes who are already branded with an everlasting infamy for the share which they have taken in the guilty triumphs of *The Edinburgh Review* ". Whether the reverend doctor was worth all this powder and shot may be doubted. But the explosion scandalised Edinburgh.

This *Letter*, like another of the same sort aimed at Professor Playfair, was signed by one of Lockhart's favourite pseudonyms : Baron von Lauerwinkel ; the *Letter* to Playfair being further disguised by German names : Playfair being the Rev. Professor Laugner, and *The Edinburgh* the Königsberg Review.

Dr. Playfair was a minister of the Church of Scotland who, after holding a charge for some years, was appointed to the Chair of Natural Philosophy in Edinburgh University. He was one of the most valued contributors to *The Edinburgh Review* ; and in Edinburgh society, a man greatly respected for his intellectual distinction, and much loved for his goodness. In 1818 he was old—as it happened, within a year of his death. The attack on him made in this *Letter* may have been sincere in its disapproval ; but there was enough rancour in it to disgust many readers including Scott. Dr. Playfair was denounced as an apostate priest, called " the d'Alembert of the Northern Encyclopaedia ", and accused of being either a hypocrite or a renegade : " The man who can undertake for a bit of bread to wrap himself in deceit as in a garment . . . who can chuckle with impious satisfaction over the success with which he imposes on the credulity of the simple . . . that man, if such there be, is, inasmuch as eternity is greater than time, a fouler hypocrite than the most pernicious miscreant who ever practised, under the mask of kindness, upon the property or the life of his fellow-men."

The suggestion that the venerable Dr. Playfair was a kind of spiritual Deacon Brodie was more than even the strong stomach of Edinburgh could digest.

Scott's rebuke was restrained, indeed, too mild ; but his way was to reprove in charity rather than in anger. He was not yet on such intimate terms with Lockhart as to bring the note of personal appeal into his remonstrance :

" I did not approve of the personal and severe attack on Playfair, though extremely well written, and perhaps it is one consequence of such hostility that men of inferior literary consideration endeavour to distinguish themselves in an alleged vindication of others, when in fact they only seek to gratify their own envy and malignity, or to enhance their no-importance."

Scott's letter was in answer to one of Lockhart's which showed the latter in a mood of mingled resentment and alarm. He and Wilson were being forced to swallow a dose of medicine that was, if anything, more unpleasant than any they had administered to others. They had been attacked in an anonymous pamphlet, *Hypocrisy Unveiled*, in which Lockhart was accused of infidelity—a thrust that must have wounded him sorely ; while Wilson was accused of writing " obscene parodies " on the *Psalms*. They both sent, through *The Scotsman*, challenges to the anonymous writer, which were not taken up. Wilson was in a state of hysterical fury. Scott gave wise counsel ; that " the one true anti-dote " to such poisonous attacks lay " in so bearing yourself both in life and in literature as to command the esteem and approbation of the good and the wise to whose opinion, in the long run, that of the rest of the world never fails to become conformable ". But Lockhart was some way yet from winning that esteem.

His work, however, even at this period was not all smoke and fire. The mocking devil in him could be amusing ;

could in short become a " de'il " in the Scots form ; for in Scotland the word " de'il " can be used almost with affection.

Lockhart discovered himself as a poet, with a special talent for humorous verse. He wrote, under the name of William Wastle, a long and hilarious poem : " The Mad Banker of Amsterdam ", which began its appearance in *Maga* of July 1818. He had the necessary dexterity in rhyme and rhythm and sufficient high spirits for such composition, and if the poem rambles far and wide from its supposed subject, the rambling is entertaining. His own memories of foreign scenes inspired the description of a typical Dutch beauty :—

> The mistress of Mynheer must be a bouncer,
>   Fat is the chief commodity he seeks,
> It must take scores and scores of yards to flounce her,
>   She must have pounds of chin and pounds of cheek ;
> She must have fists would knock a bullock down, sir,
>   The μεγαθος και καλος of the Greeks ;
> If she sits down upon the grass she leaves
> A mark as broad as any of her beeves.

A widow of these ample charms captivates the Banker : they make their wedding-tour on a canal boat, in which are also the narrator and a friend, among :

> A score of peoples, kindred, tribes and tongues
> All exercising in one way their lungs. . . .

The narrator and friend dine with the Banker and his bride and sing for their supper by gossiping about Edinburgh celebrities.

The Scorpion could sting himself, when he chose :

> Then touched I off friend Lockhart, (Gibson John)
>   So fond of jabbering about Tieck and Schlegel,
> Klopstock and Wieland, Kant and Mendelssohn,
>   All High Dutch quacks like Spurzheim or Feinagle ;
> Him the Chaldee ycleped the Scorpion—
>   The claws, but not the pinions of the eagle
> Are Jack's ; but though I do not mean to flatter
> Undoubtedly he has strong powers of satire.

The poem meanders amusingly through reflection and

description, often entirely forgetting the Banker ; and why or how he is mad is never exactly made clear.

At one stage, the Banker would appear to have come on a visit to Edinburgh. Lockhart, the true serious poet, now holds the pen : as in the description of Mary Stuart :

> Look on her whose beauty hath become
>   A by-word to all nations—in the prime
> And flush o' her days—the rose of Christendom,
>   Shedding such lustre over this cold clime
> As never Southern knew—she struck men dumb
> With the sun-dazzle of her regal charms,
> And stooped, a goddess, to young Darnley's arms.

He could see in Mary's royalty a quality innate and essential, not an adornment to be assumed or laid aside ; she cannot be thought of merely as a woman, lovely and hapless ; she is always the tragic queen :

> Wearing her majesty as it had been
>   A thing she fain would quit, but in her eyes
> Enthroned, immovable, sublime, serene
>   Woven in her essence by her destinies.

The description of " the tragedy of Fotheringay " (of which his grand-daughter was to write) is altogether meet and noble ; of the " evening of tranquillity " when Mary had passed beyond agony.

Lockhart enjoyed many disguises. One was coolly borrowed from a real person, a Dr. James Scott, a worthy surgeon-dentist in Glasgow, nicknamed *The Odontist*. Under this name was published, in the issue of *Blackwood's* of September 1819, one of Lockhart's best-known poems, " Captain Paton's Lament " ; one of his most endearing, in its mixture of affection, gentleness and humour :

> Touch once more a sober measure, and let punch and tears be shed
> For a prince of good fellows, that, alack-a-day is dead ;
>   For a prince of worthy fellows, and a pretty man also,
>   That has left the Saltmarket in sorrow, grief and woe ;
>   Oh ! we ne'er shall see the like of Captain Paton no mo.

Lockhart had a genius for the vignette or the swift pencil-sketch. The good Captain lives, in the round ; he walks into full view, a true son of Glasgow, on the plainstanes and in the Saltmarket, with the Kirk in the background. Lock-hart, of course, was an artist in line as well as in words ; he saw men and scenes with the artist's eye for essentials ; and this liveliness of description was the salt and savour of his first book : *Peter's Letters to His Kinsfolk*.

The creative force in him was stirring ; it found, in the next few years a more satisfying expression than the *Blackwood* articles and reviews had provided. This release and fulfilment may in part explain the gradual conversion of Lockhart from a satiric young devil to a man of acute but no longer malignant judgement, talent and expression. A pent-up energy was diverted into better channels than those of the reviews in *Maga*.

Chapter 5

LOCKHART : ESSAYIST AND POET.
1812–1823

I

I N a letter to William Blackwood (undated, but from
the date of the subsequent contract, probably late in
1818), Lockhart wrote of his new project :
" I saw James Ballantyne yesterday, and sounded him
about Dr. Morris. He seems to say he would stake all his
credit on the Dr's success. Scott also writes in great terms
touching the Doctor. On the whole I do think that the
writing of the book might be accomplished and would be
singularly pleasant in the doing : 3 volumes, 12mo, size of
Waverley. 1st Vol : Edinburgh : town described : Education Scotch and English—Bar—Society—Portraits of the
Professors and Barristers—*Edinburgh Review*—Mackenzie-
Scott's *Tales of My Landlord* discussed—Scott's merits as a
Tory writer in Scotland—A Visit to Abbotsford—Dilettanti
—Wilson, Hogg. Vol. 2nd. Glasgow ; West Country :
Residence at a Manse—The Life of the Clergy—Sacraments
—Presbyteries—All graphically done but with kindly feel-
ing. Chalmers, Balfour, Moncrieff, McCrie. Comparison
of Scotch and English Churches—and peasantry. Marriages
etc.
Vol. 3rd. To be written chiefly by Wilson, and to con-
tain accounts of the Dr's tours of the Highlands, Tweeddale
and along the Clyde.
" All this to be done immediately, *currente calamo*, on
smooth paper ?
" What do you think on't ? I think it would do much
in every way, and reflect much credit, if successful, upon
your magazine. Let me therefore hear what you say."
Blackwood apparently thought well on't, for in April 1819
Lockhart wrote to him formally accepting his offer of £500
for the first edition—of 2,000 copies—of the Letters of
Dr. Morris, or, as they were called : *Peter's Letters to His*

Kinsfolk. The title recalled that of Scott's *Paul's Letters to His Kinsfolk.*

Whether or not there *was* ever a " First " edition is still one of the minor problems of book-collecting. He who would find it may have to search the book-shop at the foot of the rainbow or in Serendipity Street. Most collectors possess the " Second " edition. A third was speedily called for and produced. It would have been a typical Lockhartian jest to talk of a first and have a second edition imprinted. What really matters is that the book was something new, highly diverting and as a gallery or portfolio of period-portraits, invaluable.

Lockhart was credited with having himself reviewed the book before publication, in the February *Blackwood's* ; but if he did, he did not indulge in self-praise though he might permit himself a lively publicity.

" Though it is said on the title-page that the volumes are to be sold by all the book-sellers, yet, strange to tell, a single copy is not to be found among all the bibliophiles of Edinburgh. These gentlemen are really very remiss, and seem not to know their own interest. They seldom think of selling a new publication till it has become an old one . . . For our part we are easy . . . for all writers of any eminence send their works instantly down ' To the Editor of *Blackwood's Magazine* ', and as that well-meaning, ill-used man reads but little, we, his Contributors, have all the presentation copies to ourselves."

The new book had, it would appear, been discussed at one of the Noctes Ambrosianae ; lots having been drawn, the review fell to one " Mordecai Mullion ", which is as good a name as any. The plan of the book is described, long quotations are given, but there is no unseemly laudation.

" To make any lengthened comments on Dr. Morris's style would be superfluous after the very copious extracts which we have given. He is singularly free from the passion for fine writing which affects most modern tourists." It was an adroit introduction.

Scott was cordial. " I have much to say to you about Dr. Morris," he wrote (in April 1819), " being delighted with his purpose of publishing his Tour." The letter was one of invitation to Lockhart, to visit Abbotsford, travelling from Edinburgh by the Blücher, the coach which was " almost as convenient to Abbotsford as the Field-Marshal is to Europe ".

Scott's interest in *Blackwood's Magazine* and Blackwood's books was of the utmost importance. " Get Scott and you get everything "—Lockhart had written to William Blackwood in the early days of *Maga* just after the appearance of *The Chaldee MS.* " Be extremely cautious in giving to him names or power unnecessary. But secure him :

" 1mo—to write a paper in No. 2.

" 2ndo—to speak against the exclusion of your magazine should such an inquisitorial and absurd measure be talked of in a faculty meeting.

" 3tio—not to say any ill of you, your magazine, or, essentially, of the ' Chaldee ' itself. On him everything depends."

Scott was long established as the *arbiter literarum* of Edinburgh.

Peter's Letters, then, set sail under a favouring wind from Abbotsford. In July 1819 Scott wrote again, thanking Lockhart for a presentation copy :

" I think the Doctor has got over his ground admirably, and the general tone of the book is perhaps too favourable to the state of public society and of individual character . . . But it was in every point of view right to take this more favourable tone, and to throw a Claude Lorraine tint over our Northern landscape. We cannot bear the actual bare truth, either in conversation or that which approaches nearest to conversation in a work like the Doctor's."

His only regret was that there had not been a Dr. Morris, fifty or even twenty-five years earlier, to catch the likeness and report the talk of the men of those previous generations.

Peter's Letters make a glorious lucky-bag of memories and impressions. Lockhart's many moods found expression. He could " remember and be glad " ; he could draw a true sketch or a caricature ; indulge his mischief or his affection. He was, later in life, to depreciate this work in words that may be read as apology for all the sins of his reckless youth :

51

" Nobody but a very young and a very thoughtless person could have dreamt of putting forth such a book " ; adding that the *Letters* " were not wholly the work of one hand " ; but he accepted responsibility.

There are acerbities in the *Letters*, and a certain amount of coat-trailing, but there is nothing to shock us as do the *Blackwood* reviews. It has been truly said that much of Lockhart's best criticism lies in his *obiter dicta* : there is some in these *Letters*—notably in regard to Wordsworth.

" In listening to Wordsworth it is impossible to forget for a single moment that the author of *The Excursion* is before you. Poetry has been with him the pure, sole business of life . . . The large, dim, pensive eye that dwells almost for ever upon the ground, and the smile of placid abstraction that clothes his long, tremulous melancholy lips, complete a picture of solemn, wrapped-up contemplative genius." The poet in Lockhart recognised the greater poet in Wordsworth ; he recognised in Wordsworth that sense of peace for which he himself longed.

Of Scott he wrote that he was " the very poet of active life ", before whom life, in all its variety, lay " bright and expanded as in the glass of a magician ". He realised the largeness, the universality of Scott's genius : " Whatever subject be mentioned, he at once steals a beam from his mirror and scatters such a flood of illustration upon it that you feel as if it had always been mantled in palpable night before." Lockhart, more than any other, noted the otherworldliness in Scott's power—something even more than magnanimity : " The eye and the voice, the words and the gestures, seem all alike to be the ready unconscious interpreters of some imperial spirit that moves irresistibly their mingled energies from within."

On the adverse side Dr. Morris dealt severely with *The Edinburgh Review*, chiefly for its sins of commission against his own admired authors : among them, Charles Lamb. But its condemnation of Wordsworth was still more grievous an offence :

" What we cannot understand, it is a very common and indeed a very natural thing for us to undervalue ; and it may be suspected that some of the merriest witticisms which have been uttered against Mr. Wordsworth have had their origin in the pettishness and dissatisfaction of minds unaccustomed and unwilling to make either to others or to themselves any confessions of incapacity. . . .

" The spirit of this facetious and rejoicing ignorance has become so habitual to the Scotchmen of the present day that even they who have thrown off all allegiance to *The Edinburgh Review* cannot divest themselves of its influence." He has touched on one of the weaknesses of the Scottish character—the complacency of invincible ignorance.

The Edinburgh Review " praised only where praise was extorted "—and never generously. Added to these faults was the graver one of irreligious mockery. There was need, Dr. Morris thought, of an attack ; and had the Blackwood company but gone prudently about their campaign, victory would have been easily won and cleanly won. Unhappily, too many of them " were very young or very inexperienced men " whose zeal for literature far out-ran discretion, courtesy or judgement. With much knowledge they had too little wisdom. In fact, " their veneration for intellectual power was too great—exactly as that of the Edinburgh Reviewers was too small."

Such immaturity of wisdom with over-zealous intellectualism was, however, forgivable. But *Blackwood's* young men had " stained, in plain language, the beginning of their career with the sins of many wanton and malicious personal satires . . . Since that time, experience and reflection seem to have taught them many lessons concerning the folly and vice of this part of their giddy career—but they have still not a little to learn before they can be made fully sensible of the true nature of some of their trespasses."

So Lockhart made his act of contrition : made it, too, for his confederates, in deploring the attack on Coleridge's *Biographia Literaria* which had appeared in one of the first numbers of *Maga*—and for which not he but Wilson was to blame. He now paid, through Dr. Peter, generous tribute to Coleridge :

" If there be any man of grand and original genius alive at this moment in Europe, such a man is Mr. Coleridge." *Peter's Letters* made a book original in conception and valuable in execution. It is the work of an artist endowed with strong visual perception and memory, and the capacity to awaken the perception of his readers. It is full of portraits and of interiors vivid as a Dutch painting. The description of Blackwood's " great lounging book-shop ", for instance, is delightful.

In portraiture, Lockhart could describe his rival, Jeffrey, without bitterness, though certainly with mischief :

" It is a face which any man would pass without observation in a crowd because it is small and swarthy, and entirely devoid of lofty, commanding outlines—and besides his stature is so low that he might walk close under your chin and mine without ever catching the eye . . . The lips are very firm, but they tremble and vibrate . . . in such a way as to give the idea of an intense, never-ceasing play of mind. There is a delicate kind of sneer almost always upon them . . . But what speaking things are his eyes . . . Once kindled with the heat of any passion how they beam flash upon flash . . . Their repose is even more worthy of attention . . . They seem to take a pleasure in banishing every ray from their black, inscrutable glazed tarn-like circles."

The impression left is that of a melancholy monkey.

The account of a visit to Jeffrey's suburban villa, Craigcrook, is an excellent picture of social life. There is some detail interesting to gastronomes : champagne was drunk with the dinner, not as a dessert-wine.

Claret was served with the dessert.

Already, in 1819, Burns' suppers were in vogue, and Dr. Morris attended one such function in the Assembly Rooms in George Street. The oration in honour of The Immortal Memory was something of a " cauld harangue "—but gave the Doctor an excuse for dilating, in his next Letter, upon the genius of Burns (to whom Lockhart *in propria persona* was always generous) and for attacking Jeffrey and his *Review* for their attitude towards the poet :

" It is an easy thing for those who have comfortable homes to rail against the dissipated habits of a poor wandering poet, compelled to waste his best days in degrading drudgeries, and night after night to find himself surrounded

in his own narrow dwelling by all the depressing and con-
tracting squalor of penury." The Doctor also made a
mellow apology for conviviality. The austere and "high-
brow" can know nothing of the "full hearty swing of
jollity. How can they ever sympathise with the misty
felicity of a man singing :

'It is the moon ; I ken her horn.'

I think no man should be allowed to say anything about
Burns who has not joined in this chorus, though timber-
tuned, and sat till daylight, though married." (A jewel of
a phrase—" misty felicity ! ")

Peter's Letters may rank second (though at long distance)
to Lockhart's masterpiece,—the *Life of Scott*, and as prelude
to that great symphony. As a book it has double value
and significance ; for not only has it the fascination of revealing Lockhart, but it is a brilliant picture of Regency
Edinburgh. It might also be regarded as an incipient
Autobiography. It has salt and savour ; it is full of zest,
sometimes a wicked zest, but always antiseptic with style
and vitality.

II

There must have been much gossip and guessing about
the authorship of *Peter's Letters* ; probably much correct
guessing. The first of Lockhart's works to be published
under his own name was his volume : *Ancient Spanish Ballads :
Historical and Romantic*. Some of these appeared, originally
in the *Magazine*, and the volume was published by Blackwood in 1823. A new edition was issued nearly twenty
years later, in 1841, by John Murray.

It has been said (by J. H. Millar in his *Literary History
of Scotland*) that the *Spanish Ballads* " first of all made the
public take Lockhart seriously as a man of letters ".

They were Lockhart's most objective creation. Opinion
as to the merits of *Peter's Letters* was influenced by the feeling and prejudice of the reader ; but the *Ballads* could be

read with a purely literary pleasure ; and they still give enjoyment even to those who know nothing of their originals, and must take them on their own merits.

Lockhart's interest in Spanish literature began, as we have seen, in his Oxford days ; his intention now was to communicate that interest to English readers, and give them (to quote his own Introduction) : " some notion of that old Spanish minstrelsy which has been preserved in the different *Cancioneros* and *Romanceros* of the sixteenth century ".

His Introduction is a scholarly essay on the style, language and nature of the *Ballads*, and on their historical background in the conflict between Spaniards and Moors. Lockhart as a literary historian might have written a book or books of great and enduring value.

When one has no knowledge of Spanish it is impossible to discuss the *Ballads* as translations, in point of accuracy or reflected colour and form. But it is both possible and easy to enjoy them as poems ; and to discover in them all, or nearly all, of the qualities that make up Lockhart's greatness : his zest and virility, the sense of rhythm, of organic movement ; and the inner qualities of his hidden self— " the sense of tears in human things ".

The magic is apparent in *The Wandering Knight's Song* (a version of a sixteenth-century *Canciero*).

My ornaments are arms,
My pastime is in war,
My bed is cold upon the wold,
My lamp yon star :

My journeyings are long,
My slumbers short and broken ;
From hill to hill I wander still,
Kissing thy token.

I ride from land to land,
I sail from sea to sea ;
Some day more kind I fate may find,
Some night kiss thee !

The translation of the *Ballads* was not Lockhart's first return to the literature of Spain that had captivated him in first youth. In 1822 he published an edition, with notes, of Motteux' translation of *Don Quixote*. His Introduction is a brief promise of his supreme talent in literature, the biographical, and has some notable criticism.

He appreciated to the full the twofold glory of *Don Quixote* : its comic genius and its sublimity : " One of the greatest triumphs of his skill is the success with which he continually prevents us from confounding thc absurdities of the knight-errant with the generous aspirations of the cavalier. For the last, even in the midst of madness, we respect Don Quixote himself. We pity the delusion, we laugh at the situation, but we revere, in spite of every ludicrous accompaniment, and of every insane exertion, the noble spirit of the Castilian gentleman."

A final remark of Lockhart's on *Don Quixote* has an interest connected with his own writing. He points out that Cervantes was an old man when he wrote his great romance, and adds : " Nobody has ever written successful novels when young, but Smollet."—Lockhart, when young, wrote four novels ; none of them achieving much success, though all of them deserved some approbation, and one of them was a near-masterpiece. Had he returned to fiction in his maturity, would he have written a great Scottish novel ?

Chapter 6

THE HAPPY ENCOUNTER:
LOCKHART AND SOPHIA. 1817–1820

I

IT was always apparent that in Lockhart at least two
selves dwelt: the one " all energy and darting wit ",
the other " all kindness and tender domestic feeling ".
The latter was evident very early, in the boy stricken by
the death of a brother and sister, and was discovered by
his friends at Oxford, even when the devil-self was active
too. Edinburgh and *Maga* and the company he kept there
might have developed that devil-self to dangerous strength.
But while he was at his worst eminence, he met the man who
was so beneficently to influence him, and the woman who
was to be the half of his heart and life. Scott and Sophia
recognised his depths of kindness, his loyalty; and to
that benignant self Scott appealed in a moral crisis, and
won his cause. Sophia by her own tenderness and trust
guarded and nurtured that self, by her merriment too, and
mischievous humour that could meet Lockhart's wit. She
was very far from being a " child-wife " of insipid sweetness, being strong as well as gentle, wise as well as merry.
In fact, she recalls the old rhyme about Sunday's child as
being : " Fair and wise and good and gay." A gentle
simpleton would have bored Lockhart ; a woman who was
brilliant without kindness would have ruined him by en-
couraging his own pride of intellect. Sophia was exquisitely
balanced ; utterly right for him.

He must tell his own tale, at least in part. Under the
cloak of Dr. Morris, he described a visit to Abbotsford :

" This far-famed river . . . with the turrets of the great
poet's mansion immediately beyond it, and the bright foliage
of his young larches reflected half-way over in its mirror."

His portrait of Scott is memorable—of Scott the poet and
dreamer, as well as the humorous observer :

" The common language of his features expresses all

manner of discernment . . . He smiles frequently, and I never saw any smile which tells so eloquently the union of broad good humour with the keenest perception of the ridiculous." Then, when he chanced to quote one of the *Ballads* : " his eyes seemed no longer to glance, quick and gray, from beneath his impending brows, but were fixed in their expanded eyelids with a sober, solemn lustre. His mouth . . . instead of its usual language of mirth or benevolence or shrewdness was filled with a sad and pensive earnestness."

Lockhart introduces himself with admirable tact and courtesy. It has been well said that he slips into the room like a modest and welcome guest. He met Scott first in 1818 during the General Assembly of the Church of Scotland in May—always an occasion for encounters and introductions. They chanced to dine together with Mr. Home Drummond of Blair Drummond, and after the ladies had left the table, Lockhart sat by Scott. They talked of the former's tour in Germany and his meeting with Goethe.

Scott soon put some work in the young man's way, by declining for himself, on plea of over-work, the writing of the historical part of the *Edinburgh Annual Register,* for 1816, and suggesting to the publishers, Messrs. Ballantyne, that Lockhart might be given the task. The friendship was begun that was to prove so strong and deep and affectionate. Lockhart visited 39 Castle Street, and it is through his eyes we see the study there : the small back parlour with windows on the patch of garden that was all a town house could expect to have ; the walls " clothed with books . . . some of them rare and irreplaceable, in most meticulous order ". The volumes in use lived close to the desk on " some thing like a dumb waiter ". When one was borrowed, its place on the shelves was filled by a block of wood of the same size, bearing the name of the borrower : —a good device. The room was rich in the subdued colour of morocco bindings, " all stamped with his device of the portcullis and its motto : *Clausus tutus ero* (an anagram of his name, Walter Scott). There was only one picture,— a portrait of Claverhouse ; a Highland targe set round with dirks, for further ornament ; and a fox's tail mounted in silver to serve as book-duster. There was a book-ladder on top of which lay, most of the time, that notable personage Hinse of Hinsfeldt, " a venerable tom-cat, fat and sleek and no longer very locomotive ", looking with equanimity and tolerance upon Maida the hound on the hearthrug by Master's footstool. When Maida chose to leave the room he signified his intention by thumping with his paw on the door, opened at once by a well-trained master. Thereupon Hinse descended from his perch to lie on the rug by the footstool, " *vice* Maida absent on furlough ". Thus was domestic peace preserved. Scott used to talk to those companions, vowing they understood his every word.

At this point in the *Life*, Lockhart states his credo on the ethics of biography : " I never thought it lawful to keep a journal of what passes in private society, so that no one need expect from the sequel of this narrative any detailed record of Scott's familiar talk. What fragments have happened to adhere to a tolerably retentive memory, and may be put into black and white without wounding any feelings . . . I shall introduce as the occasion suggests . . . but I disclaim on the threshold anything more than this ; and I also wish to enter a protest, once for all, against the general fidelity of several literary gentlemen, who have kindly forwarded to me private lucubrations of theirs designed to Boswellize Scott."

There was, in Lockhart's view, a danger that readers unfamiliar with the background and the interlocutors, might misunderstand conversation thus reported, and misinterpret " sportive allusions into serious statement . . . In proportion as a man is witty and humorous there will always be about him and his, a widening maze and wilderness of cues and catchwords "—too easy for outsiders to misconstrue.

He has said of Scott's table-talk that, while it was generally praised for its " hearty good humour " and sense and sagacity, it was, by some superior persons, found lacking in brilliance. Lockhart admitted this criticism—and showed it to be no true depreciation. Scott's quality, in talk as in writing, was far beyond the merely brilliant and intellectual. Edinburgh society was, however, at this time and

for long afterwards, consciously and complacently intellectual ; the table-talk " such as might be transferred without
alteration to a professor's note-book or the pages of a
critical Review . . . It was the talk of a society to which
lawyers and lecturers had, for at least a hundred years,
given the tone "—for, since 1707, Edinburgh, though always
a Capital, was no longer the seat of a Court and nobility.
The absence of the Scots aristocracy (who were in the main
anglicised) meant a certain lack of urbanity, in social intercourse, and of that easy worldliness that does not argue
over-much, or seek to impress by a show of learning.   Scott
had more than a touch of this urbanity, warmed by humour
and humanity, and his great sanity of mind.

The first visit to Abbotsford followed an invitation sent
by Scott, in September 1818, to Lockhart, at Mr. Murray's,
Bellshill, Holytown, where he may have been on a visit,
or on circuit.   Scott wrote :

" Dear Sir,
" You were so good as to give me the hope of seeing you
here this vacation.   I am very desirous that, if possible,
you would come here with our friend Mr. Wilson, on
Thursday, 8th October, as Lord Melville is to spend a day
with me, and I shall be happy to introduce you to each
other.   Do not say me nay, but arrange matters so as . . .
to stay a day or two."

So Lockhart set forth upon his journey, like a hero in
a romance.   He was handsome enough for such a rôle,
and Sophia's first impression of him cannot have been
slight.   He came with a very considerable intellectual
reputation : which is not, admittedly, essential in a hero
of romance, but was a distinction in the eyes of Scott's
daughter.   She may have found him, at first, a little difficult ; for he was shy in company.   Even Scott, the easiest
of hosts, wished for him " a little more facility of manners ".

His background was beyond criticism ; that of a family
" of lang pedigree ", and he came of known folk.   " It is
not indifferent to me that his father represents the family
of Wicketshaw, very old cadets of that of Lee," Scott wrote,
on the wedding-day, to his cousin James Russell of Ashestiel.

This invitation was of no small honour and importance, to be the guest of Scott, and fellow-guest with Lord Melville, at that time First Lord of the Admiralty, and of almost regal authority in Scotland. Already, Scott's active benevolence and watchful wisdom were in play. Having welcomed J. G. L. and Wilson, he added : " I am glad you came to-day, for I thought it might be of use to you both, some time or other, to be known to my old school-fellow here, who is, and I hope will long continue to be, the great giver of good things at Parliament House. I trust you have had enough of certain pranks with your friend Ebony (Blackwood), and if so, Lord Melville will have too much sense to remember them."

Never were caution and reproof more gently administered. Lockhart's memory lingered, with wistful affection, upon this visit : " I now recall as if I had heard and seen them yesterday, the looks and words of eighteen years ago."— Thus he wrote, in his house in Regent's Park, re-creating those golden days at Abbotsford : when Scott chose his evening walk by the bowling-green near his coachman's house, where he could hear the man lead family worship ; when the household gathered round the dinner-table with much good talk ; and he himself looked on the moonlit waters of Tweed and Gala from the window of his turret room. He remembered the dancing in the new drawing-room thus festively handselled and warmed ; and breakfast next morning with Scott cutting himself slices from a brown loaf to eat with kippered salmon. In the afternoon they went to Melrose and Dryburgh, and returned to find : " Mrs. Scott and her daughters doing penance under the merciless curiosity of a couple of tourists . . . rich specimens . . . tall, lanky young men, both of them rigged out in new jackets and trousers of the Macgregor tartan "— both, as may be guessed, American. Scott contrived, with his inimitable dexterity and courtesy, at once to welcome and to evict them ; and to soothe his wife's wrath at having been asked—not only Scott's age but her own ! The scene was dissolved in laughter ; and at dinner, Scott was heard to murmer : " For a' that, the loons would hae been nane the waur o' their kail."

Americans, however, were not all impudent or unwelcome. One who was warmly bidden to come and who came with courtesy and deference was young Washington Irving, who had made for himself a pleasant popularity with his *Sketch Book* of travel in England. At Scott's request, Lockhart gave this book favourable notice in *Blackwood's* ; and years afterwards, he used Irving's own account of his visit, in the *Life*.

Young Irving met the family : " Sophia, then a fine girl about seventeen," her younger sister Anne, and her brothers Walter and Charles, of whom the latter acted as guide to Melrose. In the afternoon, Scott took his guest walking on the hills with the dogs, where they were met by Sophia and Anne, free from the schoolroom, who came " bounding lightly like young fawns, their dresses fluttering in the pure summer breeze. . . . They joined us with countenances full of health and glee. Sophia the elder was the most lively and joyous, having much of her father's varied spirit in conversation, and seeming to catch excitement from his words and looks."

Charlotte Sophia (to give her her full name) was born on 24th October, 1799 ; Charlotte for her mamma, Sophia from an old family friend, Mrs. Dumergue who was also her godmother. She was baptised into the Scots Episcopal Church by the Rev. Daniel Sandford of St. John's Church, Edinburgh, later Bishop of Edinburgh. Her other godmother was Scott's own mother, her godfather the Marquis of Downshire, Mrs. Scott's guardian. Dr. Sandford baptised also Walter, who was born in 1801, and Anne, born in 1803, and given in the kindly old Scots fashion the name of her paternal grandmother Anne Rutherford. Charles, the youngest, born in 1805, on Christmas Eve was, for some reason, made a Presbyterian babe, being baptised by the Rev. John Thomson, the artist-minister of Duddingston. Scott had long shown allegiance as an adherent, if not a confirmed, communicant member, of the ancient and suffering Episcopal Church of Scotland, the Faithful Remnant, the " shadow of a shade " as he called it by the mouth of Pleydel. Whether or not he himself was confirmed, his daughters received that sacramental rite ; Sophia just before her marriage. Mrs. Scott, though of French birth, had been baptised and brought up as an Anglican.

Lockhart has described the family atmosphere of the house in Castle Street—doubtless from Sophia's memories ; where the children had free access to the study, and papa was never a remote or formidable figure. He was comrade and playfellow as well as loving and beloved father, watchful and wise. One has indeed an impression, and more than an impression, that he was much more deeply in the confidence of his children than their mother. Scott was never a growling genius, and youthful chatter did not appear to check his inspiration. Sophia and Anne grew up, like Bridget Elia, in a profusion of books ; encouraged to read, trained to listen, never forbidden to ask questions. Lockhart recorded that Scott " had a horror of boarding-schools, never allowing his girls to learn anything out of his own house, and chose their governess Miss Millar . . . with a greater regard to her kind good temper and excellent moral and religious principles, than to the measure of her attainments in what are called fashionable accomplishments ". If " the young curiosity was excited, the intellect, by whatever springs of interest, was set in motion ", then he was well satisfied. In one matter he shared his son-in-law's prejudice : " He detested and despised the whole generation of modern children's books in which the attempt is made to convey accurate notions of scientific minutiae."

The Scott girls were nurtured on literature, their minds and imaginations stored with poetry and legends ; their memories trained by the learning and recitation of verse. They listened (most blessed of bairns) to their father's tales of Scotland's past, except on Sunday. Scott in renouncing Presbyterian gloom in the matter of Sunday observance retained a due reverence for the day of worship ; and on Sunday he told his children stories from the Bible. When he was a grandfather, he wrote down his stories from Scottish history for small Johnny Lockhart ; but, to our great loss, did not so recall the stories from Scripture that he told his own bairns.

In an age when children were severely disciplined the young Scotts enjoyed a golden age of liberty. Their father had few rules, and these sound. Lockhart has told us that, like the ancient Persians, he insisted on the virtues of truthfulness and courage, that are so closely intertwined. " Without courage there cannot be truth, and without truth there can be no other virtue." Courage could be shown in good horsemanship, and he delighted in his children's fearlessness and good hands, especially Sophia's. " As soon as his eldest girl could sit a pony, she was made the regular attendant of his mountain rides."

One fact that is presented, both explicitly and implicitly, is that in the Scott family papa came first. With all respect to Lady Scott who, in her youth, had charm, and who was, within her limits, a devoted wife and mother, this was a " second-best " marriage for Scott ; but it gave him four children all responsive in trust and affection, none of them unworthy, even if none inherited his full mind. Of his sons, Walter the soldier was to show the soldierly virtues of loyalty and sense of duty, warmed by a great deal of his father's benignity ; Charles had a delicious quiet humour, of the most endearing kind, and given health and length of life might well have distinguished himself in at least some minor way of literature. Of Anne too this may be said, with even more probability. She had wit and sparkle, a liveliness of mind that (like Lockhart's) might have had an edge to it ; in some ways, she and her brother-in-law were close akin. Had she lived even a decade beyond her thirtieth year she might have turned her adroit pen to writing domestic novels, or at least sketches. Her letters give promise of some such fulfilment. But Sophia appeared to those who knew them to have most of her father's mind and heart and spirit. His magnanimity appeared again in her, and her virtues were intellectual as well as moral. She may have lacked the creative mind (though how much may have been suppressed by domestic cares and joys so closely interwoven, and by physical delicacy it is difficult to estimate) ; but the faculties of appreciation and criticism were well developed. She was alive in mind ; and she was the loved and responsive companion of two great minds, in her father and her husband.

Sophia's girlhood may be seen in occasional glimpses

in the *Life* ; and more directly in that delightful volume of *Family Letters* which she and Anne wrote to their governess Miss Millar when that worthy and much-valued lady left them, at the end of schoolroom days, for a new series of situations—for she was not easily settled or satisfied. But after Castle Street it must have been hard to discover a schoolroom where she could be completely happy.

In one early letter (in 1817) Sophia has given a report of the progress of Abbotsford : " They are building the last story and it looks beautiful." In other letters we hear of papa's having bought more land so that the estate now extends to the Eildons ; and of the well-known painting by Wilkie : " We are all drawn in character, Anne and I as two milkmaids with pails upon our heads, Papa sitting, and Captain Ferguson standing, looking for all the world like an old poacher who understands his trade."

The two girls had at least one fashionable accomplishment : they played the harp : " Papa has got us a most delightful new harp from London, the other day. It, and the stand for the books, cost £119, so you may think that it is a very handsome thing " ; then a scrap of gossip : " We had Lady Byron for a day at Abbotsford. She is very pretty and very melancholy." (Scott could achieve what was almost impossible—friendship and sympathy with both partners in that amazing and disastrous marriage.)

These letters are, for the most part, cheerful in their news and lively in their gossip, but the onset of Scott's malady makes sad reading in one—in 1819. He was suffering from the excruciating cramp of the stomach and from jaundice : " One attack remained unmoved for thirty-six hours during all which he was not five minutes free from the most dreadful agony." The worst, however, was over, and cheerfulness breaks in with the news that Walter is likely to pass into the army, and that Charles is doing well at the Royal High School. There was plenty of gaiety for Sophia and Anne :

" We had so many invitations that, if we had accepted a quarter of them we might have been at two or three places a night, but we kept on the side of moderation. Anne is grown up a very handsome girl and is much admired. She is improved very much upon the harp, indeed Mr. Pole says that if she would practise she would be one of the best players in town "—but Anne, the " lively, rattling girl " as Lockhart called her, did not always choose to practise. Anne had great charm ; only a little marred by a turn for satire (for which her father reproached her) and for a little affectation. She was once overheard saying to Lady Anne Scott, daughter of the Duke of Buccleuch : " I do wish I were Lady Anne too—it is so much prettier than Miss." This is the sort of indiscretion that brothers and sisters can and will deal with, and thereafter she was nicknamed " Lady Anne".

Sophia's account of her father's suffering left untold the tale of her own fortitude and tenderness ; but Scott has recorded that in her honour ; writing, afterwards, to the Duke of Buccleuch that : " Poor Sophia was alone with me for some time, and managed a half-distracted pack of servants with spirit and sense and presence of mind far beyond her years." Hers was the rare kind of strength that can forget personal fear and anxiety in active compassion : " Pardon the side compliment ", Scott went on, " to Your Grace's little Jacobite to whom you have always been so kind." The eldest in a family, if a girl, is usually disposed to " mother " or manage her juniors and sometimes her parents too ; and Charles especially had a trusting affection for " Fia " as he called her. But she was far from being a solemn little ray of sunshine, of the type so justly disliked in certain types of moral books. There was enough fun and mischief—even of gentle malice in her to give salt and savour to her sweetness. She could gently mock Walter when he was gazetted as Cornet in the Hussars and, as it were, assumed charge of the British Army : " He is too happy, and the only thing that is to be feared is his dying of pride and conceit before he joins "—but she adds : " We shall miss him very much," and in a later letter reports his writing " most capital letters " from his barracks in Cork.

In one letter Sophia mentions the new *Tales of My Landlord* : " Are they not excellent ? "—and refers to another recent publication : *Peter's Letters to His Kinsfolk* as " one of the most clever, and at the same time rather severe books that has been written for years. This is Papa's opinion "—

and probably her own. It is the first hint of interest in the clever and severe young author.

The friendly beasts appear in her letters as well as the human members of the household : as, the new pony Queen Mab, presented by papa. There is a brief obituary : " You will be sorry to hear that poor old Lady Wallace died the other day to the distress of the whole family " : her late ladyship being the old pony. One letter apologises for Sophia's having neglected her Italian studies : " At present they are quite at a stop, and although with the new Year (1820) I made the customary good resolutions, still the new leaf remains to turn." Then comes the announcement that could well explain a certain neglect of studies :

" I wish to be the first to tell you that I have at last made up my mind to marry Mr. Lockhart. Anything that I may say to prepossess you in his favour in the present state of my feeling towards him might well appear to you overdrawn, but Papa has the highest opinion of him, and his opinion is worth all the world to me." Sophia was wholeheartedly in love, but was not without a touch of feminine vanity : " That I might have made a much higher marriage in point of rank and wealth I have little doubt but I am not one who can be persuaded that happiness can depend upon these two alone." Perhaps Sophia was—a very little—her mother's daughter as well as her father's ; perhaps she was reflecting maternal opinion. Lady Scott's first comment, on being asked for approval of the marriage, may have been in effect : " I suppose it is well enough, but you might have done better for yourself my dear, and brought a title into the family." Lockhart's own account of his engagement is brief and reticent. He wore his heart in fetterlock, *coram publico* : " About the middle of February (1820)—it having been ere that time arranged that I should marry his eldest daughter in the course of the spring—I accompanied him and part of his family on one of their flying visits to Abbotsford, with which he often indulged himself on a Saturday during term."—On these Saturday mornings Scott would appear as usual in Court, in wig and gown, but wearing under the latter, instead of his sober and urban black, a country coat of green.

Scott told his son Walter—on 17th January : " Mr. Lockhart has made his formal visits to Mama, and so forth. I think Mama would have liked a little more stile [*sic*] but she has no sort of objection to the affair. Indeed, the principal persons being pleased, I do not see there is much to be said, as they will begin with a competence, and with prudence may end with wealth."

During their engagement there was an interchange of letters between Sophia and her dear Mr. Lockhart (as she continued to call him—agreeing with Emma in her use of " Mr. Knightley "). Sophia's first letter to her love (happily preserved at Abbotsford) is very proper ; almost prim if we (and Lockhart) did not know Sophia.

" Dear Sir," she wrote, sitting at her desk in the drawing-room of 39 Castle Street, " Although I fear I am doing very very wrong in writing to you without Papa's knowledge, yet after what passed to-day I cannot be happy till I do it. Believe me, we do not know each other sufficiently to have any reasonable prospect of happiness. Though my name is Sophia Scott I know well that I am not in the least clever, and fear, greatly fear that you give me credit for talent and information beyond what I possess. When I told Papa of your letter to me at Abbotsford it went no further than himself, so neither Mamma, brothers or sisters know anything of it. That Papa had no serious objection I firmly believe, but only thought (and you must say with reason) that we were about to take a step, one of the most important of our lives, without considering sufficiently whether our different tempers and dispositions could make us happy through life. And now, Mr. Lockhart, for God's sake if you love me do not be so unhappy ; it makes me quite wretched to think that you are so, and to feel that I, who would do anything for your peace of mind, am the cause. Do not answer this, as I know that any further correspondence of this kind, unknown to Papa, would be very wrong, and believe me to remain yours very sincerely, Charlotte Sophia Scott."

These letters are undated, but they are not difficult to arrange in order. Sophia's " keep away, come closer " bidding was read by Lockhart as he wanted to read it, and as Sophia hoped he would read it. The following letters were written with full approval of Papa and Mamma ; Lockhart had been accepted by them as well as by Sophia, and there was no longer the faintest shadow of impropriety in her addressing him. But he remained : " Dear Mr. Lockhart." Only after marriage did he become " Dear " or " Dearest John " or, often, " Lockhart ".

Lockhart's first love-letter is, as we should expect, controlled in expression—but there is no lack of that deep and loyal tenderness and gratitude that made the foundation of a singularly happy marriage. All the good in him, his steadfastness, his entire affection, were given to her :

" My dear Sophia,
" Charles has just been dining with me, and as he says the packet I sent yesterday has not yet been sent, I cannot resist the temptation of talking with you on paper one moment more. And yet I have nothing to say except how much I am obliged by your kind letter which went to Glasgow and only came to me here this morning. Everything you say is exactly what I could have wished to hear, and I trust Mama's plans will all be easily matured, after a moment's conversation on Friday evening. I feel myself in a strange—a very strange state at present, and can scarcely pretend to be quite myself. When I look back a few months and compare what I am now with what I was then, how is it possible that my heart should not overflow with tenderness. My dearest Sophia you have put great trust in me. God grant I may never cost you a minute's pain in return for all your kindness. If I can put any faith in my knowledge of myself, you are sure of always possessing whatever happiness my love can give you. I wish I had other things to lay at your feet—but I have no fear for my part—all will be very well, and we shall be very happy. Most affectionately yours, John Gibson Lockhart."

All was indeed very well, and they were very happy.

This letter may have been in reply to one from Sophia which told of her being obliged to leave town for Abbotsford, with Mamma ; " It is very provoking to be obliged to go without seeing you "—but they would all be in town again on Friday when, she hoped, Lockhart would come to see them. In another note we hear of Mamma's plans and of Papa's being in London ; " In the first part of his letter to me he complains very much of not having heard from me, but in Mamma's he says that he is very sorry that he has done so, as he has that moment received two long letters from me which gave great satisfaction . . . He went to the theatre last Saturday and was very much amused. Mrs. Siddons acts so very well in *The Jealous Wife*." There was play-going in Edinburgh too : " Mr. Raymond and I were the best of friends possible during the whole evening. (You had better return quickly.) He has persuaded Mamma to take a box for his play, and offers to delay bringing it out till her return from the country, as she thought that might prevent her being present the first night. Mamma talks and intends going to Abbotsford on Saturday or Sunday."

Lockhart would appear to be out of Edinburgh—probably travelling on circuit, or perhaps on his Yeomanry duty, for Sophia adds : " It is so long since we have seen you, and I trust that you now feel and look quite strong again." He had been unwell—and there had been kind and anxious little notes :

" Captain Lockhart [J. G. L.'s younger brother] gave but an indifferent account of you this morning, and by your not being out in the forenoon I fear you are not so well." (The distinction between " morning " and " forenoon " is clear to a Scot ; the former is the earlier.)

The theatre plan matured : " Mamma has taken a box for tonight, and likewise one for tomorrow night, and as her Ladyship purposes to remain till the curtain drops both nights, I think we shall both have enough of Liston."

The prettiest of all Sophia's letters conveys—under a veil of demure discretion, a clear picture of a girl in love—walking round and round the hill, looking from under her bonnet for a sight of her sweetheart :

" I am afraid that I cannot promise to be at home for certain tomorrow forenoon, as I must go to chapel in the forenoon with Anne, and afterwards with Mamma, unless the day should be bad, but I hope you will come to us in the evening. We are to be quite alone. I cannot think how we missed seeing you today, as Anne, Miss Clephane and myself walked three times round the Calton Hill "— with never a glimpse of J. G. L. One hopes that no intrusive visitor dropped in that Sunday evening and that Mamma, Anne and Charles withdrew discreetly to the back drawing-room, leaving Sophia and Lockhart alone ; sitting, perhaps on the graceful Empire sofa, in its grey-green covering, that now stands in the Upper Hall of the Signet Library.

Sophia was a good girl to go to church twice : the chapel was probably St. George's (now St. Paul's and St. George's where Scott's pew can be seen). It may be that Lockhart also felt devout that Sunday.

Theirs was not a long engagement, and with frequent meetings there was not much need for letter-writing. But in April 1820, only a week or two before the marriage, Lockhart had to go on service, as a Yeoman, in Glasgow and district. There had been a call-up of Regulars and Yeomanry alike to deal with the serious Rising, in the West of Scotland, by the Radicals ; which came very near being revolution.

" I take up my pen now ", wrote Lockhart from Glasgow, " only because it is very uncertain whether I may have another opportunity. Here we are—excessively dull and wearisome, never knowing where or what we are to be about an hour hence . . . I have never been allowed to go as far as Germiston . . . I saw Violet, however, for a moment yesterday . . . There seems now to be no doubt that there had been a serious and well-arranged plan on Monday last. On Wednesday evening, the greater part of the roads leading from Glasgow were in the hands of the Radicals, and various places of encampment in the neighbourhood were resorted to by the weavers from the villages. The drum was beat, such was their audacity, within a mile of the Barracks. But on the whole, the arrival of so many broad-backed Yeomen, etc., had the effect of chilling the ardour of all but the very hottest . . . and the spirit of all soon began to subside. In short, they returned home, dispirited, and many of them were immediately arrested. Indeed the jails are all full now . . . The numerous

72

executions which must occur in a very few weeks may be expected to produce a salutary effect, but meantime, till they are over, there is no prospect of entire tranquillity. I think it is likely we shall not be home till the end of the week, but we are all kept in total darkness—for mystery is in all professions, but I see it is the very essence of the military . . . I wish you would write to me, my dear Sophia . . . Now do—you can't think how I should be refreshed with a few lines here, for upon my soul I am heartily sick of everything. I wrote Papa t'other day when I wrote you, and am writing Mr. Croker to-day . . . Do write to me, my dearest."

Sophia did write, and he replied with thanks for her letter " and all your kindness ", telling her of his wretchedness in being kept from her. " There is so much that I should have spoken about to you." He was living in Great King Street, in Edinburgh, and was to bring her there as his wife, and was anxious about probable deficiencies of furnishing and arrangements : she must " have the goodness to take the trouble of supplying your own wants afterwards. I am so ignorant on these matters that I really don't know what should be in the house where a lady is, but I rely on Violet's word who assures me that there is all that is necessary for a little time at least. So, my dearest Sophia, do just put up with things, and we shall lay our heads together and remedy all evils and wants. I am sadly vexed, however, that Lady Scott should talk of going to Abbotsford so soon and for so long a time."—Could she not postpone this departure until after his return to Edinburgh ?— " Nothing is more plaguesome than the way I am compelled to spend my time here, nothing to do but never knowing whither I might be sent . . . But I daresay I feel all this a thousand times worse now than I should have done at any other time. My thoughts are always with you." Lockhart's experience is curiously modern ; there have been innumerable bridegrooms in recent years who could return from service only on the eve of the wedding day. It was a grim experience, this quelling of the rising. The country was in no happy state. Labour conditions were bad, the condition of the poor was piteous ; the Throne was regarded with very lukewarm loyalty, and Britain was still suffering, five years after Waterloo, from the results of the long war with France. In those days when a man might be hanged for sheep-stealing or lesser theft, there was no question as to the punishment for revolt. The leaders were regarded as traitors, and suffered the last penalty. It may well be that Lockhart's brief but poignant experience of this rising stiffened him in his Tory opinions.

Presently, however, he was back in his house in Great King Street, writing to Sophia ; too late to see her, for Lady Scott had persisted in her plan of going to Abbotsford. Need she ? One has the impression of placid selfishness ; her chosen routine must continue. And there is singularly little reference to her in Sophia's letters ; nothing about Mamma's suggestions or advice. Even in the matter of the new home, it would seem to be Violet, Lockhart's young and pretty and cherished sister, whose help is sought.

Lockhart wrote, then about his love's absence : " I don't remember being so downcast for a while—however, as Baillie Jarvie hath it, there's a braw time coming. On Friday we meet, my dearest, I trust to part no more. But I know you don't like speeches and you will know I can't make them." This was a true eve-of-the-wedding letter with plans for the honeymoon—to be spent in Perth, Crieff and Stirling and then at the Lockhart country-house, Germiston, near Glasgow . . . The Yeomanry campaign was over :

" We had a hard ride or two at night and in rain, and I wanted sleep a good deal, but I think I came into Edinburgh with a good deal more beef on my bones than I carried with me, and am as well as possible and almost as happy as I could wish to be."

Very soon, about a fortnight later, he was quite as happy as he could wish to be, as happy as mortal life could permit.

II

Meanwhile, Papa in London was writing to and about the young couple. To Morritt, the Squire of Rokeby, one of his own closest friends, and in years to come of Sophia and Lockhart and of their children also, he wrote : " Sophia's marriage promises happiness as much as our dimness of sight enables us to guess. Lockhart is a very handsome young man and remarkably clever, well disposed and well principled . . . To me, as it seems neither of my sons have a strong literary turn, the society of a son-in-law possessed of learning and talent must be a very great acquisition . . . All I fear on Lockhart's part is a certain rashness which I trust has been the effects of youth and high spirits, joined to lack of good advice, as he seems perfectly good-humoured and very docile. So I trust your little friend Sophia has a very fair chance of such happiness as this motley world can afford."

His letters to Lockhart himself, though concerned primarily with Wilson, contrived indirectly to give his future son-in-law the good advice he needed. Scott was an expert in administering a wholesome powder smothered in jam ; or in persuading one patient to swallow his medicine *pour encourager les autres*. Wilson was at this time a candidate for the Chair of Moral Philosophy in Edinburgh University, a post for which he was eminently unfitted, and to which he was appointed, on political grounds, and after much shameless " lobbying " by Scott and others. Scott's part in it at least proves (which is hardly necessary) that he had a kind heart.

Scott approached Lord Melville on Wilson's behalf, and found him " extremely well disposed to be friendly. He asked, between joke and earnest, whether our friend would be able to restrain his gaiety within the bounds of a teacher of ethics. I said that Wilson had his levities like all of us, but that I was sure they must have been most calumniously magnified by rumour, if they had reached his ears in any shape more discreditable than as the levities of a man of genius."

" Levities " may appear to us something of a euphemism for Wilson's brutalities in *Maga*. But Wilson must look to his own credit and that of his friends, must control his irascibility, " leave off sack and live cleanly as a gentleman ought ". Implicitly Scott bade Lockhart : Take this counsel to your own heart.

There was also the practical advice that the candidate must make friends of the Mammon of unrighteousness in the persons of the Town Council (the phrase being not Scott's but the author's; but Scott doubtless appreciated that particular parable). Among the baillies was a prosperous grocer, known as Palladio Johnston from his predilection in architecture. He had been a schoolfellow of Scott's, and naturally enjoyed Lady Scott's custom; so: " If my wife canvasses him, she may do some good on the man of cheese."

It may appear an odd and not altogether praiseworthy mode of electing a Professor, especially to the Chair of Ethics; but it was successful. Wilson was appointed, and became famous for the eloquence and fervour of his discourses.

From London, Scott wrote to " Lady Scott of Abbotsford to be " at the end of March saying that he hoped to be home again, with his new honours (the baronetcy) bright upon him, by the end of April and that the wedding might safely be fixed for 28th or 29th April. It was to take place in the Castle Street house—in the old Scots fashion that rarely had weddings celebrated in church : " All this you will have to settle without my wise head, but I shall be terribly critical, so see you do all right."

Finally he wrote to Sophia herself, just before leaving for home, six days before the wedding—that he was bringing her gifts of jewellery from various friends, enough to make her " quite an Indian princess "—so many that instead of adding to them, he proposed sending her a cheque for £50— " for pocket-money etc. which you will find convenient in your new situation . . . This will keep you always easy, and teach you the comfort of having a few guineas at your own command."

It was like Scott to be so understanding. Sophia would not have the embarrassment of having to ask her newly married husband for small sums at once. There was news also of " a certain veil of Flanders lace floating in the wind for a certain occasion, from a certain godmother, but that is more than a dead secret "—the only detail we have of Sophia's wedding-dress. The letter ends with a reference to her and Anne's Confirmation.

SOPHIA SCOTT (AFTERWARDS MRS. LOCKHART)
From a portrait by W. Nicholson, R.S.A.

After the wedding Scott wrote to Lady Abercorn : " My house seems lonely to me since she left us, but that is a natural feeling that will soon wear off. I have every reason to think I have consulted her happiness in the match, as became the father of a most attached and dutiful daughter who never in her life gave me five minutes' vexation." She was—chief of his dearly-loved children, his *dimidium cordis*. He added complacently : " Lockhart being a very handsome man, they make rather a pretty couple, and as they marry for love and with very fair prospects in other respects, their present lot seems to be enviable . . . I suppose by-and-bye some kind suitor will carry off my black-eyed maid, and then the old folk will be lonely enough."

The wedding took place on 29th April 1820 ; the formal announcement in *The Scots Magazine* for May described the bride as " eldest daughter of Sir Walter Scott of Abbotsford, Bart." We must wish that someone, Lady Scott or Anne, had written a detailed description in a letter, of what the bride wore, and how she looked and how it all went off. It was perhaps a little like Emma's wedding to Mr. Knightley : " Very little white satin, very few lace veils "— but at least the bride had her lace veil ; and like that imagined wedding this real one resulted in complete happiness for the couple.

As to looks, Sophia in her portraits appears sweet of face, animated and intelligent, if not, strictly speaking, beautiful. The miniature in the National Portrait Gallery of Scotland gives her the charming colouring (not uncommon in Scotland) of dark hair with blue eyes and a clear, fair complexion and of somewhat a delicate look. Family tradition describes her as fair, in contrast with " the black-eyed maid " Anne. She was, physically and mentally, very much her father's daughter, and, it is said, transmitted a look of him, especially in the shape of head and forehead, to her daughter Charlotte.

The young couple went off on honeymoon, and at the end of this brief tour came to visit Lockhart's parents at Germiston, near Glasgow : an old estate that had once been part of the endowment of the Archbishop of Glasgow. After the Reformation it passed into lay ownership, and came, eventually in 1690, into that of Robert Dinwiddie, one of Glasgow's wealthy merchants. The Dinwiddies were an important family among the Glasgow gentry in the eighteenth century that had dealings with America ; and one of them was Lieutenant Governor of Virginia before the War of Independence. He is mentioned in Thackeray's novel, *The Virginians*. The last Dinwiddie laird of Germiston was Robert, son of Laurence, who died in 1819, and was succeeded by his cousin, William Lockhart ; son of Dr. Lockhart by his first wife, Elizabeth Dinwiddie, sister of Laurence. She brought these two names—Laurence and Robert—into the Lockhart family. William had, indeed, been born at Germiston—in 1789. Another Laurence— though with no Dinwiddie blood in him—succeeded William ; for this half-brother, junior to him and to John, was his heir when he died in 1856.

The house was about two miles from Glasgow Cross, then the centre of the city ; a distance which in 1820 made it suburban if not altogether rural. It is pictured in *Old Country Houses in Glasgow* as a large, square two-storied building pleasantly proportioned, with a pillared door ; only just a small mansion rather than a large villa ; surrounded by lawns and beyond these, no doubt by fields and plantations of trees, well secluded from the highway. It looks comfortable and homely—and it proved so for Lockhart and Sophia not only on their wedding visit but many times afterwards. The Lockharts adopted their new daughter with as much affection as Scott showed his new son, and she in turn became a kind elder sister to Violet and the younger boys.

Chapter 7

FAMILY LIFE

I. PRELUDE ABOUT ANNE

ANNE, the black-eyed maid, was now the daughter at home, and she moves into the foreground of the Lockhart family picture as well as that of Abbotsford and Castle Street. With no sister at hand, she must write letters to impart gossip and confidences. Miss Miller had the benefit !

The letters give news of the family : Charles had left school and gone as pupil to Lockhart's old friend, " Taffy " Williams in Wales, to be sadly missed by Anne, now the only young thing left at home. Life was, however, busy and varied, with a stream of visitors coming to Abbotsford, including Joanna Baillie whom Anne greatly liked :

" No one would ever guess by her behaviour that she was an authoress " (which is meant as a compliment to Miss Baillie's good sense and good manners, authoresses being generally regarded as freaks if not nuisances). Anne was not unlike her new brother-in-law, with a touch of satire in her wit : as when she referred to Walter having met in Dublin a former acquaintance : " still, though much against her will, a blooming virgin ".

Her letters tell of gaieties in Edinburgh and comparatively quiet weeks on Tweedside ; the four or five years following Sophia's marriage were a brief golden age in the chronicles of both the Scott and the Lockhart households— before Scott's financial disaster and the collapse of Lady Scott's health.

The latent Jane Austen in Anne often holds the pen : as in her description, in more than one letter, of two sisters, Mrs. Ross and Miss Agnes Hume, who would appear to have been afflicted, at one time, with severe piety : Mrs. Ross, Anne reported, had " recovered from her fit of goodness ", while Agnes " last time I saw her was in blue satin with a flower in her hair, and had even some thoughts of

79

going to the Bachelors' Ball ". The lapse continued :
" Agnes is no longer holy and wears a white silk bonnet "—
which certainly does not betoken unworldly thoughts ;
while Mrs. Ross " has so many children she really has not
time to be good ". This would bear out the theory that
excessive goodness is found only in spinsters and childless
widows. The final touch to the portrait of Agnes is in two
perfect sentences—worthy of Jane Austen :

" Agnes is no longer good. She dresses in white satin,
and goes to Balls."

Gossip and surmise must have been active concerning so
attractive a girl as Anne. But there is little or no hint of
any true romance,—in Anne's own letters, or her father's,
or Sophia's. She had so brief a girlhood. After 1825—
when she was only twenty-two—the clouds began to gather.
From 1826 until her father's death in 1832 she was the
devoted daughter, nurse and companion ; her gaiety and
spirit not wholly quenched until near the end, but youth
gone.

In these few bright years, however, she was happy as
daughter and sister and aunt.

She is her sweetest in her new part of aunt. She wrote
frequent reports of the small John Hugh, of his recovery
from teething troubles, his progress in health and beauty
as he grew out of his fragile babyhood, and gave promise
of what was to be so sadly unfulfilled—a radiant childhood :

" He is, of course, a great beauty," wrote Aunt Anne,
" and as great a wit. He makes Lockhart very idle for he
does nothing but play with him all day, and teach him all
sorts of absurd speeches."

Little Johnny's birth had been announced to Miss Millar
by Sophia herself : " In spite of all my bad health before,
I think you would say that my little boy is as pretty a
baby as you ever saw, and what is still better, he is very
healthy."

He—John Hugh Lockhart—was born in the house in
Great King Street, on 14th February 1821 ; after his
christening he was to be taken to Germiston—and be
brought back to the new house that Lockhart had taken

in Northumberland Street. Never was child more dearly loved ; he gave Scott a title he prized even above his baronetcy—that of Grandfather.

II. LOCKHART, SOPHIA AND JOHNNY

Scott was again in London at the time of Johnny's birth, and wrote to Lockhart with immense thankfulness—for Sophia had indeed suffered grievously. Her pregnancy had been complicated by bouts of the malady which she, unhappily, inherited from her father—cramp of the stomach. " I am inexpressibly relieved on account of my dearest Sophia," wrote Scott . . . " I trust in God her recovery will be as perfect as her confinement has been tedious . . . Pray contrive amongst you to let me hear from you daily . . . and tell me if the boy that makes me grandsire is dark or fair, and above all if he can gripe hard as a Scott should."

To Sophia he wrote with heart overflowing with tenderness : " You are now, my dearest girl, beginning a new course of pleasures, anxieties and duties, and the best I can wish for you is that your little boy may prove the same dutiful and affectionate child you have always been to me, and that God may give him a sound and healthy mind with a good constitution of body—the greatest blessings which this earth can bestow . . . Give your bantling a kiss extraordinary for grandpapa." He added characteristically : " I hope Mungo approves of the child, for that is a serious point." Mungo was the Lockharts' dog ; they were continuing the tradition of a dog on the hearth ; and it was indeed very important that the old dog should like the new baby. Scott gossiped about animals in the same genial way he did about human friends ; and he told Sophia now that " there are no dogs in the hotel where I lodge, but a tolerably conversable cat who eats a mess of cream with me in the morning ". As he often did, he has here achieved, without effort, the exact word. For a cat to be " tolerably conversable " is all that any reasonable human can ask. Scott who " spoke to a'body as if they were his blude relations " could make even the most aloof of cats conversable, to say nothing of the emollient powers of cream.

In another letter he wrote : " I expect by your description quite a cherubim of a grandchild, though not, I hope, representing those who, we are told in the prayer-book, eternally do cry."

The baby had the dark Lockhart eyes : " I suppose, as the song says, he got them from his daddy."

Scott's anxiety was alleviated, but he thought that no one could take such good care of Sophia as he could, so he wrote bidding Lockhart : " try to amuse her and get her to go out often in the carriage ". She was his " little lady and love " and he would " take your attendance as very kind "—hardly a necessary injunction to the most devoted of husbands, but kind papas are like that.

This spring of 1821 was a climax both of joy and of wretchedness for Lockhart. On the domestic side there was this new bliss ; on the other, where his own darker self was active, a misery that was not without shame. The devil in him may have been making a last desperate struggle for mastery.

He was in serious trouble, with a malignant adversary but he was not guiltless. Scott told the matter in a letter to his brother Thomas :

" You would like Lockhart if you knew him ; he is very handsome, full of spirit and fire, both of genius and temper . . . He has got into an awkward scrape which notwithstanding all his efforts has had a termination very unpleasant to his feelings. Being abused, by name and in print, on his supposed connexion with *Blackwood's Magazine*, he came up to town to punish a person of the name of Scott, author of the said abuse . . . The fellow, being absolute dunghill, would do nothing but shufle [*sic*]. Lockhart remained in town several days after having posted him publicly, went to Court, and so forth, and heard nothing of him. But when Lockhart had returned to Edinburgh, Scott began again to clap his wings, and finding that he was scouted in society, he fastened a sleeveless quarrel upon Christie,

a young man who had carried him Lockhart's message . . .
Scott was that dangerous animal a coward made desperate,
and they met, when Christie shot him through the body.
He is still very ill, and it is matter of deep affliction to
Lockhart whose friend was thus, though most unwittingly,
placed in the predicament of being a principal in his
quarrel."

It is a miserable story from which only one man emerges
with clean hands, and that is the man who fired the shot—
Christie, Lockhart's *fidus Achates*, who was, by the point of
honour, forced to fight. The affair began when this John
Scott wrote and published (in *The London Magazine*) three
articles attacking, virulently, *Blackwood's Magazine* in general
and Lockhart in particular ; he accused J. G. L. of being
Editor of *Blackwood's*, of forging testimonials to his own
publication, and of having written the scurrilous reviews
of Coleridge. He refused to believe Lockhart's denial of
these charges. Christie, with another loyal friend, James
Traill, called on Scott who demanded an explanation from
Lockhart. This was refused. Scott was the offender,
having published the attack ; apology and explanation
were due from him—but were refused. Lockhart, believing that Scott would give satisfaction in a duel came to
London, and carried on negotiations through Christie.
Scott again demanded from Lockhart an assurance that he
derived no money from the sale of *Blackwood's* ; this Lockhart refused to give—and Scott, as the aggressor, had no
right to ask. Lockhart wrote to him, calling him liar and
coward—terms that were almost bound to lead to a chal-
lenge—but none followed. Then Lockhart published a
statement declaring that although he was a contributor to
Blackwood's he was not the editor, and derived no salary
from any share in the management. By some mishap the
printed copy sent to Scott lacked this particular and definite
assertion. Scott fastened on the discrepancy, was answered
by Christie, and the outcome of this final interchange was
a duel, provoked by Scott, between him and Christie.
Lockhart, meanwhile, despairing of any issue, had returned
to Edinburgh. It has not been pointed out so far that he
had a compelling reason for going home. His wife was

very near her time, and her pregnancy had been very difficult. There was cause for anxiety, even for fear.

The letters of that month of February are poignantly interesting, especially those of Sir Walter Scott ; for often, in one letter, appear references both to the joy and the misery of the moment, the birth of the baby, and the duel.

These letters of Sir Walter's make sad reading ; whatever John Scott might be, even if utterly unjustified in his conduct (and there must be two sides to every such case), the tragic ending of the story makes the contemptuous references deplorable, and utterly unworthy of the most magnanimous of men. But Sir Walter was sometimes, if very rarely, a good hater. He wrote to his son Walter about this " foolish scrape with a blackguard who . . . blustered when at a distance " but " sat down under the handsome appellations of scoundrel and liar ".

Sir Walter's visit to London at this time (caused by the business affairs of Lady Scott's sister-in-law, Mrs. Carpentier) brought him into direct touch with Christie, and it was he who gave Lockhart an account of the tragedy. The duel was fought at Chalk Farm. Scott fired at Christie, who then fired into the air. Both seconds (Traill for Christie, P. G. Patmore for Scott) then compelled him to fire again—and to take aim. He fired and wounded Scott. Christie and Traill had their adversary carried to an inn, sent for a surgeon, and did everything in human power to save him. But after some faint signs of rallying, he died. The three—Christie, Traill and Patmore were found guilty of murder, at the coroner's inquest. Christie escaped to France—but returned to stand his trial, with Traill, at the Old Bailey. They were found not guilty ; and that verdict stands on the strictest judgement of the case. Christie's honour and valour, his selfless fidelity remain without shadow of stain.

Lockhart's behaviour may have been technically correct, but only by a large effort of charity and compassion can he be absolved. If John Scott was scurrilous in attack, he was attacking that which was itself foul, the cruel criticisms of *Blackwood's*. He may or may not have, in his heart, believed Lockhart's denial. But much that Lockhart had written did deserve censure. Like most critics, he disliked having to swallow his own medicine. The best that can be said of the affair is that it may well have proved the turning-point in his life ; the moral crisis.

Sir Walter, becoming his wise self again, did not fail to realise this. His letters to Lockhart told of Christie's fortitude, and of Mrs. Christie's steadfast courage. There was no pity for John Scott when, for a few days, he seemed to be recovering ; even when he died, very little pity—or sense of contrition, and Sir Walter could assure Lockhart that the tragedy could not affect him " as a man of honour ". But he gave wise counsel : " You have now the best possible opportunity to break off with the *Magazine*, which will otherwise remain a mere temptation to your love of satire . . . Christie and I have talked over the matter, and it is his opinion as well as mine . . . Do not promise, but act at once, with positive determination."

Whatever Lockhart's own reflections, he could not forget that his turn for satire had led—though he was not deliberately the provoker—to a man's death ; to another man's bearing a burden of apparent guilt. It had led to an issue worse than anything portended by the gravest warnings. Now it was time for him to put away—not childish but heartless things, and to become the man he was meant to be.

III. THE HAPPY YEARS BEGUN

The darkness of the duel episode lifted, there is a sunny landscape. Anne's letters continue to reflect the Lockhart family life, at moments, and there are letters between Lockhart and Sophia during their infrequent separations, Lockhart was still a practising advocate, and had to be absent from Edinburgh on circuit, from time to time. Sophia would then take the baby to Abbotsford or to Germiston, where they would both be cherished and petted. Sometimes she left town a little in advance of her husband, to give Johnny the benefit of what a nurse-maid in one of E. Nesbit's stories called " the new-laid air ".

If these letters between husband and wife do not rank among the world's great love-letters, they may undoubtedly be counted among the happiest and most delightful of intimate epistles. One of the earliest was written while Lockhart was on the Highland circuit : "Mr. Mackenzie, the comely advocate, is here with me, and we go together to Inverness to rejoin the great Donald Horne and the chief of the Maclachlans, none of whom have ever been five hours sober since the morning they left Edinburgh. But I ", went on Mr. Lockhart virtuously, " have been a better boy, and I hope you have been a better girl. If not, amend speedily. If so, continue in your sobriety, and don't set a bad example to the young squire in my absence " (the young squire was then about three months old). He went on :

"When I am made Advocate Depute, I think I shall bring your ladyship along with us. I wish you had come hither, if only for the sake of the old Highland nurse of this house. She is about 99 years old,—privileged completely—drinks tea and punch every night in the drawing-room, tells stories and sings ballads . . . The old girl dances everything from reels to quadrilles "—and expected her partners to kiss her, a duty which Mr. Lockhart would appear to have performed with due courtesy.

This letter ended with loving messages, " not forgetting the Baby who, I trust, is daily more beautiful to behold, and more heavy to dandle ", and with one of the most ingenious apologies ever offered for bad handwriting (though in fact Lockhart's hand-of-write is more than tolerable) : " The room is cold, my hand shakes, the pen is Highland." (One feels somehow that there ought to be something about in dreams beholding the Hebrides !)

This letter was probably " crossed " by one from Sophia, at Germiston written on 22nd April 1821, and sent to Inverness. It was addressed to " My dearest John ", and told of a comfortable journey, of a good Baby who slept most of the way, " then treated us to a tremendous loud sob. However we got him comforted before we arrived at Germiston where he appeared in great beauty and was very much admired . . . Your mother said he put her more

in mind of the little boy Archy she lost than anything.
The Doctor is divided in opinion where the likeness lies,
but is very fond of him, and your grandmother has him in
her arms for a long time every day." Sophia and Johnny
between them so charmed the family that they overcame—
but only just—a certain theological displeasure. Great-
grandmamma did not approve of the baby's having been
"christened in the English form with their crosses and
abominations", for in her view the Episcopalian form of
worship was not a bit better than the Roman Catholic.
"The old lady told me she hoped you and I intended to
bring up our eldest son to the Scottish Kirk." There must
have been a good deal of head-shaking when the elder
Lockharts heard of that prelatical, Episcopal baptism. " I
am afraid ", confessed Sophia, "the Doctor is still a little
angry with you." He was too courteous a host and too
kind a father-in-law to mention any controversial matter
to Sophia ; " but your mother says he speaks of it often
to her, and talks, sometimes, of speaking to you, but you
know he is so good-natured that the next hour he forgets
he has made any such resolution ".

Life at Germiston was, except on the Sabbath, far from
being strict or dull. It was a comfortable, leisurely mode
of life, with visits made and returned, and with playgoing.
Sophia and her pretty young sister-in-law, Violet (who
became a pet with her as already with brother John), went
to see *Hamlet* : " I almost think I like Young's acting of
that character better than Kemble's. Mrs. Siddons made
a most delightful Ophelia." It was all very happy, and
her only fear was that Baby and she might be killed with
kindness before Lockhart came to take them home.

In July there were letters from Abbotsford. Lockhart
was still in town, the session being not yet ended. They
had now been given their own home on Tweedside—
Chiefswood, near Melrose, which was within easy walking
distance of Abbotsford : " pretty Chiefswood " as Johnny
was to call it when he acquired the gift of speech. Sophia
was very housewifely :

"You will laugh at me when I tell you I could not
resist walking over to Chiefswood the very same evening

87

I arrived, and found everything looking beautiful. I was there the whole of Saturday, and saw everything unpacked . . . I think you will be pleased with the arrangement of the things . . . It will be quite ready for us to go into when you come."

The letter ended with various commissions ;—would he bring the little flower-baskets and the water caraffes ordered from Brown's, and would he pay the dentist's bill ; and bring a bottle of leeches which would be " so very useful in the country "—when bleeding in one form or another was so common a remedy. Baby sent kisses and : " I do not like at all to be separated from you . . . dearest Lockhart."

Chapter 8

THE HAPPY YEARS CONTINUED :
EDINBURGH AND CHIEFSWOOD

THESE early years of marriage are documented for us not only in letters but in diaries—though here very briefly. Sophia used, as a rule, *The Ladies' Polite Remembrancer* for entering her own and her husband's engagements ; small pocket-diaries in leather covers, that were full of useful information as to hackney-coach fares and the Kings and Queens of England, and also of elegant extracts, poems and charades and even an occasional moral tale, perhaps about the vanity of riches which may have been a solace when bills came in and household accounts refused to be balanced.

The Lockharts' engagements were chiefly dinner-parties and assemblies ; the dinner-hour being then in the late afternoon or very early evening. In Edinburgh the dinner-hour was influenced by the sitting of the Courts of Session—which rose, usually at four in the afternoon. For many years, until well into the century, it stayed at six or half-past six, which meant a long, sociable evening ; often a long drinking session. Scott is credited with having set the fashion for the men to leave the table decently sober though benign, and join the ladies in the drawing-room for tea or coffee, music—Scots or Italian songs (Scots if Sir Walter had his choice) accompanied on the elegant harp, the spinet or the pianoforte. As the century advanced into Victorian opulence, dinners became longer and more elaborate with a formal succession of courses. There was abundance of good French wine ; claret being still the common Scots drink.

One must wish Sophia had entered in her diary more than a note of the dinner-parties ; had added a list of the company, something about the food, the dresses, the music or the charades that entertained the company afterwards, the dinner-table talk, the stories and compliments. Most housewives cherished some family recipes and Sophia may have had French as well as Scots traditions in her kitchen and still-room. She carried some of hers to London, for in one of her letters written to J. G. L. when he is at home in their London house and she is at Brighton with Johnny, she sends instructions for her cook to make double quantities of marmalade, as some is to be given to a friend, Mrs. Terry, who has no notion of how to make that Scots delicacy.

Scott's daughters were well trained in hospitality and Sophia had her father's warmth of friendliness. The Lockharts' own dinner-parties must have been agreeable ; for even those who admitted Lockhart's stiffness, reserve, shyness—call it what you will—in general society, found him amiable, gentle and amusing in the more intimate gatherings he enjoyed. He loved gossip and could tell a story well. R. P. Gillies in his *Memoirs of a Literary Veteran* recalled a party at the Lockharts', when Sophia sang, to the harp, her father's favourite ballads : *Kenmure's On and Awa'*, and *Bannocks O' Barley*. " The music dies not though the harp be broken "—it is a good sentence on her life and character.

Apart from private parties there were the assemblies— still very formal, excessively well conducted, concerts and the theatre. On one evening of March 1823 Lady Scott and Anne dined with the Lockharts before going to Mrs. Siddons' Benefit. On another occasion there was an At Home for the Terrys before their evening performance.

The musical zenith may have been passed with the great days of St. Cecilia's Hall (which was now no longer a concert hall), but it was still a musical society and a fair standard of accomplishment, both in singing and in harp or piano-playing, was expected of a well-educated woman. Henry Mackenzie recalled that in his youth unaccompanied singing by the ladies was the custom. They sang as they sat round the table or by the fire, nearly always the old Scots songs. He remembered too the progress or procession of instruments in fashion : first the guitar, then the lute, though it had no long vogue, then the harp ; followed by the key-instruments, the spinet and pianoforte.

There is a letter from Lockhart to his friend and colleague on *Maga*—Maginn, the lively, versatile Irishman—who had apparently written to ask advice about the prospects of a music-teacher coming to Edinburgh. Lockhart replied that a lady who could teach singing as well as pianoforte was sure of having many pupils. " The standard is rather higher here than in most provincial places." He advised the lady to come in October, when the winter season began. It ended in April. (The social calendar was set by the Courts of Session.)

In these years in Edinburgh Lockhart had his law-work ; sometimes going on circuit, when Sophia would take Johnny on a visit to Germiston or to Abbotsford. He had increased his literary work which was more and more absorbing his time and energy and interests. His " rapidity of pen ", according to Gillies, " was marvellous " ; thirty-two columns, a whole printed sheet, being an ordinary day's work, " and now and then a law-paper " as well. His novels were written between 1820 and 1824. He was breaking away from *Maga* ; trying to find himself in liter-ature in forms other than the satiric ; reading widely, living as far as possible a scholar's life ; grateful for the com-parative seclusion of Chiefswood in the summer. Had he lived at Abbotsford he would undoubtedly have been driven to frenzy by the turbulent stream of invaders.

As a rule Sophia preceded her husband to Tweedside, staying at Abbotsford and going over to Chiefswood to see that all was in order :

" Babs and I made out our journey here quite well, and found all well indeed. I never saw Papa and Mamma looking better. I went to Chiefswood and was quite delighted with the manner it had been kept in in our absence. Cock-a-Pistol [1] has really been very active in his department, and the garden and grass plots are in excellent order . . . I am going there to-morrow to give directions for the waste piece in front of the house to be put in order and sown with grass . . . I saw a full-grown fruit tree against the wall covering all the ugly part of it between the nursery windows and David's window. It seems Cock-a-Pistol

[1] This was the gardener, James Scott, nicknamed from his dwelling-place near Melrose where the Battle of Melrose had been fought in 1526.

91

seized upon it when it was rooted up at Abbotsford, and by taking the greatest care of it, there is not much fear of its not answering perfectly." The letter was full of news about house and garden ; Sophia was " house-proud " and the cottage must be as near perfect as she could make it. Abbotsford was still in process of growing into its immense size. The family were alone, for once, and were concentrating upon spoiling Sophia and Johnny.

" You may expect to see me with a face like a full moon if eating and sleeping have their usual effect. Mamma absolutely crams me every two hours, and the Great Unknown sits every evening with his watch upon the table for fear, by some mistake, supper should be delayed beyond half-past nine, and the whole family not retired to their rooms by ten. Mamma and Papa are quite delighted with our darling boy on further acquaintance (indeed how could it be otherwise ?), and take the greatest notice of him." Johnny was then at his happiest and healthiest ; and he was full of comic and endearing ways, reigning supreme over the hearts of men and dogs.

" The whole family have united in their efforts this last week to make him say Papa, but I am sorry to say as yet without success, as the little monkey will not try, he is too happy with the multitude of dogs to think of learning anything."

Sophia hoped Lockhart would arrive in time for Miss Edgeworth's expected visit ; but " indeed, dearest Lockhart, I do not like to be absent from you at all, and however kindly I am treated (and I never saw Mamma so well and kind before), I feel your absence deeply, particularly when I go to my room at night and do not find you to tell you all I have thought and felt during the long day ".

There had been some family worry among the Lockharts, about Dick, the youngest but one of the family, who at this date was fifteen and being difficult ; a young cub to be licked into shape. Sophia was elder-sisterly, almost motherly, proposing that he might come to them for a time : " I am sure we could do his manners much good at least, and I should think a little absence from home would be of use to him. I hope, dear Lockhart, that any fear of this being a plague to me will not prevent you being of use to your brother that can be in our power, as I can truly say I should be happy to assist you in such an undertaking."

Robert, the brother next above Dick in age, was a little difficult too : " I do not like him near so much as the rest," Sophia commented, " but I think we might do much for him." Lockhart had all his life a strong sense of family affection and family duty. He kept a brotherly eye on the younger members of his family, had an indulgent fondness for his pretty little sister, Violet, and it was not the least happy feature of his marriage that Sophia was so warm-hearted in her sympathy. The elder Lockharts regarded her with deep affection, all the more as the next marriage in their family, William's, the Doctor's only son by his first marriage, was not so happy.

In the summer of this year (1822) Sophia went to Germiston to meet William and his bride. He had married, on the 16th of April, Mary Jane Palliser, daughter of Sir Hugh Palliser whom he had met at Bath. The story might well be an episode in one of Jane Austen's novels, and asks for her delicately satiric touch.

J. G. L. reported the affair to Sophia in a letter of 18th April, from Germiston : " I found all exceedingly well, though no doubt my grandmother is a good deal more confused than she was at Christmas. At times she seems to imagine it is you William is going to be married to,— at others, she is full of fears that the Captain's Lady will never come up to Sophia "—in which the old lady showed excellent foresight. This letter was full of gossip ; circuit journeys would appear to have been far from dismal. Legal company was genial : " all fair drinkers, and the claret very old and very good. I was awakened next morning at 6 by Succoth bawling for oranges to soften his mouth ". They had stayed in Inveraray, dining one night at eleven o'clock, and not retiring to bed until a quarter past three next morning. On Sunday—" we dined at the Castle at 8 p.m. Judge, jury an enormous rabble. No ladies but Miladi la Duchesse and Miladi John, quondam the cutty Glassel." The Duchess he found " very beautiful still " ;

93

Lady John Campbell " a lively, clever, bluestocking monkey. She and I used to be friends long ago, and we renewed our flirtation as violently as you could have wished. Duke a great man for his bottle, and the party broke up at 4 "— for brief slumbers before a sheep-stealing trial on Monday which lasted until midnight. (The Duke was George William, 4th Duke of Argyll, son of the beautiful Elizabeth Gunning, " the double Duchess " who was the widowed Duchess of Hamilton when she married the Duke of Argyll. His own Duchess was Elizabeth, daughter of the Earl of Jersey. They had no children, and the Duke was succeeded by his brother Lord John. The clever Lady John was the daughter of John Glassel of Longniddry.)

Returning to the topic of William's wedding, J. G. L. reported : " It took place on Monday evening last. Laurence picked out of the Captain [William] that it was with great difficulty he could get down to Scotland at all, —so anxious were the Pallisers to hail the affair. Perhaps they took Billy for a gay deceiver, and yet he is not so much either of a Romeo or a Lovelace as to warrant any very lively suspicion."

The family verdict was that William had been " caught ". As owner of Germiston he was worth catching. The bait had been a pretty face, and no doubt a forthcoming manner ; a flirtation at a ball had been allowed, if not forced, to develop into an engagement and speedy marriage. Sophia had a good deal to say about her new sister-in-law as time went on.

Meanwhile, from Abbotsford she announced the approaching confinement of Lady Morgan : not the literary lady but her namesake, the donkey at Chiefswood ; also the safe accouchement of the cow and welfare of the calf.

She could give Lockhart some details of William and his bride, having had a gossip-letter from Violet—who was " quite in raptures not only with Jane but Sir Hugh and the whole family ". Lady Scott had been unwell, and Sophia had been her nurse : " This has been a very dull week, but she has begun to get well, and we are in hopes she will be so for some time. We would truely [sic] be too happy a family for this world if we had not this dreadful

curse." Sophia more than once expresses this feeling—
that without the dilution of some anxiety their happiness
would be too intense.

In the following July, she was staying at Germiston, and
met the bride : " William and his wife were on the steps
to receive me, and I think after passing the evening with
Jane, even without having any great discernment, may give
her character. She is very beautiful ; one moment the
languid fine lady, and the next a boarding-school romp.
I think naturally she is quick, but from the way she had
been brought up she has never exerted herself except for
outward show, and certainly has never opened a book of
any sort in her life. William and she have been trying
since they came down to get through *The Fortunes of Nigel*,
and are only now finished with the first volume." The
honeymoon couple were still unreticent in their endear-
ments : " I never saw a happier man than William, he
is so vain of such a beautiful creature being in love with
him, and you never heard such speeches as she makes to
dear Lockhart . . . They behaved very well when I saw
them, but there never were such scenes of kissing and love
and romps as take place between the pair." From the
first his marriage did not improve William. He was already
giving offence " by little mean actions, and not asking any
one of the family to the house as yet ". Sophia was observant
and amused and a little ironical.

She was enjoying country life with its gaieties, including
" a grand dinner given by Dr. Rankin " where she observed
" a very great flirtation " between her host and " an old
maid, a Miss Euphemia Glasford ". Johnny was thriving
in the country air : " You never saw him looking so pretty
as he now does, walking upon the walks in the garden,
catching flies after his own manner." But she was home-
sick for Chiefswood with her own " dearest Lockhart ".

Scott's own letters about this time give a picture of family
life. He wrote to Miss Edgeworth—whose visit had been
postponed, that his daughters were " neither of them at
all made up or got up, and rather under than over educated,
I was so terrified for their becoming lionesses at second hand
that I left them in good measure to their own natural gifts.

Both are naturally shrewd and sensible, and the elder has a sort of quiet and sincere enthusiasm about her own country which will entertain you."

These early years of full and happy family life appeared to Lockhart in the later, shadowed years when he wrote the great *Life*, to be bathed in a golden and tranquil light. He recalled the summer of 1821 as " the first of several seasons which will ever dwell in my memory as the happiest of my life ". At Chiefswood he enjoyed the tranquillity he needed ; and he and Sophia could when they chose, join in the " brilliant and constantly varying society " at Abbotsford which, unrelieved, would have been intolerable. Even Scott, most benignant and tolerant of hosts, sank, at times " under the solemn applauses of learned dulness, the vapid raptures of painted and periwigged dowagers, the horse-leech avidity with which underbred foreigners urged their questions, and the pompous simpers of condescending magnates ". At such moments Chiefswood offered a refuge. One evening, Scott would announce to his guests with apologies that he must be absent next day on business ; and early in the morning would take horse and ride over to Chiefswood. The young Lockharts were awakened by " the clatter of Sybil Grey's hoofs, the yelping of Mustard and Spice, and his own joyous shout of *reveillée* ". He would sit down under an ash-tree to await his hosts, companioned by his own dogs and the Lockharts' ; after breakfast, borrow a room for study, write and dispatch a chapter of *The Pirate* ; then join Tom Purdie in the woods. Sometimes the more worthy guests were brought over, of an evening, to the cottage. " And surely he never appeared to more amiable advantage than when helping his young people with their little arrangements upon such occasions. He was ready with all sorts of devices to supply the wants of a narrow establishment " ; one being to sink the wine in the well, and proclaim this method of cooling far superior to the use of ice ; another to have dinner out of doors,— which at once got rid of the inconvenience of very small rooms and made it natural and easy for the gentlemen to help the ladies, so that the paucity of servants went for nothing."

CHIEFSWOOD

From a painting by M. L. Robinson

Though Lockhart was adding to his professional income by his writing, it was necessarily a modest way of house-keeping at pretty Chiefswood ; but with a zest and sweet-ness that lured Scott as strongly as his kindness of heart urged him thither. He was, indeed, as Lockhart realised, recapturing some of his own happiest moments—" trying to live over again, for a few simple hours, his own old life of Lasswade ".

Sixteen years later Lockhart recalled those idyllic days with the anguish of heart that remembrance of lost happiness can bring ; for not only was Scott dead after long agony, but Sophia herself was gone : " she whom I may sadly record as, next to Sir Walter himself, the chief ornament and delight of all those simple meetings,—she to whose love I owe my own place in them,—the one of all his children who, in countenance, mind and manners most resembled himself, and who indeed was as like him in all things as a gentle, innocent woman can ever be to a great man, deeply tried and skilled in the struggles and perplexities of active life ".

There are periods in every life that seem to take on immortality ; to be held as in a crystal of pure happiness, unflawed by present fears or following griefs. We look back, see ourselves in that enchantment, and say : " I was happy then " ; and know that such certainty is a pledge of renewed and immortal joy. Lockhart had that flash of vision.

These years were recorded in letters full of gaiety and gossip, of small problems and amusements, of shared laughter and excitement. Lockhart, still in Edinburgh [1] after Sophia had gone to Abbotsford, reported that he was living very quietly, enduring his " desolate condition " by keeping himself busy, and succeeding tolerably " except at this time in the morning, for example, and supper time—but we shall all be soon together and in our glory ". He added some domestic news ; the maids were well-behaved and attentive enough, but he had met " a gay chap in a plaid of many colours going upstairs t'other night about 8 or 9 o'clock ", and hoped his intentions were honourable. Sophia was sceptical : " But now I have no faith in man." She would

[1] They were now living in Northumberland Street.

97

continued to shine with its own, enduring warmth and radiance ; producing, in the occasional separations, the most delightful of married letters.

II

Lockhart was in London in the spring of 1824, and wrote with a mixture of amusement and weariness of the round of breakfasts and dinners and incessant company. " I always see ten or twenty new lions in the day, and am quite knocked up long ere I get to bed, and in short live in a kind of fever." But he was young enough and worldly enough to enjoy the fever. He breakfasted with Samuel Rogers, the banker-poet (or poetaster) and lion-collector— " one of the pleasantest satirists certainly I ever talked with ", who asked about Sophia " most tenderly " : dined with Lydia White, the celebrated bluestocking, when " everybody spoke the very citadel of twaddle and thirtieth-rate literary humbug ". By way of contrast he had another dinner—" in a sponging-house with Theodore Hook, Terry, Sir Godfrey Webster, Dr. McGinn [*sic*], Elliston the player, etc. etc.,—the Court, they call it, of Theodore King of the Goths ". Again by contrast was a dinner with Charles Ellis to meet Canning ; and another with the old family friends, the Doumergues : " I never saw a better dinner or a more vulgar company. . . . The wines were really out of all sight the best I have seen here,—for in general Edinburgh beats London hollow as to this department." The Scots palate was sound, and the Scots cellar well stocked, especially with the good wines of France. He visited Wilkie the artist, who regarded the Scott family almost as deities—" not forgetting Minerva Sophia, Jupiter Great Unknown, and Little John Hugh Cupid Esq." The latter continued to delight his family, and was no doubt largely responsible for the " strong symptoms of homesickness " that afflicted his papa. " Everybody is very kind and flattering here, but I must have your Ladyship with me the next trip I take to London."

He went on to Bristol to visit that oldest and best of friends, Christie, who was in law-practice there ; finding him " much better in health and spirits than he has been for many years ". How much he must have suffered in both from the tragedy of the duel Lockhart perhaps did not realise. An engagement to dine with Canning on the 8th of May (Lockhart was writing on the 20th of April) meant a long stay in London—" so many days doomed to pass over us even yet ere we meet ".

On the way to Bristol he had passed through Bath which he regarded with a satiric eye : " I contemplated with scorn and derision the crowds of sedan chairs and gouty chairs on wheels drawn up opposite to some Dowager's door. The moment the coach stopped, all the ladies and gemmen of this high circle ran to the windows." With a sketch by Violet in his mind Lockhart looked for William's father-in-law, Sir Hugh Palliser, " but could not please myself with a nose to suit Violet's sketches "—which sounds as if Violet had a touch of his own satirical talent.

This letter was crossed by one from Sophia at Germiston ; a cosy and happy one full of news of Johnny ; who was refusing to kiss any of the maids except " Peggy the cook, who happens to be the best-looking ". (Might not her position as custodian of the cupboard be an equally valid reason, for a small boy who, it is likely, had a fondness for sugar candy, dried fruits, ginger-bread and other delights ?) For excuse the young diplomat urged " John Hugh's mouth too small "—for indiscriminate kissing. He was a little afraid of the poor old great-grandmother, now wandering in her wits, but retained his adroitness, pleading " John Hugh's hand dirty " when told to shake hands with her.

Laurence (the brother next in age to J. G. L.) was about to move into his manse at Inchinnan. He alone of Dr. Lockhart's sons followed his father's calling. He had been presented to the parish of Inchinnan, Renfrewshire, through the benevolent influence of Sir Walter with the patron Campbell of Blythswood. His house-warming party was to be postponed until J. G. L. came home. Sophia's longing for reunion matched her husband's ; but—" I am quite happy, dear John, to think you are so much amused, and

see so much, and expect to have many a curtain story when
you come back to me, which I am truly glad to think you
will not be very long of doing." She could promise a
happy surprise for him in Johnny's improved health and
remarkable advance " in his speaking and sense ; you have
no idea what an absurd body he has become, or the amusing
remarks he makes ".

He had reached the stage of playing " pretend " games ;
his favourite of the moment being to call himself " Wee
Papa " and to set forth for " Ondy "—as his small tongue
rendered " London "—half a dozen times a day. His
family were expected to weep on his departure and laugh
on his return, which is what all good families should do.
" He told me to-day that when you came back you was to
take him on your knee and tell him what you did when
you was a good boy,—for you flourish in all the endless
stories I have to invent for him."

Life at Germiston was quiet, with few visitors ; but on
one occasion Dr. Lockhart " picked up " and invited for the
following day " a party of five, two of whom are ladies,
and not one of whom your mother has seen, called upon,
or even heard of ". Such exuberance of clerical hospitality
was disconcerting. " I expect we shall have some entertainment," commented Sophia. The boys, Robert and
Dick, were still something of a problem, but Lockhart
and Sophia appeared to " manage " them better than
their parents could and Scott used his influence on their
behalf.

" When you come down we shall determine what should
be done for your brother ", he wrote to Lockhart ; and he
had many practical suggestions to offer. But young Dick
was to remain a problem for some time.

The year 1824 brought a grief to Sophia in the loss of
her second baby, a daughter, who lived only two days ;
she was born on Saturday the 31st January, and, as Scott
told Maria Edgeworth : " The poor little stranger left us
on the Monday following, and though Sophia is very patient
in her temper, yet her recovery is naturally retarded, and
I am sorry to say she has been attacked in her weak state
by those spasms which seem a hereditary disorder in my

JOHN HUGH LOCKHART ('HUGH LITTLEJOHN')
From a portrait by Margaret Carpenter

family." But in time, and with kind cherishing, she made a good recovery.

This year saw the great fire in High Street. Anne wrote about it to Miss Millar, the old governess, and achieved or perpetrated a pun :

" Lockhart has been out day and night with the Yeomanry, and though he kept his spirits up by pouring spirits down, he was very ill afterwards from fatigue." She added that some of the " unco guid " of Edinburgh believed the burning of the Tron Kirk in the fire to be a judgement on the minister, Dr. Brinton, who had committed the grievous sin and scandal of subscribing to the Edinburgh Musical Festival of that year. Anne gave another account of the disaster in a letter to her brother Charles—at Brasenose College—telling of the near-destruction of Parliament House and of the Bank, of the burning of David Allan the artist's house, but the fortunate saving of his pictures. In this same letter she described a night of wind and tempest at Abbotsford when she had sat up all night reading a novel, and told a true ghost story—often told again by Scott himself. " Papa insists that he saw Lord Byron in the Mall last Sunday, but that he vanished when he came up to him." It was a strange case of second-sight. It is not good to have such a vision—and Scott must have recalled it when the news came of Byron's death.

In 1825 Lockhart was again in London ; his business and its results will be told in the next chapter ; it was to lead to his appointment as Editor of *The Quarterly* and to the new life in London. Scott wrote introducing him to Joanna Baillie :

" You will like him very much if you can make him lay aside a reserve which is unpleasant to new acquaintances ; in his own house and with his own family, he is one of the pleasantest persons possible." Sophia was to spend the time of his absence at Abbotsford,—

> Till she be as fat as a Norroway seal
> I'll feed her on bannocks of barley meal.

Scott did not approve of an invalid regimen. " Betwixt indolence of her own and Lockhart's extreme anxiety and indulgence, she has foregone the custom of her exercise, to which, please God, we will bring her back by degrees . . . I have been telling her that her face which was last week the size of sixpence has, in three or four days, attained the diameter of a shilling, and will soon attain its natural and most extensive circumference of half-a-crown." He had great faith, as regards both her and Johnnie, in " the black Doctor and the red nurse " ; otherwise the pony and the cow at Abbotsford. He still clung to hope for the beloved little grandson whose mental development was so far ahead of his physical. His very delicacy in part accounted for this, for he was much with his parents, who read to him and talked to him, and encouraged him to be clever.

" But an only child is like a blot at backgammon, and Fate is apt to hit it." Scott was never without foreboding : " The parents are so much wrapt up in him that it makes me tremble when I look at the poor little fellow," he told Miss Clephane.

The shadows were still slight—a cloud no bigger than a man's hand and Lockhart's full career as a professional man of letters was only now about to begin. But looking back, we, knowing the future, can see that the happy years were ending. Life was to bring riches of experience yet, in both joy and sorrow ; but the golden age, serene and tranquil, would soon be a memory.

Chapter 9

THE SECOND TRIUMVIRATE :
LOCKHART, CROKER, MURRAY

I. LOCKHART AND CROKER

L OCKHART, between 1819 and 1825, was beset by many
influences. At times he appears the central figure in
a ring, or set of a dance ; the other dancers moving
and receding, trying, as it were, to draw him into their
own pattern. There is the Blackwood set, chiefly Wilson
and Hogg ; there are Scott and Sophia. He dances to
both, is drawn to both ; finally drawn over to Scott and
Sophia, and almost entirely away from the other pair.
But there is another figure in this dance of influence who
was to remain there for the rest of Lockhart's life, always
close, though never dominant : John Wilson Croker, that
strange, compelling personality, of great gifts and little
amiability, who came near, at times, to dominating the
House of Murray to which Lockhart was soon to give his
service.

Croker was born in Galway in 1780 ; Irish by birth and
upbringing but of Devon stock. He took his degree at
Trinity College, Dublin, proceeded to Lincoln's Inn to
read law, was elected M.P. for Downpatrick, and, in 1809,
was appointed Secretary to the Admiralty. From that
year, which saw the beginning of *The Quarterly Review*, until
1854 he was a regular contributor to *The Quarterly*, except
during the years 1826–31. There were few numbers without an article by his pen. With John Murray the Second
and with his son, John the Third after him, he was to bring
Lockhart into a second triumvirate.

He was a rigid, almost a stark, Tory ; a staunch Churchman of the intensely Protestant Irish type ; a most painstaking scholar ; and a critic with a pen like a scalping-
knife. Disraeli portrayed, or caricatured, him as Mr. Rigby
in *Coningsby*. Lockhart, at first, deferred to him ; then, for
a time, turned away from him ; then came back into an

intimacy that was rarely without rebellion yet held the two men closely together. Their correspondence began in 1819 and continued until the last year of Lockhart's life.

It began with Croker producing a new Tory periodical, *The Guardian*, which Lockhart helped, both as contributor and as publicity agent. He wrote to Croker, from Edinburgh, on 27th November 1819:

"I have this morning received the handbills and distributed them . . . I write this merely to suggest . . . that our poverty and stinginess have introduced among us of the North a fashion that may . . . be unheard of in the South. This is that the first numbers of all periodical work, and especially of newspapers, are distributed pretty largely gratis. My acquaintance with this city extends to the legal part of its population and the literary part—but not among the citizens; therefore I can say nothing about them"— but he could, none the less, suggest a representative list of those who might profitably be sent a copy of the new paper; the list included the bookshops: Constable, Manners and Miller, Hill, Blackwood, Waugh and Innes, Laing, Brown, Black, McCredie, for these were "the chief lounges in Edinburgh", being clubs as well as shops; though there were clubs also,—the New and the Albyn.

Succeeding letters dealt with J. G. L.'s contributions, often, apparently, consisting of news-paragraphs and legal notes. "I am greatly at a loss to know what I can do for the paper", he wrote in January 1820, "that may be of any value to it. *Jeux d'esprit* you have by the score, and most of them quite admirable. Now here we are away from the focus of interest, and our jokes would come cold compared with those you can so easily throw off on the spur and in the inspiration of the moment."

He could provide something better than second-hand quips. His account, of the serious and tragic Rising of that year, already described in his letters to Sophia, was a full and graphic bit of reporting. In January everything was quiet in the West of Scotland, and Lockhart, after spending Christmas and New Year there, with his family, could find "the claret and the good folk as copious and as cool as ever". But in April came that week or more of campaigning with the Yeomanry. He wrote, then, to Croker of the gathering of " the weavers of Strathaven and some other villages ", who " marched with muskets and pikes, but not being joined as they had expected, their men lost heart and went to a neighbouring Justice of Peace with an offer to surrender ".

There were excitements for the Volunteers. They had to search all the villages for arms, and one evening " we had a glimpse of 300 drilling with muskets, and galloped round to come up with them, but the county was full of canals, and we had to ride 6 or 8 miles, which gave them time to vanish into coal-pits, etc." After the collapse of the Rising, " instead of looks of resolution and savage audacity " there were seen " fear and sullen submission. The executions that must soon take place, may be expected to produce a most salutary effect, but in the mean time rescues are likely to be attempted, and until they are all hanged there can be no tranquillity here."

The end of the Rising left him full of foreboding : " I . . . have little doubt the audacity of our northern rebels will, some time or other, lead them to a regular insurrection. Of the issue of that there can be no doubt, but it is a very dark prospect at the best, enough to make the gayest of us serious."

What should equally have made the gayest of them serious was the misery of condition that had led to this revolt ; for in these days before the social conscience of the country awoke, life in the mines and factories and mills of South-West Scotland and Northern England was truly the dark, satanic thing of Blake's vision.

This long letter was the beginning of the political correspondence between Lockhart and Croker. In the following years there were to be many letters filled with gossip of Government doings, all the in-and-out of parties ; forgotten matters that are dead and dull now. But this has a sombre significance.

The personal element soon became more apparent : with a letter of thanks for Croker's good wishes to Lockhart and Sophia ; and with a note of sympathy from Lockhart when Croker and his wife lost their only child, a boy. " It is fortunate ", wrote Lockhart, " that those whose feelings are the most keen have possession of that strong sense of duty and that energy of will without which the measure of these faculties would only add to their inflation." That is a point not always recognised by those who pride themselves on their emotions. The letter is sincere ; and if somewhat formal is naturally so, between men who were not yet intimate friends and coming from one unaware that a like grief lay before him.

The personal note became more frequent as the friend-ship grew. Croker's advice and countenance already meant a great deal to Lockhart. Croker's influence, through his Government post, he valued, and on one occasion sought on his own behalf. In February 1822 a few plums of legal appointments were ripe for falling, and Lockhart hoped to gather one. He wrote to Croker by Sir Walter's advice : " There is now a considerable commotion among us law officers here, and three or four things must be going and Scott says he thinks I am entitled to have a try for one of them." This was the Sheriffship of Lanarkshire, the highest legal and judicial office in the county, and Lockhart thought he might have some claim to it " as being a member of one of the oldest families in that county, and connected in one way or other with all its best gentry ".

Even in those days when men matured early, Lockhart, at twenty-six, was full young to attain such eminence. But he thought the all-powerful Lord Melville and the Lord Advocate were not ill-disposed towards him, though he feared " they may think they will expose themselves to some vile Whig splutter if they give me any open mark of attention. They have nothing to say but that I, when very young, wrote three or four savage squibs against old Play-fair and Jeffrey, but it's wonderful, and no one knows this better than you, how such trifles may be swelled into affairs of moment when that serves the purpose of enemies, and perhaps serves the purposes of people calling themselves friends."

This plum did not fall into his hands ; to his disappoint-ment at the time, though he bore it well :

" Not having expected anything, I have met with no

sort of disappointment. The truth is that this hungry race must be enough to destroy the patience of the best-natured man in the world,—and I believe my Lord Melville is a very good-natured one. I shall take care that he be not in future pestered by me or through my means." After which, he proceeded to give cheerful gossip about Scott :—
" *The Fortunes of Nigel* go on rapidly and promise great things . . . I cannot help thinking that this will be a far superior book even to the best of the later works he has written . . . ten times better than *The Pirate* . . . But perhaps the country folk may enjoy the bustle of life in London in *Nigel*—and you prefer the steppes of the Orkney Isles on the same principle . . . Scott is, as usual, in great feather, writing like a Turk, and eating and drinking that his soul may live."

Lockhart's talent for amusing gossip was developing. He wrote about Maria Edgeworth's visit to Abbotsford and to Chiefswood : " I have seen very little of the celebrated lady. She seemed very angry one day she was dining here, on discovering that my wife drove in her garden-chaise two donkeys, by name Lady Morgan and Hannah More, but I can't say which of the god-mothers had her sympathy." The ironic eye he turned on Miss Edgeworth was to become most friendly, and the " celebrated lady " was to take Lockhart and his children, as well as Scott and his family, into her warm affections.

Croker was to write a review of *The Spanish Ballads* in *The Quarterly* and Lockhart was grateful. Scott would have done it : " He is so good-natured that he likes anything a friend does "—so did not qualify as an impartial critic. " Besides, his style is so well known (to say nothing of revealing secrets which are but rarely kept) that the only effect would be a laugh at my expense—perhaps, (what I should like still less) at his."

But one of the most interesting, even poignant, letters of this first section of the correspondence with Croker was written in the days of indiscretion.

Within three months of the Scott–Christie duel, with Sir Walter's admonitions clear in his mind, Lockhart published, under the pseudonym of John Bull, an *Open Letter to Lord*

Byron ; [1] then spent some agonising weeks, wondering whether the secret of his authorship would be discovered. It was a clever, but not a discreet, publication. It was written in reply to a *Letter* from Byron to John Murray, attacking in general the canting tone of English criticism, and in particular the strictures recently passed by the Rev. W. L. Bowles on the *Life and Poems of Pope*. "John Bull" attacked Byron's attack arguing that he himself as well as his critics had assumed this very attitude of cant and humbug.

He made a particular attack on Byron's cult of publicity, his self-defence, self-pity : " The world had nothing whatever to do with a quarrel between you and Lady Byron, and you were the last man that should have set about persuading the world that the world had or could have anything to do with such a quarrel . . . What business had you to suppose that the world cared a single farthing about any such affair. It is surely a very good thing to be a clever poet ; but it is a much more essential thing to be a gentleman . . . To quarrel with your wife overnight and communicate your quarrel to the public the next morning in a sentimental copy of verses, to affect utter broken-heartedness and yet to be snatching the happy occasion to make another good bargain with Mr. John Murray "—did not stamp the poet as a gentleman. " This is a part of your humbug . . . on the success of which I can by no means congratulate you."

He further attacked the stanza in *Childe Harold*, " Ada, sole daughter ", as being written " to humbug women and children into an idea that you were very much distressed with being separated from the sweet little Ada. We all know now that you have been enjoying yourself very heartily for four or five years, among ladies and misses of quite another kind."

Having read that epistle, it is easy to understand—if hardly to admire—the panic in J. G. L.'s letter to Croker.

" I feel very, very much obliged to you—but was never more surprised than by your letter. I will not indeed deny

[1] *John Bull's Letter to Lord Byron :* ed. Alan Lang Strout (Univ. of Oklahoma Press, 1947).

to you that I wrote that letter but how I should have been accused or even suspected, I cannot for my life divine, and so far from avowing it, I promise you I would pay a tremendous fine rather than bear the blame of it for a week. I place, as you see, the most implicit reliance on your friendliness. I pray you to do everything in your power to stop the report if it be a report. I cannot imagine how it has arisen—but I am quite sure no one has any knowledge of the thing. My only suspicion is that Murray has extracted from Wright (what he promised *in initio* to conceal most sacredly) the name of the agent . . . I cannot say how much I am distressed with this thing—not on my own account, God knows, but on Scott's. I wrote this thing when in Inverness-shire, and he has never heard of it, I hope never will. Do say whatever is strongest and most effectual to save me from a great pain. I am a most unfortunate fellow. I have written to Murray to deny the letter.[1] No, I have not written Murray, I trust everything to you."

That Croker may have failed him at this crisis may be the explanation of a letter to John Murray, which will be quoted in the next section. There was a stormy passage for Lockhart outside the harbour, before he entered haven. Objections had been made against his appointment to *The Quarterly Review* ; he was paying, in full, for the follies of his *Blackwood* days :

" I understand ", he wrote to Croker, " that Mr. Barrow and Mr. Hay (of the Colonial Department), being consulted by Murray, have advised him against doing a thing which in fact, and as he ought to have told them, is done. I can easily gather that these gentlemen consider me as a man of squibs and of squibs alone, and that they lay to my charge all the abuse that ever appeared in *Blackwood*, and above all, a sort of connection with Blackwood which has had no existence, I having in reality ceased to write almost at all in his paper, for many years back. . . . You know Murray far better than I can be supposed to do, and are, of course, quite aware what impression is made on his mind by things of this kind. I know him sufficiently to

---

[1] This sentence is, in the original, scored out.

be certain that one word from you can dispel the darkest
cloud that ever disturbed the serenity of his mind. . . .
For myself I was well prepared for all that has happened,
and am prepared for much worse ; but I confess that on
my wife's account I should be very glad to have as little
to fight with among those who ought to be friendly as
may be—considering how plentifully I am provided in
enemies."

So Lockhart wrote his Apologia for the least seemly part
of his life ; and paid for the pleasure he had taken in writing
bitter things.

And at this point we must turn back in time, to the
beginning of the House of Murray with which, for the
rest of his life, Lockhart was to be so closely connected ;
to John the First, its founder, whom he never knew, and to
John the Second—one of the second triumvirate.

II. MURRAY AND LOCKHART

The House of Murray was, almost from the first, a
dynasty ; recognised as such as early as the days of John
the Second, son of the founder, who was invested with the
imperial title and known as The Emperor of the West ;
also as Glorious John ; also by Byron's name for him, The
Anax of Publishers. The founder, John the First, was born
(like Henry Mackenzie) in 1745. He became an officer in
the Royal Marines, and retired in 1768, at the end of the
Seven Years War. His father, a Writer to the Signet, in
Edinburgh, had added " Mac " to his surname, but this
was dropped by his younger son, John.

Life on half-pay was flat and unprofitable, and the young
officer decided to begin a new career. He set up as a
bookseller at 32 Fleet Street, and became, also, a publisher
in a small way. Among his publications were the first
volume of Isaac D'Israeli's *Curiosities of Literature*, Mitford's
History of Greece, and the *Memoirs* of Lord Lovat ; with a
new edition of Lord Lyttelton's *Dialogues of the Dead*, and
of Horace Walpole's *Castle of Otranto*. In 1771 his business

was enriched by a legacy from an uncle, and it continued to prosper in a quiet and steady way.

John Murray married twice, his second wife being the sister of his first ; and of this second marriage, John the Second was born in 1778. John the First did not live to see his son grow to manhood ; he died in 1793, aged only forty-eight. Young John was still a schoolboy, at the Royal High School, Edinburgh, and for some time the business was carried on by a faithful assistant, Samuel Highley, who was presently made partner. Mrs. Murray married again, and young John was rather a lonely youth, which probably developed his manliness and independence. It was, besides, an adult century, when the young matured early if they had any mental capacity. By the time he came of age, John was a person of character and decision. Three years later he proposed to Highley, who had been an honest but un-enterprising partner, that their agreement be terminated, and this was amicably arranged. Young John carried on the business in Fleet Street without his " drone of a partner " as he called the worthy Samuel ; he continued his father's association with booksellers in Edinburgh ; and his friend-ship with the elder D'Israeli which was, later, extended to the latter's son, Benjamin, born in 1804.

Chief among the Edinburgh associates was Constable, who was then " in high feather " to borrow Lockhart's phrase for Scott. He was a pioneer in periodical literature in Edinburgh ; having acquired the much-respected *Scots Magazine* in 1801, started *The Farmer's Magazine* in 1800, and in 1800 also produced the famous or infamous (accord-ing to your politics) *Edinburgh Review*. This last had, as contributors, Francis Jeffrey (who became editor), Lord Brougham, Sydney Smith and all the Whig intellectuals.

A great deal was happening in Edinburgh, in the literary world. Scott was publishing his poems with Constable : *Sir Tristram* in 1804 and *The Lay of the Last Minstrel* in 1805. Murray was agent for these and other Constable books in London, and gradually undertook more and more of Con-stable's affairs in the south. In the summer of 1806 he visited Edinburgh, strengthened his friendship with Con-stable, and continued another friendship which warmed into a romance : with Miss Elliot, daughter of an Edinburgh publisher. They were married in the following year.

For all the cordiality of this visit, relations with Constable did not remain happy or secure. " The man that is crafty in counsel " had a tendency to draw on Murray's funds, offering in return bills and promissory notes ; a habit which did not commend itself to a canny young Scot in London. John had a healthy dislike of too much paper-money. Constable at this time became closely connected with James and John Ballantyne, with whom, in 1805, Scott entered into a partnership that was to have disastrous results : binding himself to produce his books for them, and investing in their business most of his capital.

Murray and the Ballantynes had a scheme for issuing a series of the British Novelists, from Defoe to those of the eighteenth century, to be edited, with preface and notes, by Scott ; but this remained unfulfilled. It was, however, a token of what was to be done by Murray and his son, in the way of popular editions ; in this they were pioneers.

The schism between Murray and Constable was finally brought about by the *Edinburgh Review*, of which it was said, in a masterpiece of understatement, that its " criticism was rude, and wanting in delicate insight ". One example of this lack may be found in Jeffrey's review of Wordsworth's *Excursion*, beginning : " This will never do," of which he boasted that it would crush the poem.—" He might as well say that he could crush Skiddaw," commented Southey. The *Review* became more and more aggressive and alienated Scott, who had, at first, been well disposed to it. In 1808 he found himself attacked by Jeffrey in an acrimonious review of *Marmion*, and he wrote, in November of that year, to his brother Thomas :

" Constable . . . has behaved to me of late not very civilly, and I owe Jeffrey a flap with a fox-tail on account of his review of *Marmion*." The flap was a hearty one, and the fox-tail nothing less than a new Review, on Tory principles, about to be published by Murray. Scott wrote about it to his friend, the antiquarian, George Ellis :

" Let me touch a string of much delicacy,—the political character of the Review. It appears to me that this should be of a liberal and enlarged nature . . . but stern in detecting and exposing all attempts to sap our constitutional fabric. Religion is another slippery station ; here also I would endeavour to be as impartial as the subject will admit of." As for literary criticism, he said : " There is policy as well as morality in keeping our swords clear as well as sharp, and not forgetting the gentlemen in the critics." There were two deplorable extremes of criticism : that which prevailed before the coming of *The Edinburgh Review* had been " extremely mawkish ", giving a " dawdling, maudlin sort of applause " even to mediocrity. Thus, when " the Edinburgh folk squeezed into their sauce plenty of acid " they produced a novel and popular dish. As always (*vide* the Lytton Strachey school of the 1920's), the minor talents copied the greater, and Scott found that the imitators of the new style had " *outréd* the matter still farther and given us all abuse and no talent "—which stands as a sound condemnation of much criticism in his and in our own day. On the need for " decent, lively, reflecting criticism teaching men not to abuse books only but to read and judge them " Scott and Murray were in agreement. The forthcoming Review had been discussed when Murray visited Scott at Ashestiel. The editor was to be William Gifford, and to him also Scott wrote ; referring to Murray as " a young bookseller of capital and enterprize, and who has more good sense and propriety of sentiment than fall to the store of most of the brethren ". The new editor's " team " was to include George Ellis, the scholar and antiquarian, Hookham Frere the Grecian, nicknamed "Aristophanes " from his translation of that dramatist, Richard and Reginald Heber, Malthus the economist, Will Erskine and Scott himself.

The Quarterly Review duly made its appearance at the end of February 1809. The first number was much more literary than political in contents.

Scott's contributions were : a review of Burns's *Reliques* . . . *Letters and Poems* (edited by the Rev. R. H. Cromak) ; a review of the translation of *The Chronicles of the Cid* by Southey, and (probably) one of an *Essay on the Early Life of Swift*.

The portrayal of Burns is vivid : " In general society Burns often permitted his determination of vindicating his personal dignity to hurry him into unjustifiable resentment of slight or imagined neglect . . . the dignity, the spirit, the indignation of Burns was that of a plebeian, of a high-souled plebeian indeed . . . but still of a plebeian, untinged with the slightest shade of that spirit of chivalry which, since feudal times, has pervaded the higher ranks of European society. The lowness of his birth and habits of society prevented rules of punctilious delicacy from making any part of his education." The man who was at ease in the world, who could " speak to a'body as if they were his blude relations ", had perceived the aggressiveness of the man who, in colloquial phrase, had a chip on his shoulder.

In the following decade, Scott was to contribute many reviews : the most famous being that of Jane Austen's *Emma*, in the October issue of 1815. The new magazine was safely launched, and was to sail under the captaincy of Gifford for fifteen years.

During those fifteen years Murray flourished as a publisher, and *The Quarterly* justified his hope. He moved from Fleet Street to No. 50 Albemarle Street, where the brass plate inscribed " Mr. Murray " still adorns the door. No. 50 was Murray's home ; almost a private club, for there foregathered in his drawing-room and library many of the writers and statesmen of his own and his son's generation. His dinners became famous. No. 50 was the centre not only of his career, and that of his authors and contributors, but of his domestic life. To-day, when it consists of offices, it still retains a dignity and tradition wholly domestic ; it seems almost to be haunted, as Abbotsford is haunted, by memories too vivid and substantial to be ghostly.

John the Third was born in 1808, and was nurtured on printer's ink, on which he throve so greatly that he lived until 1892 ; his life spanning every phase of a great century, from Georgian to Victorian England, from the Napoleonic Wars to beyond the Jubilee of George the Third's illustrious granddaughter ; from Scott's day and Byron's to that of Swinburne and Meredith, Wilde and Shaw.

As a child of six he enjoyed a remarkable, indeed a double "Shelley-plain", for he saw, in the drawing-room of the house in Albemarle Street, Scott and Byron meeting for the first, but not the only, time. They met again almost daily, while Scott was in London. The little boy retained a clear picture of Byron : "rather a short man with a handsome countenance", with rings on his fingers and a brooch in the frill of his open-necked shirt. His lameness was very marked, especially on the stairs. "It was a curious sight to see the two greatest poets of the age, both lame, stumping downstairs side by side." Byron's voice was deep and impressive, and "bore some resemblance to that of Mrs. Siddons" (!). John the Third was, like his father, to be the friend as well as the colleague of Lockhart, who came, in age, between father and son. He was to carry the publishing house and the *Review* to within sight of modern times; when he died his son, John the Fourth, succeeded him, and John the Fifth had then been long enough upon this earthly scene to make the continuance of the dynasty secure.

To return, however, to Glorious John, the Emperor and Anax, his reign in those early decades of the century was full of splendours. He published Byron and Jane Austen, each of matchless, though somewhat different quality ; he had a share in publishing Scott, and he did publish most of his periodical writing. He brought Scott and Byron together in the flesh, to their mutual pleasure, and he introduced Jane Austen in her work to Scott whom she so warmly admired and who was so fully to value her originality. Besides these, there were many other names of distinction on Murray's list ; there was, too, a great deal of pioneer production ; and in himself Glorious John was one of the most majestic figures of a tremendous age ; with a touch of flamboyance that toned well with his background. He had *panache*.

As well as publishing the most gorgeous genius of the age, he discovered and produced talents of a more homely practical sort, and of the utmost propriety ; notably Mrs. Rundell in her *Domestic Cookery*, which was the forerunner of Mrs. Beeton's masterpiece, and which may be studied happily and profitably for suggestions as to the domestic background at Albemarle Street. It would seem probable and only right that those famous literary dinners should owe their substance to the recipes of that excellent lady. Her book was printed in Edinburgh for John Murray, in 1809 and again in 1810, and the copyright was accepted as surety for the purchase of the house in Albemarle Street.

Among other, equally practical and famous, works was Mrs. Markham's *History of England*, which became indispensable to every well-conducted schoolroom. On this book the historical education of generations of young ladies in the nineteenth century was founded. " Mrs. Markham " (whose real name was Mrs. Penrose) set the fashion for the dialogue form of instruction ; it was almost history-through-fiction ; Mamma, who could answer all the questions set by Richard and Mary, is a personage and a personality.

By the end of the first quarter of the century Murray was in the full tide of achievement. He had published masterpieces of poetry and fiction, household books, various works of minor but authentic interest ; his *Review* was read and discussed, and now firmly established. He thought of a new venture. There was room, he considered, for a Tory daily paper, and he proposed to found one, calling it *The Representative*. Among the supporters of the scheme were the two Disraelis, Isaac, already well known in the literary world, and young Benjamin, whose achievements in literature and politics lay ahead of him, but whose infinite energy of mind and character was already manifest. John the Second appointed him ambassador between himself and his chosen editor—who was J. G. Lockhart. The embassy failed. Lockhart declined the offered post. Journalism was still a risky calling, and not altogether well-seen. Lockhart wrote to Murray, in October 1825, of an " inexpressible feeling . . . in regard to the impossibility of my ever entering into the career of London in the capacity of a newspaper editor. I confess that you who have adorned and raised your own profession so highly may feel inclined . . . to smile at my scruples." But journalism was a game, almost a gamble ; and " if such a game ought to be played I am neither young nor poor enough to be the man that takes the hazard ". (He was 29 ; a young man still, but past the recklessness of first youth, and was, besides, married and *rangé*.)

This decision may have been taken on Scott's advice ; certainly with Scott's approval, for the latter himself wrote to Murray :

" There is nothing in life that can be more interesting to me than his prosperity, and should there eventually appear a serious prospect of his bettering his fortunes by quitting Scotland, I have too much regard for him to desire him to remain, notwithstanding all the happiness I must lose by his absence and that of my daughter.—But the present offer does not present such a prospect. I cannot conceive it advisable that he should leave Scotland on the speculation of becoming editor of a newspaper." There was a possibility—but hardly more—of a reformation in journalism : " It is very true that this department of litera- ture may, and ought to, be rendered more respectable than it is, but I think this is a reformation more to be wished than hoped for." There was also, in Scott's view, a risk of Lockhart's losing, in such a post, " a considerable portion of his respectability in society ". Lockhart's immediate prospects, in Scotland, were good : " His situation in publick estimation and in private society is as high as that of any one at our Bar, and his road to the public open if he chooses to assist his income by literary resources."

Lockhart, Scott knew in his heart, needed stability, moral and social, as well as financial. He must not break his present career unless for a post where he would stand well in the eyes of men. Such a post was very soon offered him. (*The Representative*, as it happened, was a bow at a venture and fell far from its aim.)

Gifford had through ill health almost given up his work as editor of *The Quarterly* in 1823, and until his resignation in the following year, Croker acted editor, assisted by Sir John Barrow. In 1824 J. T. Coleridge was appointed ; but owing to his increasing legal duties, was unable to hold the post for long. In 1825 Murray was in search of a new editor who should be of proved capacity, mature in intellect but young in years. Lockhart was all these things, so again

The Emperor sent young Disraeli on an embassy to Tweed-side. This time he was successful. Lockhart was appointed Editor of *The Quarterly Review* in October 1825.

The appointment was not made without dissent and criticism, of an active and hurtful kind. Lockhart was still haunted by the ghosts of his *Blackwood* indiscretions. Scott again came to the rescue, writing warmly to Murray on Lockhart's behalf ; reminding him the offer of *The Quarterly* had been made to Lockhart, not sought by him, or for him by Scott ; referring to the old scandals :

" When he was paying his addresses in my family, I fairly stated to him that while I might be pleased with his general talents and accomplishments, with his family and with his views in life, I did decidedly object to the use he and others had made of their wit and satirical talent in Blackwood's magazine . . . Mr. Lockhart then pledged his word to me that he would withdraw from this species of warfare, and I have every reason to believe that he has kept his word with me . . . It seems extremely hard that the follies of three or four and twenty should be remembered against a man of thirty who has abstained during the interval from giving the least cause of offence . . . I cannot help thinking that five years proscription ought to obtain a full immunity on their account. There were none of them which could be ascribed to any worse motive than a wicked wit . . . Lockhart is reckoned an excellent scholar, and Oxford has said so ; he is born a gentleman, has always kept the best society, and his personal character without a shadow of blame. In the most unfortunate affair of his life he did all that man could do, and the unhappy tragedy was the result of the poor sufferer's afterthought to get out of a scrape." Already, in Scott's view (and though not impartial he was a wise judge), the debit side of Lockhart's account with God and man was being reduced, while on the credit side were many items. He had an excellent talent, including the primary journalistic one of adaptability :

" I never met anyone who had such ready command of his own mind or possessed in a greater degree the power of making his talents available upon the shortest notice and upon any subject." Moreover he was (as one hardly expects of an impetuous mind) " remarkably docile and willing to receive advice or admonition from the old or experienced ". His strong filial sense may have fostered this attribute.

It was a serious matter for Lockhart to be opposed at this point. He had given up his legal work in Edinburgh, let his house and taken lodgings in London. From a letter to Murray, of 27th November, he would appear to have suspected Croker of malign interference ; as noted in an earlier section, his appeal to Croker may have failed.

" Mr. Croker's behaviour has indeed distressed me, for I had always considered him as one of those bad enemies who make excellent friends . . . The correspondence that has been passing between him and me may have been somewhat imprudently managed on my part. I may have committed myself in it in more ways than one. It is need-less to regret what cannot be undone ; at all events I perceive that it is now over with us for the present."

Croker was pledged to work for *The Quarterly*, but it is obvious that at this stage his defection would not greatly vex J. G. L. :

" I believe that his papers in *The Review* have (with a few exceptions) done the work a great deal more harm than good . . . There was always the bitterness of Gifford without his dignity, and the bigotry of Southey without his *bonne foi*." There was, in fact, a break in Croker's writing for *The Quarterly* between 1825 and 1831. Thereafter he wrote copiously. But in spite of the break, he and Lock-hart were bound close together till the end of Lockhart's life—for good or ill, in loyalty, in intimacy, sometimes, it may be, in aversion.

Scott asked Lockhart for a reassurance that he had honoured his pledge " to break off that sort of satirical warfare ". He had not, till now, cared to ask " how far that was strictly complied with, or how far your roguery had carried you again among the Ambrosians ". The matter once cleared, and the appointment secure, Lockhart must not go to the other extreme of submission, or play " the old man and his ass " of the fable.

" You must just harden your face against all this nonsense, or consider it as penance for past folly." In another
letter he spoke of Lockhart's friendship with Theodore
Hook, of whom, and his paper *John Bull*, Scott dis-
approved :

" You must take devilish good care of your start in
society in London. I do not look on Theodorus as fit
company for ladies, and if you even haunt him much
yourself you will find it tell against you especially when
the paper comes to be read. He is raffish, *entre nous*."

Lockhart may have replied to this, in his heart at least,
with Lamb's defence of his odd friends, those " good and
loving burrs ".

The affair was happily settled at last, and on 2nd December Scott noted in his Journal : " Sophia dined with us
alone, Lockhart being gone to the west to bid farewell to
his father and brothers. Evening spent in talking with
Sophia on their future prospects. God bless her, poor girl,
she never gave me a moment's reason to complain of her.
But oh, my God, that poor delicate child, so clever, so
animated, yet holding by this earth with so fearfully slight
a tenure. Never out of his mother's thoughts, almost never
out of his father's arms when he has but a single moment
to give to anything."

The shadows were falling on that bright and tranquil
domesticity of which Sophia once wrote to her husband
that they might have been too happy for mortal capacity
were it not for this fear for Johnny. The little boy had,
at one time, appeared to be growing from fragile babyhood
into sturdier boyhood. But he was, and his grandfather
knew it, " doomed to know not winter, only spring ", and
so brief a spring.

Next day Scott attended the farewell dinner given in
Lockhart's honour : " The company most highly respectable and any man might be proud of such an indication
of the interest they take in his progress in life."

On the 5th of December he wrote in the Journal :
" Lockhart and Sophia left us early, and without leave-
taking ; when I rose at eight o'clock they were gone.
This was very right. I hate red eyes and blowing of noses.

Agere et pati Romanum est. Of all schools commend me to the Stoic."

The shadows were falling around him. The night of his financial disaster was very near, in which he was to bear himself manfully. *Agere et pati* was his aim and achievement.

So, in the dark of a December morning, Lockhart and Sophia took coach and away. The first chapter was over in their life-story ; what was to come was to be a tale of mingled joy and sorrow ; but still, and to the end, a tale of true love and faith.

Chapter 10

LOCKHART AS NOVELIST

THESE five years between his marriage and his departure to London were, for Lockhart, a period of reformation, almost of conversion. He found himself, began to be what he was meant to be. This was due in large measure to the influence of Sophia and her father and to the almost perfect domestic happiness in which his heart's affections were satisfied. Scott's comment, made more than once, that Lockhart in his family life was wholly lovable, with his reserve broken, his bitterness dissolved, only repeated what Christie saw in him—saw not only in retrospect at the end, but in their youth together.

There was another fulfilment, or partial fulfilment also, in his work. The energy released in *Peter's Letters*, where the portraits and sketches are truly creative, and in the verse translations of *The Spanish Ballads* turned, for a brief while, into the channel of fiction. Lockhart wrote four novels between 1820 and 1824 : *Valerius, a Roman Story* ; *Adam Blair* ; *Reginald Dalton* ; *Matthew Wald* : all readable, all well-written but oddly unequal and none revealing him as a born novelist ; yet satisfying in him some need of self-expression. *Reginald Dalton* is amusing in parts ; *Adam Blair* comes nearest being a great novel and is worthy of a place among the minor Scots classics ; *Matthew Wald* is a strange, dark tale with no other to match it, unless perhaps Hogg's *Confessions of a Justified Sinner* ; a comparison that might suggest the question of whether Lockhart revised Hogg's manuscript.

Valerius and *Reginald Dalton* are easily classified, though both were pioneer novels in their day. Every now and then in the last century some one has felt it his duty to write a novel about ancient Greece or Rome. Lockhart was one of the first to hear that call. There have also been many novels about Oxford, with some sort of plot worked into the pattern of nostalgic memories. In this form also Lockhart was an innovator.

Valerius is more of an exercise in fiction, a very well-written exercise, than a novel of organic interest. Scott approved of it as " most classical and interesting at the same time, and cannot but produce a very deep impression. I am quite delighted with the reality of your Romans."

Henry Mackenzie, reviewing the book in *Blackwood's* in April 1821, found this reality something of a defect :

" Perhaps the adherence to the severity of the Roman character may account for the want of the pathetic in this story." Certainly the reader remains throughout in the condition of Margery Fleming's mother-turkey :

> But she was more than usual calm,
> She did not give a single dam.

One is fortified by the reflection that the characters are, as the Scots schoolmistress said of the Old Testament personages : " A' deid onywey." A good historical novel ought to arouse an imaginative sympathy strong enough to break down the barriers of time ; Lockhart's fails in this. Andrew Lang made a good point in saying that it reads like a translation from the Latin, and that conversely " as one reads *Valerius* one is always turning it into Latin prose ".

The story is that Valerius, a Roman Briton, meets and falls in love with a Roman girl Athanasia, whom he discovers to be a Christian ; who is imprisoned and in danger of martyrdom, and whom he rescues in a gallant and exciting manner ; marries and brings safely to Britain. He is himself converted to the new Faith. There are various complications, caused chiefly by the beautiful but wicked Rubellia, who tries to capture Valerius' cousin Sixtus. This marriage is almost forced on the youth by his stern father until Rubellia is revealed in her true character, as wicked, cruel and a trafficker in witchcraft. There are one or two faithful and comic slaves in the best Terentian manner ; and there is Sixtus' tutor, Xenophrastes, the Stoic, who is " guyed " by the author through Valerius. It has been suggested that Lockhart wrote " advocate's prose " ; and in his descriptions and presentations of character it is often easy to see the advocate addressing the jury, appealing to their emotions. There is a deliberate attempt at raising a laugh in the portrayal of Xenophrastes.

The characters are conventional : a gallant hero, a beautiful and virtuous heroine, a villainess, a number of subordinate characters mostly amiable. The descriptions are vivid in detail ; especially of the gladiatorial games and the martyrdom of the old Christian, Thraso, and of the secret assembly of a little group of Christians who are betrayed, surprised and captured. It ought to be more moving and exciting than it really is.

It might be compared not unfavourably with Kingsley's *Hypatia* which for so many readers, even willing and determined, remains one of the great unreadable novels. A more fascinating comparison is with Walter Pater's *Marius the Epicurean*, where the hero is, like Valerius, a young pagan, attracted by the new Christian faith. The difference between the two heroes reveals the utterly diverse minds of their respective creators. Pater was allured by the charm of the old paganism, as he found it in the poetry of Virgil and Tibullus and the Italian legendry ; equally allured by his own conception of Christianity in its mystery and tranquil beauty. So he made his hero waver, and linger on the borders between the two lands of opposing faiths. Lockhart was simply and sincerely Christian in belief ; paganism in every form was error, at its best an imperfect understanding of God. Christianity was true ; once that truth was revealed there was no temptation to linger in the old ways. The atmosphere of the dying pagan world is not conveyed, in spite of the accuracy of detail—whereas in *Marius* we dwell in a dream of Rome and the Italian countryside. In *Valerius* we are not shown the mind of the convert, or any struggle in his soul ; Valerius is converted swiftly, by example : that, first, of the old martyr Thraso ; and that, supremely of the Life revealed in the Gospel which Thraso gives him to read. His confession might be that of the Centurion at the foot of the Cross : " Truly this was the Son of God."

A sound judgement was given by Lockhart's friend Gleig, in his article in *The Quarterly* after Lockhart's death :

" The truth is that *Valerius* belongs to that class of novels which scholars hardly care to take up, and which mere readers of fiction cannot appreciate." He coupled it with *Reginald Dalton* as an example of the near-success or splendid failure in fiction :

" As the machinery of *Valerius* had been made use of to exhibit the author's acquaintance with Roman manners and customs in the reign of Trajan, so it appears as if in *Reginald Dalton* Lockhart's chief aim had been to describe undergraduate life as it was at Oxford during the earlier terms of his own academic career . . . Lockhart's strength did not lie in the direction of novel-writing. He could tell a story admirably ; he could not write a novel."

Professor Saintsbury, though a sympathetic admirer of Lockhart both as man and as author, pronounced a like verdict :

" Lockhart had every faculty for writing novels except the faculty of novel-writing." He found *Reginald* amusing but exaggerated : " the obvious work of a man who supplies the defects of a ten years memory by deepening the strokes which he does remember ".

Yet *Reginald* is full of charm and has so many virtues that it is somewhat baffling to find that they do not add up to make a good novel. Much of its charm is in evocation and recollection ; Lockhart might well have written one of the great autobiographies of literature had he chosen to recall his own youth directly. As it is, *Reginald Dalton* offers good entertainment for amateurs of the old-fashioned novel with a meandering plot, a runaway marriage, a wicked baronet (unfortunately converted to very dull morality, and only Sir Charles, not Sir Jasper), an amiable hero going slightly astray but soon returning to paths of virtue, a lovely heroine of mysterious parentage, a nearly lost inheritance, a duel, and many other activities. It is better in parts than as a whole.

Since *Reginald Dalton* appeared—in 1823—there have been many novels of Oxford life ; the one most comparable with Lockhart's being Newman's *Loss and Gain*. They have, in common, nostalgic memory. Newman's Oxford does not differ greatly from Lockhart's. But Newman sees it with the added wistfulness of an exile. He had to renounce

Oxford when he made his submission to Rome ; and he showed the anguish of that sacrifice in his description of his hero, Charles. There is nothing in *Reginald Dalton* to match the beauty and poignancy of the scene where Charles visits, for the last time, Christ Church meadows, throwing his arms round the willows and kissing their trunks ; gathering some of the black leaves to carry with him as memento. But *Loss and Gain* is the history of a soul that Oxford has nurtured ; *Reginald* only a pleasant tale of youth.

In his best novel, *Adam Blair*, Lockhart achieved a minor masterpiece, and something entirely unexpected, for which his previous work seemed to offer no preparation. It is not merely Scottish in interest ; in some ways it has affinity with the Russian fiction of the latter part of the nineteenth century.

The plot was given him in a true story told by his father, which may be read in the sober but fascinating records of the Church of Scotland, the *Fasti Ecclesiae Scoticanae*. It happened in Cathcart, near Glasgow, where, in the mid-eighteenth century, the Rev. George Adam was minister ; a man of piety and devotion, much loved by his people ; so much, that when he fell into the sin of fornication, and confessed it to his fellow-clergy, there was less scandal than sorrow and compassion. He was deposed, as was inevitable —but only for a year. " Such had been his exemplary character and great usefulness that his elders [*anglice* vestrymen] unanimously petitioned the Presbytery that the sentence might be removed. He was reponed to his office and charge." This story Dr. Lockhart told very well ; it possessed his son's imagination until he could re-create it.

Adam Blair is minister of a country parish ; a widower with one small daughter. He is greatly esteemed by his flock and has among them two specially good friends ; old John Maxwell, one of his elders, and Mrs. Semple, a benevolent old lady who is described with humour and affection : " She was one of that once numerous class of ladies in Scotland who, virtuous and religious and every way estimable as they may be, do a great many things as if they believed the stomach to be by far the most important part in the construction of every human being. For instance, if she heard of a long-absent son or brother returning to any family in the village, her first speech was sure to be : ' Poor bodies, poor bodies, I'm very glad to hear it, I'm very heartily glad to hear it. I hope they'll have something comfortable in the house. It would be a burning shame if they had not a good supper the night " ; and the end of the speech would probably be a whisper to her butler : ' Thomas, tak' down the cauld pye to John Anderson's wi' my compliments.' "

The novel is not a long one ; indeed it lacks light and shade, and might well have been richer in character-studies. Adam himself, and the heroine, his partner in sin, Charlotte, are formal and tragic types rather than human figures. But their story is told with tragic force. Charlotte, a friend of Adam's dead wife, comes on a long visit to the manse. Mutual sympathy and compassion between her and Adam end in their discovery of mutual love ; there is a brief realisation of happiness—a dream from which they are awakened by a summons to Charlotte. She is married, unhappily, to a gentleman described (in one of Lockhart's characteristic phrases) as " one of that numerous division of the human species which may be shortly and accurately described as answering to the name of Captain Campbell ". They have, for a while, been separated, and the husband is abroad. But now he sends his agent, one Strahan, a brutal type, to conduct Charlotte to his home, a small, lonely castle on the shores of Loch Fyne. Adam sinks into despair. A fellow-cleric, the shrewd and kindly Dr. Muir, gives him good counsel : " Pluck up your heart, my man, and put on your ain face again, and beware of sinking into your dumps, and gang about your work among your folk as usual, and take my word for it, ye'll no' repent it." Adam tries to obey ; but good counsel is forgotten and resolution overthrown by a letter of wild appeal from Charlotte. Adam set forth on a mad journey to the castle on the loch-side, and reaching it, cries out to Charlotte at her window :

" It is I, Charlotte, it is your friend, it is Adam Blair that has come to see you."

Charlotte cries in return :

"Oh, Adam, God has heard my prayer, God has not deserted me. But now, I was alone; now I have you with me and shall fear nothing."

For all the melodrama, there is the true note of compelling passion. The lovers are driven together. Charlotte gives Adam supper and wine; and tells him the story of her suffering from the insults of Strahan, of her utter misery : "Had she never told that story, perhaps Adam Blair had never been a fallen man."

That night, they are lovers without joy. Adam wakens to a passion of remorse deeper than his love. He flees from Charlotte and from the house and walks far away, to a hidden glen where he sits brooding beside a dark tarn.

"No living thing was near when Adam Blair took his seat upon one of the great, shapeless fragments of stone that . . . lean their bare masses over the dismal waters ; and though the bright sky of noontide hung far above in its beauty, the black mirror below him reflected nothing of its azure. Blair sat there gazing upon the pool . . . Once and again he strove to frame his lips to prayer, but the syllables stuck in his throat . . . He felt as if he were wrapt in some black and burning cloud which would not let in one ray upon his misery of thirst and scorching, and became at last bewildered with a crowd of the most sombre fantasies. Black, loathsome creatures seemed to sit close beside him on either side, polluting the breath ere it reached his nostrils, scowling upon him with faces of devilish glee . . . He strove to utter the Name of his Maker, but ere he could open his mouth the holy Name itself passed away from his recollection, and they stooped nearer and nearer to him and peered into his eyes with looks of triumph as if they had read his thoughts, and knew he was baffled from within."

Lockhart took no light view of what a modern novelist has called " the most popular of the deadly sins ". Adam comes to the verge of suicide, in his despair ; is saved by Charlotte ; and swears never again to attempt self-murder : "I shall wait God's time. God grant it be not long. God shield me from presumptuous sin."

He falls into a fever ; and recovers only to hear of Charlotte's death, caused by her own unbearable anguish.

Her husband comes home, and in his brief encounter with Adam shows not only dignity but a touch of nobility :

" Go back to your own country and guard yourself better. The grave has swallowed up all my resentment. I hope you have not had so near a look of it for nothing."

Meanwhile, Adam's friend and comforter old John Maxwell, has followed him to bring him home. They reach Glasgow on the day of a meeting of Presbytery, called, though Adam does not know it, to deal with the scandal he has caused. He himself insists on attending, in order to demit his charge. As he enters, he hears Dr. Muir pleading for him ; and then the good Doctor addresses him : " I thank my God ! Adam Blair, speak, look up, let them hear your voice. Speak solemnly in the hearing of God and your brethren—Adam Blair, are you guilty or not guilty of this uncleanness."

" The unhappy Blair laying his hand upon his breast, answered quickly and clearly : ' Call me no more your brother—I am a fallen man—I am guilty.' "

It was a harsh age. The Kirk was rarely merciful to the weak and the fallen who were then, and for many years to come, publicly admonished by the clergy for even a whiff of the popular sin. It might have been expected that Adam's brethren would deal zealously with him. But their mood is one of compassion ; they are full of horror for the sin, of pity for the sinner. Had he pleaded aberration of mind they would have accepted the plea. It is Adam himself who demands that the sentence of deposition be pronounced.

There is the same gentleness among his people when he returns to live among them, not as clergyman, but as a peasant, working on the small croft once held by his grandfather. The picture of Scottish country life is a kind one. Years pass—and Adam is persuaded by his former brethren to let himself be reinstated in the office of the ministry. He accepts, and ends his days in peace.

It is a melancholy story—and melancholy not only in the central tragedy. There is little joy, even tranquillity in it. But there is a sense of pity and of chastity deeper than any conventional morality, that lifts it far above melodrama.

Adam Blair knows that he has sinned against himself, against Charlotte, against the Body of Christ of which he is a member. He desires to make atonement ; it is not inflicted upon him. It is a story of contrition, not of punishment ; in which it is a contrast with a better-known novel with a like theme—Hawthorn's *Scarlet Letter*. There, the tragedy is one of persecution and punishment far beyond what the fault has merited ; inflicted with sadistic fervour by the community on the offender. *The Scarlet Letter* is a study of cruelty.

In an earlier age, the theme would have been told as a ballad, not as a novel ; and the narrative has a hint of the ballad-quality in it.

Having looked into the depths of human passion, Lockhart was impelled to look once more, and into murkier deeps. His last novel, *Matthew Wald*, is the study of a mind possessed by the passions of love and hate, with hate predominating and driving its victim to madness. Matthew, who tells his own tale, is dominated by his love, from boyhood, for his cousin Katharine ; and, when she falls in love with a worthless rival, by hatred and jealousy. (The rival is Lord Lascelyne : the wicked baronet of melodrama, raised to the peerage !)

To give even an outline of the plot would break the bounds of a reasonable chapter, for it is " a demned outline ". There are many episodes, many minor narratives, some exceedingly well told : as the account of the murder in Matthew's lodging in Glasgow, which is completely irrelevant to the main theme, except as forming part of Matthew's experience of horror and violence.

Matthew is qualifying as a surgeon. Like many a Scots student he takes a post as tutor, in the household of Sir Claud Barr, an invalid and once-wicked baronet whose past has some importance in the plot. Matthew is friendly with the old nurse, Mammy Baird, who tells the story ; which is another example of Lockhart's talent for the short story or episode. Sir Claud, in his youth, had brought home from abroad a lovely girl Joan : called " Perling Joan " by the servants, from the lace trimming of her black satin gowns. Mammy Baird recalled her fondly : " Sic a dancing, gleesome bit bird of a lassie was never seen ; and ane could not but pity her mair than blame her for what she had done . . . " She never put powder on her hair, neither ; oh, proud, proud she was of her hair. I've often known her comb and comb at it for an hour on end ; and when it was out of the buckle, the bonny curls fell as low as her knee."

Perling Joan is forsaken ; Sir Claud, yielding to family pressure, makes a suitable marriage. Joan goes away with her baby, it is supposed back to her own people. On the day when Sir Claud brings his bride home— " As fast as fire ever flew from flint, a woman in a red cloak rushed out from among the auld shrubbery at the west end of the house, and flung herself in among the horses' feet, and the wheels gaed clean out ower her breast, and crushed her dead in a single moment. She never stirred. Poor thing ! She was no Perling Joan then. She was in rags, perfect rags, all below the bit cloak ; and we found the bairn, rowed in a check apron, lying just behind the hedge. A braw, heart-some welcoming for a pair of young, married folk."

The child has been brought up in her father's house, on sufferance ; Matthew knows her as Miss Joanne ; admires and likes her. He meets his lost love Katharine again, when she visits the house, with her husband Lord Lascelyne. Sir Claud's death, before very long, ends the domestic arrangements. Joanne goes to live with Mammy Baird in her cottage ; Matthew qualifies in medicine, settles down in practice, and finds himself mildly in love with Joanne. They marry and are happy for a time. Mammy Baird dies, and leaves to Joanne a locked casket, in which are discovered letters from her father to her mother, addressing her as his wife. On the strength of these Matthew brings a lawsuit, to prove Joanne a legitimate daughter and heiress of Sir Claud ; he wins his case, and gains half of the estate for his wife. All appears to be going well ; he is a good doctor, well-liked and prosperous. He stands for Parliament and is elected.

Before going to London to take his seat, he spends some time in Edinburgh with Joanne, where they meet Matthew's aunt, Katharine's mother ; hear of Katharine's unhappiness in marriage. Lascelyne is unfaithful to her and insults her by forcing her to meet his mistress. All the old fires of jealousy and hatred blaze up again in Matthew and he is in dangerous mood.

In London they have a mysterious neighbour who remains a recluse. A little boy is sometimes seen in the garden, but no master or mistress of the house. Matthew's curiosity is aroused, and one evening, seeing a light in one of the windows of the mysterious house, he crawls along the branch of a tree in his own garden which reaches over to the neighbour's ; he leans too far over, falls, and is stunned. When he recovers he is brought into the house, sees its mistress—and recognises Katharine. She tells him she has left Lascelyne, taking their little son with her. Matthew is driven to frenzy by the tale of her suffering :

" I cursed him, madman that I was, I cursed the hour in which she saw him. I cursed him like a fiend."

After a passionate scene they are reconciled, and Katharine falls into his arms, weeping. At that point they are discovered by Joanne, who, anxious about Matthew, has searched both gardens, seen the lighted window and entered the room.

" Suddenly a piercing cry was uttered quite close to us. Joanne was within the chamber door. She had seen with her own eyes the agony of that tenderness and she saw no more. One convulsion chased another over that delicate frame. Wild reproaches, melancholy wailings there were, but they were all sunk immediately in the screams of her untimely travail."

Joanne dies in that travail. Matthew's next meeting with Katharine is by his wife's coffin. She tries to calm his frenzy of grief and remorse, and has almost succeeded when a servant brings a message from Lascelyne. The latter has traced his wife, and now accuses her of seeking Matthew's protection. He now has cause for divorce, and he will separate her from her child. Matthew forces the servant to lead him to Lascelyne, whom he provokes to a duel. They fight with swords :

" I rushed upon him, sir, as if I had been some horned brute . . . He stabbed me thrice, thrice through the arm . . . I felt his blade as if it has been a gnat, a nothing. At last my turn came—I spitted him through the heart—I rushed on till the hilt stopped me—I did not draw my steel out of him—I spurned him off it with my foot . . . I dipped my shoe in his blood."

Rushing madly back to Katharine, Matthew exults in his deed. " I held out the red blade before me—the drops had not all baked yet—one or two fell upon the floor."

" ' Speak, Matthew. What is this ? Speak. Ha ! God of mercy, there is blood upon that sword ! '

" ' Ay, blood, my cousin, blood.'

" ' My husband ! My Lascelyne ! '

" I heard no more. Heavens and earth that I should write this down. One shriek—one, just one. Fainted ? Swooned ? Dead ! oh dead ! I remember no more."

It is melodrama at its thickest and best. Lockhart should have written detective-stories of the most lurid kind. There follows a strange chapter of troubled imaginings, half memory, half dream, in Matthew's crazed mind ; then a scrap of speech from a keeper in a madhouse. It would all seem to end in gloom. But there is a postscript or epilogue, written by one young man to another ; both of them apparently friends of Matthew in his old age, long after his recovery from madness, and after his natural death. To them he has appeared a benevolent friend and host, a man much esteemed, living in tranquillity and comfort. His own narrative has been bequeathed to one of these young men who sends it to the other, with the comment :

" That a man . . . who was, whenever any of us met him in society, the soul of the party—that this man should have been in reality the habitual victim of the darkest and most melancholy reflections, was, undoubtedly a thing not likely to be suspected by observers so young and thoughtless as we both were when we first knew Mr. Wald."

Matthew Wald, in fact, forestalls *Dr. Jekyll and Mr. Hyde*, and it is one of the freaks of literary fame that it should be forgotten while Stevenson's fable has caught the imagination and personified an idea. Lockhart's novel is full of faults. Scott perceived the chief of these when he wrote " a painful tale very forcibly told—the worst is that there is no resting place—nothing but misery from the title-page to the finis ".

The very violence of passion crushes and blasts sympathetic emotion. Matthew is fascinating as a psychological study, but as a real human personality he does not exist : nor do any of the other characters involved in the tragedy.

As a novelist Lockhart remains an enigma. He could write so well ; he could tell a story dramatically, describe a scene vividly, search deeply into a tortured mind and heart. Yet even at his best, even in *Adam Blair*, he did not write a complete masterpiece ; and his four novels are singularly detached from each other. There is not a Lockhart novel, recognisable in type, as there is a Trollope, a Dickens novel. The verdict of Gleig and of Saintsbury is true—he was not in essence and substance, a novelist. But in the four novels he wrote he did express something in himself, did release and shape some energy of imagination ; it was a necessary phase in his own intellectual progress.

PART 2

YEARS OF MATURITY

Chapter 11

THE NEW LIFE

I. FAMILY MATTERS : JOHNNY IN BRIGHTON

THE Lockharts lived, at first, in furnished rooms in Pall Mall, conveniently near Albemarle Street, then, for a time, at Wimbledon. About two years after their going to London they settled in their permanent home : 24 Sussex Place, Regent's Park : still a pleasant region, and at that period spacious and retired from the noise of town. There was the park and there were gardens where a child could play. Abbotsford was still a second home, and Scotland was to see the Lockharts every year. Brighton became a favourite resort. It had, perhaps, passed its zenith of Regency fashion and elegance, but its popularity was securely founded. The bracing air from sea and downs, the regimen of bathing, approved more and more by doctors, the easy journey, and the charm of the place itself all attracted visitors of every type and class, especially the middle class who were beginning to enjoy annual holidays by the sea.

Sophia began taking Johnny to Brighton in the hope that air and sun and sea would strengthen, perhaps even cure him. It was a fragile hope now ; for spinal disease was manifest, and Johnny had to spend most of his days on a sofa.

Sophia was, her father thought, too " doctor-loving ". It was her " most marked foible " and it brought her a gentle, paternal little note of caution against " engaging again with a pet doctor which next to a pet parson is an abomination ". Poor Sophia could hardly help her dependence upon a favourite doctor, with Johnny holding so feebly to life, and with her own health delicate. She had already chosen her London physician, Dr. Ferguson, who became one of their truest friends as well as a skilled medical adviser. His name recurs not only in Sophia's letters but in Lockhart's until the end of the latter's life.

Lockhart was already, at the beginning of 1826, deep in his new work ; Scott was writing an article on Pepys for *The Quarterly* : " I enclose the article ", he wrote to J. G. L. in January. " It is totally uncorrected, so I wish, of course, much to see it in proof if possible, as it must be dreadfully inaccurate. The opiate was busy with my brain when the beginning was written."

Scott had been ill ; the shadow of his last, long illness was not far off and the other shadows, of his financial ruin, were dark about him. Three firms, Constable, Hurst & Robinson, and Ballantyne and Scott himself were bound together in an intricate tangle. Scott refused the escape of bankruptcy. He would shoulder his own share of the burden. His letters to Lockhart were not despairing :

" Even supposing that Constable & Co. and Hurst & Robinson do not repay me a penny of upwards of £30,000 which they owe me . . . my old age will be far from destitute, and my family not ill provided for, even if my right hand should lose its cunning." It was an extra-ordinarily magnanimous letter : " While I live I shall regret the downfall of Constable's house, for never did there nor can there exist so liberal, so intelligent and so trust-worthy an establishment." Lockhart was less forgiving when the time came to write of these difficult years ; but he had to witness the suffering of his hero and of the family that were as dear to him as his own.

Scott acted swiftly. The house at 39 Castle Street was given up, and Lady Scott and Anne returned to Abbotsford, where it was possible to live in comfort with economy. Lady Scott took it ill ; she was inadequate to her husband's need of comfort at this time. In her defence it must be remembered that she was on the verge of her last, painful illness.

For Anne, this was the end of a chapter, the end of her youth, of her dancing days. She had much of her mother

in her ; loved *le beau monde* ; had a gaiety that kindled and
sparkled at the touch of grandeur ; had wit and charm
and not a little beauty of the dark and vivid type. It
might have been forgiven her if she had repined. But
Anne was her father's daughter, and came of generations
of women who could and did " thole " what life brought :
pain and illness, sorrow, poverty.

His own cares could not quench Scott's interest in the
Lockharts' affairs. He approved of their temporary home :
" It is better you have got a good house, for there is scarce
anything in London so necessary to comfort and credit.
You may scrub in your dinner as much as you please, so
you have a handsome front in a fashionable part of the
town." He approved too of the enlarging of social life ;
writing, of Lockhart, to Maria Edgeworth : " he will be
obliged to lay aside his hidalgo silence and exert himself
a little in society, and I am glad to learn he takes the trouble
to do so. He has now a great stake to play, for his talents
are of a nature singularly applicable to whatever lies before
him, and he has a great fund of applied information, and
Sophia is in every respect a safe and prudent help-mate."

There was some anxiety about Sophia in April 1826 ;
when her second son, Walter, was born, prematurely, in
Brighton. But the new baby flourished and gained strength
daily, and Sophia made a good recovery. As the second
son, he was, in the old Scots fashion, named after his maternal
grandfather " Walter—a favourite name in our family, and
I trust of no bad omen. Yet it is no charm for life "—
Scott entered in his Journal.

Sophia's letters from Brighton, that spring, before and
after the baby's birth, give a clear picture of domestic life.
Johnny at first appeared to thrive. On the night of their
arrival (" their " comprising Sophia, Johnny, Junor the
maid and David the manservant) Johnny was " sitting here
opposite me, eating an enormous piece of bread and butter "
—after a comfortable journey with only one mishap : when
Junor dropped the bandbox, fortunately without damage
to its contents.

" Do, dearest Lockhart, have a good hope. Johny [*sic*]
never would have gone through what he has done were he

not better than we think him." Sophia had a good deal
of trouble about lodgings. The hotel where they went on
arrival presented a bill so extortionate that ' I keep it as a
curiosity '. She found rooms—two bedrooms and a parlour
and a bed for David, in Marine Parade for which she was
charged £3 3s. a week, including fire and attendance.
The rooms all looked towards the sea, and " the little body "
could lie on his sofa in the window and enjoy " the same
benefit of the air as if he were on the beach ". Sometimes
he was able to drive out in one of the little donkey- or goat-
carriages that were to be had. The lodgings were not all
that Sophia could wish. The seaside landlady had come
into power. " How people can, for mere pleasure, come to
such places as this I cannot conceive, for though the sea is
beautiful it is a perfect town, and contains the most miserable
accommodation, and few of the lodgings are near the beach."
The lodgings became unbearable ; the landlady was " a
perfect horror, a man in petticoats . . . with indefatigable
legs and a tongue like a bell ". Other rooms were found,
in Preston Street, at £2 a week and a pound for Sophia's
dinner, with a landlady who was " a perfect gentlewoman
in appearance ".

The Lockharts when separated worried about each other,
and tried to be reassuring : " I long to see you, dearest
Lockhart, and trust you are a good boy, and not letting
yourself get low, to think you are drooping would quite kill
me, so do let me see you with a smiling face, for I do think
you will see your darling, even when you come, stouter."

Lockhart, on his part, deplored Sophia's efforts at economy
and bargaining : " My happiness would be much increased
if I thought you really were in a comfortable place " ; her
discomforts gave him " not only great but unnecessary
pain ". But on the whole, Brighton was a success. Johnny
enjoyed his outings, and mamma commissioned papa to
find him, second-hand in London, a little carriage ; those
to be hired in Brighton were all too large. Like many
mothers, Sophia found a new use for old garments. Her
discarded riding-habit was to be made into a carriage-
cloak for Johnny ; she had bought him a peaked cap to
shield his eyes from the glitter of sun and sea.

Johnny was well enough to have daily lessons, shared with a friend's child. His governess was a Miss McTavish : " You see you need not fear for her losing her Scotch tongue," wrote Sophia. She " liked the young woman's appearance very much indeed " ; and Miss McTavish further won her heart " by proposing to bring *Mother Goose's Tales* and *The Seven Champions* to read to the two students ". Johnny was following his father in regard to early reading.

The new Walter was duly made a Christian in the Parish Church of Brighton ; Sophia wrote to Lockhart that he must bring " some drinkables to drink the Baby's health "— as they had only two bottles of port left ; he must bring some spoons and forks, too, for the christening luncheon. Johnny was to go to church to see his brother's baptism, and was wildly excited about it. The letters were cosy.

At Abbotsford the shadows were gathering more darkly than ever. Lady Scott was grievously ill now ; too ill to know her husband or say good-bye to him when he left for Edinburgh. On the 15th of May she died. As sometimes happens, there had been a premature rumour of her death and Anne had written to Lockhart, bidding him prepare Sophia for the inevitable end :

" Mamma, thank God, is better, but last night was a very terrible one . . . God knows it is a melancholy sort of recovery, for though she may linger, yet we have no hopes of her recovery, and if it had been God's pleasure I almost wish she had been released from her suffering last night." Lockhart wrote, then, to Sophia : " I know you too well to hesitate about letting you see precisely how the matter stands, and you know me well enough to know that it is a great misery to me to have to write instead of speaking such sad tidings. You must exert yourself and be, as poor Anne seems to be, satisfied that prolongation of life under such circumstances is a cruel prayer."

Anne wrote to Sophia, on Sunday night, May 21st, 1826, when the end had come :

" Charles has arrived, and that dreaded meeting is over. I was relieved that dear Lockhart did not come. He will comfort you, and Mamma wants nothing now . . . The last three days were like a terrible dream, but before that she very often asked for you, and during your confinement was in great anxiety about you. Johnny was among the last she mentioned, at least I heard the name, though I could not make out the words, also her father, Lord Downshire."

Scott's letters at this time, and his entries in the Journal show how deeply he felt his loss, how tenderly he mourned his " thirty years companion ". She had not been his first love ; the crack in his heart had never wholly mended. But, loyal and loving himself, he remembered the affection and loyalty she had given him. In a letter to Sophia he made his only reference to any flaw in her : " Whatever were her failings they hurt only herself, and arose out of bodily illness, and must be weighed against one of the most sincere, loyal and generous hearts that ever blood warmed."

Anne found the sweetest memorial to her mother in the sorrow of the poor people about Abbotsford : " My dear Sophia, if you saw the distress of the poor servants and the poor people, though it would give you pain, yet you would feel what I do, that to be regretted by the poor so deeply is a sign that she is now in Heaven. She was always kind."—Could there be a better valediction ?

Sophia was not yet able to travel, nor could she leave her baby and Johnny ; Lockhart was held in town by business. Scott's sons were with him and Anne ; they had comfort in mutual gentleness and in kind memories. Then the sons must return to duty, Walter to his regiment, Charles to Oxford ; Scott left for Edinburgh and his work in the Courts. Anne stayed at Abbotsford with Cousin Anne Scott as companion, and with the dogs. Both she and Scott wrote about Ourisk, Lady Scott's little terrier, that had shown exclusive devotion to her in her lifetime. " Before poor Mamma died it was so cross to me that I could not touch it," Anne told Sophia. But after " all was over, the first thing I saw was Ourisk on my bed, it came out of the room immediately after she died ".

Life went on quietly, but not unhappily, for the two Annes. They sewed and worked together : " I have been employing myself when I am able in making baby clothes for two of the poor women " in the neighbourhood. Anne was continuing her mother's kindness. For her own new nephew she procured a frock and cap of the exquisite Ayrshire embroidery that is among the glories of Scottish domestic arts. There were all the sad little details to arrange, too. Scott had bidden Anne send a memento of their mother to Sophia, and something to Walter's wife Jane, and to keep the rest of the jewels and trinkets for herself. Some of the most valuable, Anne found, had been sold, in the first days of the disaster. Sophia was to have " the aquamarine set " and a gold locket with some of her mother's hair. Anne longed for her sister's companionship and counsel ; but she was being very brave and very capable, and her father praised her. " You have no idea how regularly I keep house, no bills, everything paid, but I do hate to ask for more money."

Chiefswood was let, to the Hamiltons, a brother of Sir William Hamilton, whom Anne found agreeable neighbours and as near as possible to being worthy tenants. " As she has no carriage I generally call for her to make visits, but I cannot get over the strange feeling of seeing her come out instead of you, and when Mr. Hamilton steps out of the window in a dressing-gown and slippers, I almost think it is Lockhart."

Anne liked the Hamiltons. " He puts me in mind of Lockhart, except that he torments his wife now and then "— which was, apparently, not one of Lockhart's habits. Johnny's toys were still at Chiefswood, safely locked away. Anne's major trial at this time was Mrs. Jobson, mother of her sister-in-law Jane.

" Walter and Jane have been here for a fortnight with Mrs. Jobson. Walter is in high spirits and is well, and I rather think Jane is improved but heaven help us with Mrs. Jobson. I had, I thought, expected all that was detestable, but my expectations were far surpassed, to say nothing of her vulgarity and bad manners."

Anne had resigned herself to the prospect of a quiet winter at home when the most agreeable of diversions came, in a visit with her father to Sophia and Lockhart in London ; followed by a few days in Paris ; and then a visit to Charles at Oxford, and to Mrs. Thomas Scott at Cheltenham.

They stayed in Paris for a week, at a hotel in the Rue de Rivoli, being fêted and petted, much to their enjoyment.

"Anne has seen more fine folk and heard more fine speeches than she has seen and heard in all the previous course of her life. Hitherto her head stands it pretty well, nor do I see any stronger symptom of innovation than may be inferred from a Parisian bonnet as large as a shovel "— was papa's comment. He too was happy in this visit, though painfully impressed by Johnny's fragility. Lockhart and Sophia were well and cheerful and baby Walter a healthy and beautiful child.

It was an Indian summer for Scott and for Anne ; golden days before a long, dark, seemingly endless winter.

II. THE NEW EDITOR

Lockhart's first *Quarterly*, that of March 1826, contained Scott's review of the new edition of Pepys' *Diary*.

The other articles included one on that notable eccentric Charles Waterton, whose *Wanderings in South America* was reviewed : some political articles : a review of three novels : *Tremaine ; or, The Man of Refinement : Matilda ; A Tale of the Day :* and *Granby ; A Novel :* all of which strike the modern reader as uncommonly and comically bad. The age of fiction had begun, and a flood of novels swept through *The Quarterly*. There was an article on some recently published *Revelations* by a devout and *exaltée* French nun ; with which the reviewer dealt trenchantly. Two Lives of Sheridan, one by Thomas Moore, were noticed at length— in the leisurely and ample fashion then permissible. Altogether it was a solid and varied number. Lockhart's ship was well launched.

In the June issue, Scott reviewed a *Life of John Philip Kemble* ; Lockhart himself dealt with poetry : the posthumous volume of Shelley's poems, and a verse translation of *Faust* by Lord Francis Leveson-Gower. He gave the latter somewhat modified praise ; showing his own sound knowledge and admiration of the great poet he had once met. Of Shelley's version (included in the volume of poems) he said that while there were failures and blunders enough to make one suspect " that Mr. Shelley's knowledge of the German language had been defective "—yet these could not " conceal the extraordinary merit " of many passages. " Mr. Shelley had a fine ear for harmony and a great command of poetical language . . . a fine liveliness both of feeling and of imagination, and, in short, wanted little to be a distinguished original poet but distinctness of conception and regulation of taste." He thought the discipline of translation had been good for Shelley as a preventive of " the vague and idle allegories in which he delighted, to say nothing of the *dulcia vitia* of a worse kind ". —Had Lockhart learned justice and mercy since his *Blackwood* days, or was he attracted by Shelley's scholarly and aristocratic mind, as he had been contemptuous of the young apothecary in whom he could find neither learning nor genius ?

In September, he reviewed Scott's *Lives of the Novelists*, in what remains one of the most important, most interesting and most valuable of his critical essays. It contains his theory of the novel, still a comparatively new form of literature, a rival of the drama. He was a novel-reader, and for him, in spite of the stream of trivial fiction that continued to flow past him, the novel was not only entertainment but (to borrow, ahead of time, from Matthew Arnold) " a criticism of life ". He saw it as the new form that must reflect the manners and express the thought of contemporary life :

" The business of painting our manners and lashing our vices has been truly in the hands of our novelists ever since Fielding, Smollett and Sterne produced their strong and graphic delineations. These men were to their own times what Jonson and his brother moralists had been to a preceding age, and what the Wycherleys and Vanburghs had been to another."

The novel was a form more perfected and more potent than the drama in the work of two authors. " What is *The Good-natured Man* to *The Vicar of Wakefield* ? Not very much more than *Tom Thumb* to *Tom Jones* . . . *Candide* and

The Princess of Babylon did more for Voltaire's ends than all his Theatre. . . . Had Jonson written novels, his peculiar fancy for the delineation of mere oddities might have been gratified to the utmost extent . . . *The Fortunes of Nigel* may be considered as an attempt to do what it is a thousand pities that Jonson should have left undone."

Scott had feared that novel-reading might be an allurement from the study of " useful history and real literature " (which, coming from the prince of novelists, sounds unduly deprecatory). Lockhart disagreed with this view, arguing that a vivid historical romance—such as Defoe's *Memoirs of a Cavalier* and Scott's own *Waverley* and *Old Mortality* both preserved contemporary material and stimulated the desire of many readers to turn to history itself. As for those who read only light, modern fiction, they would probably " have been, in the immense majority of cases, readers of exactly nothing at all had they lived a hundred years ago ". His sketch of the pleasures of reading indicates an intellectual level from which we have sunk deplorably far :

" Reading is a source of entertainment which, out of the actual business of life has no rival to fear. No one that has formed any intellectual habits at all can dance or sing, or look on dancers or listen to singing for many hours on end ; nor is there any cultivated audience in the world that would not, if the matter were put to a fair and honest vote, acknowledge that three hours of the best-acted play are enough."

J. G. L. was not musical, and enjoyed the theatre only in moderation, perhaps as a good husband rather than as an amateur of the drama. The portrait of him by MacLise that shows him in elegant ease by his own fireside, lying back comfortably in his chair, cigar in mouth, browsing peacefully in a large volume, probably presents him as he best liked to be. He enjoyed society—however he might pretend to grumble ; for he loved gossip and only at clubs and parties can sufficient gossip be gathered to add spice to letters and conversation. But he was essentially domestic, and as essentially, intellectual ; and took his pleasures above all through reading. It is obvious from his own articles and reviews that he read with zest—even when he proceeded, with equal zest, to demolish a book he found ill-written. When he approved he could praise heartily, conveying the warmth of his own enjoyment ; but any book was better than no book.

Lockhart's defence of the novel may well have surprised the serious-minded readers of *The Quarterly*. Since Fielding and Smollett, and before and after the splendour of the Waverleys, there had been so much foolish and worthless fiction that there was a reluctance, among the intellectual or would-be-intellectual, to admit to a taste for novel-reading. Scott himself, in his admiring and admirable notice of *Emma* in *The Quarterly*, in 1815, had thought it necessary to explain —if not apologise for—his serious regard for a work of fiction. Jane Austen in turn had been impelled to make her humorous defence of novels—in the well-known passage in *Northanger Abbey*. Lockhart had the discernment to recognise that so much genius had been poured into this form that its progress was assured ; and he appreciated the importance of this most readable kind of literature in an age when reading was a pleasure ; and men and women read for amusement as well as for instruction, and might find both in the pages of one book.

To survey these *Quarterlies* of 1826 is to see that the first year in London was a full one, with good work performed, and the foundations solidly laid of a career that was to engross Lockhart until nearly the end of his life. The domestic pattern was one of interwoven joy and sorrow : there had been much grief—the disaster of Scott's failure, the death of Lady Scott, anxiety about Anne, anguish about Johnny ; on the other hand, the fortitude of Scott himself, Anne's recovery and valour of spirit, recurring hope about Johnny, delight in the new baby. The strands of Lockhart's life were to be so mingled until the end. His private and his professional life, too, were to be intertwined. He cannot be considered only as critic and editor and professional man of letters ; nor can his whole self be found (though most of it and the best of it) in his familiar letters. Even when both sources are discovered and explored something remains elusive ; but there are moments of complete revelation, and every glimpse shows part of the truth.

Chapter 12

THE BEGINNING OF MATURITY

*T*HE QUARTERLY, when Lockhart became editor, was fifteen years old, and now solidly established as the Tory, High-Church periodical. Political opinion was as strong in London as it had been in Edinburgh ; political prejudice influenced literary judgements, and few critics saw any reason to practice moderation of statement. Religious feeling too was fervent. It was an age of churchgoing and of strong, even passionate interest in church matters. Within a few years of Lockhart's appointment the Church of England knew a renaissance, a second Reformation in the Catholic revival of the Oxford Movement. *The Quarterly* took a lively interest in that Movement and in all its results and repercussions. There was a good deal of anti-Roman feeling, along with a firm belief in the Anglican Church as Catholic and Apostolic, and loyal to the teaching of the primitive Church.

The country was at peace ; but the long years of war had not far receded. The fear of invasion was a fresh memory ; even the dread and foreboding roused by the French Revolution was no mere dream of a night safely past. The knowledge that it might have happened, might yet happen here, was at the root of ultra-Conservative feelings and policy. Republicanism was no remote theory. The Monarchy still lacked prestige and popularity.

Georgian London was a city of feuds, literary and political ; it was large enough to be a city of the world and not only of England, but it was a society small and compact enough to cultivate gossip.

Lockhart, coming of good stock with his own brilliant intellectual attainments and the magic key of his connection with Scott, could enter many doors. For all his " hidalgo airs " of pride and reserve he enjoyed company. If he never had the deep humanity of Scott, he was no cloistered or academic intellectual. He made enemies ; but he made and kept friends.

The Lockharts' circle widened, in London, but it included friends of long standing, such as the vivacious Lady
Davy, widow of the famous scientist Sir Humphry Davy.
She was born (in 1780) Jane Kerr, of Kelso, and claimed
cousinship, though distant, with Scott ; was the only
daughter of wealthy parents, and while still in her twenties
reached the position described as desirable by the " Provincial Lady " of the " Diary "—that of a rich and childless
widow. Her first husband, Shuckburgh Apreece, died when
she was twenty-seven. Her second marriage in 1812
increased the scope of her enjoyment, as, on the other hand,
it greatly added to the comfort of her distinguished husband.
They spent much of their time abroad, especially in Italy
which Lady Davy enjoyed ; and in London they had all
the *kudos* that came from Sir Humphry being President of
the Royal Society. Lady Davy's success and her zest for
life were not quenched in her second widowhood. She
was a popular hostess and a kind friend to the young
Lockharts ; Sophia she had known from her childhood.
Lockhart liked her and was amused by her, and sometimes
called her Jinny.

Sophia was of immeasurable help to her husband socially,
as well as of domestic comfort and sweetness. Her father's
true daughter, she had warmth and gentleness in her
courtesy. She had written once of herself : " Although my
name is Sophia Scott I am not at all clever "—but she *was*
clever, in an intuitive, feminine way that reproduced her
father's deep wisdom. Intellectually she could respond to
her husband without any pretence of learning ; she was
intelligent, interested in books, in the political news of the
day, in all that absorbed him. He took this for granted in
his letters, and he trusted her judgement upon books. Her
letters to him, when she is in Scotland or at Brighton or
Boulogne with the children, are full of domestic detail but
are never dull : Lockhart obviously wanted to know the
domestic details, which in itself shows an aspect of him
unknown to his detractors then or now. Sophia was sure
of his response and sympathy ; she knew he would laugh
over the children's sayings and doings, would delight in her
accounts of their health and charm. The Lockharts talked

to each other on paper, when separated, as they must have talked together at home.

Anne's letters help to build up the picture of family life. Those she wrote to Sophia in London are full of little things, sad and merry. In spite of much care and loneliness, cheerfulness kept breaking in : as when she reported her dream that there was a report in Edinburgh that Mrs. Lockhart had eloped with the Duke of Hamilton. " I hope it is not second sight." There was to be a Fancy Dress Ball at Merchiston and she would have liked very well to go " but Papa will not hear of my going . . . It is too bad of Papa, because he goes away whole days, and I am just like one of Johnny's enchanted Princesses who can't get out of the Castle."

There does indeed seem to be a spell over Abbotsford at this period, as if life were slumbering, time stayed still. The agony of death and disaster was over for a little ; meanwhile there was a sad quietude, a cessation of pain rather than serenity. Anne seems to move behind veils of mist that drift about the walls and turrets of the great house.

There were suggestions of Sophia's bringing the children to Scotland in the summer for sea-bathing ; Anne proposed taking a house in Edinburgh and having Johnny driven down, every day, to Portobello, which was then a little village by the sea, much recommended by doctors for its bracing air, and coming into fashion as a holiday resort.

Sophia did go to Scotland that summer (1827), and in July took lodgings at Portobello. Lockhart wrote her all the London gossip and news, of impending changes in the Cabinet, of the appointment of the Duke of Clarence as Lord High Admiral, and His Royal Highness's tour of the Cinque Ports, with Barrow in his suite, not Croker who formerly had accompanied Lord Melville : " No one believes Croker will keep his present place long, and it is very doubtful whether Canning will now think it worth while to give him another." When dining with the Crokers, J. G. L. heard his host—" cramming a Guardsman with his joy in not going with the Lord High Admiral the circuit of the Ports, as he is always badly headached at the sea-side.

But everyone knows that Clarence taking Barrow with him instead of Croker . . . is a sad slight "—and the spoken relief of Mr. C. was merely a cry of " Sour grapes ! " London was hot and sultry : " I wish I could get myself iced."

Sophia having been ill, and forced to spend most of her time between bed and sofa, had little news to give : " But I feel you would not be happy unless you heard all the little nothings about your little bodies from myself. They are quite well—quite the fashion of Portobello. John gets presents of flowers and fruit every day, and all the gardens are open to them." Walter was full of life and high spirits, climbing into mamma's bed in the morning, performing alarming acrobatics upon chairs and sofas, and going into fits of rage if Johnny touched any of *his* toys among those presented by kind Aunt Anne. Sophia hoped to join her own family at Abbotsford soon. As for the Lockharts, Violet had written about her own recovery from an illness (Violet remained delicate) ; she was to go to Inchinnan, to Laurence's manse, and drink the waters from a well in the neighbourhood, before having a course of hot sea-baths. Sometimes the letters crossed, and Lockhart, having heard no news for some days, wrote with anxious enquiries. He did indeed want to hear all the little nothings about his little bodies !

In return he sent many spicy little somethings : describing the ovation given to the Duke of Wellington at his Review : " The cheering was heard at Brompton and must have reached Downing Street. It was a mob of real gentlefolk too, chiefly, and I understand the scene recalled those after his return from Waterloo. To think of his being presented to that coxcomb Palmerston (who never saw a musket fired) as Commander-in-Chief ! "

A most spicy morsel was the gossip about the now-notorious Lady Caroline Lamb who had " taken an apothecary apprentice as lieutenant for her husband. They live together in the Strand in the most open scandal. She has written her *Confessions*, detailing all her amours in the most profligate style, and sold them to a blackguard book-seller. She ought to be in Bedlam."

Also " in the news " was the now elderly Duchess of St. Albans (formerly Mrs. Coutts, widow of the millionaire banker), who with her young Duke had been seen driving down the Strand in a " procession of two carriages and four, everything blazing with coronets . . . She went to introduce him to the Establishment (i.e. not the C. of E. but the Bank !) "

Letters full of gossip, preferably tinged with scandal and malice, are good for invalids and ladies leading a quiet life, and Sophia enjoyed her budgets, replying with cheerful news of " my little fellows " who were having daily bathes in the sea. " Think of your poor little bird being plumped over the head. He made a great work the first day, but now only gives one roar. What a change you will see in him he has grown so strong and sensible "—the " little bird " being Walter, that " steerin' wean " as he was no doubt often called in Scotland.

There were plans for their being settled in Sussex Place by winter : " You rejoice my heart, my dear Lockhart, by saying we are not to be separated next winter. Anything better than that, and any accommodation. I feel well you cannot do good or be comfortable without us, and my happiness depends on being with you."

One of the great and enduring events of this summer was that Scott began to write for Johnny his *Tales of a Grandfather* ; rehearsing them to this small, eager and critical audience of one, as they walked or rode slowly together about the grounds and woods of Abbotsford, or sat comfortably in the library.

Murray would gladly have published the *Tales* ; but they were promised to Cadell in Edinburgh. In December 1827 Scott wrote to his son-in-law :

" I send Johnie's three volumes with my kindest love to him and Walter. We will have a smarter one by Christmas, when he may give that to any ' Cynthia of the minute ' who chances to captivate his affections for the time."

Johnny approved his grandfather's labours, as did many other readers. There was not, as yet, a flood of juvenile literature : there were the old, strong romances beloved by both Scott and Lockhart in their boyhood, there were

JOHN HUGH LOCKHART, AGED $6\frac{1}{2}$, AND WALTER SCOTT LOCKHART,
AGED $1\frac{1}{2}$

From a portrait by D. Maclise, R.A., 1827

the fairy-tales, told by mother or grandmother or nurse by the fireside, and there were beginning to be the new, instructive books for children that were to have a long vogue. Scott was not entirely a pioneer ; *Mrs. Markham's History of England* was in demand, and one of Murray's most successful publications. Croker had also written a *Child's History of England* which Scott admired, and which would seem to have suggested to him his own volume on Scottish history : a fact that may be held to absolve Croker from many of his sins. " I am glad the *Tales* go off," their author wrote to Cadell at the end of December. " Our new set of customers not being those who take the utmost care of their books will need supplies sooner than in the ordinary case "—a point, indeed, to cheer authors and publishers, if not parents. " The next volumes ", he added, " will be more entertaining, because there will be more story and less history."

On the 1st of January 1828, Lockhart announced " A New Year gift of promise—to wit, a very plump little girl." It was the first time Sophia had had a short and easy labour ; and the little girl who came in with the year was to be an unfailing comfort and joy. She was christened Charlotte Harriet Jane ; and by her birth, though neither her parents nor her grandfather could guess it, Scott's line of succession was secured, for only thus, on the distaff side, was it continued. Sophia took the three children to Scotland, that summer, and wrote of Anne's welcoming kindness :

" I feel quite grateful to be here, Anne is so attentive to John and nurses him so well ; he never is left for an instant, and every whim gratified." Sometimes he was able to go out in his own little carriage ; but he was very easily tired. Baby and Walter were lively and well.

In the following winter—of 1828–9, Lockhart went to Abbotsford himself, on a New Year's visit. Sophia was at home with the children, much occupied with domestic matters : such as having bookshelves put up by a joiner recommended by Mr. Murray, and seeing to the repair of the pipes and drains. These had gone wrong because, as it was discovered, the joints had been fixed with putty instead of lead ; apparently jerry-building did not begin in our era of progress. Sophia was also having trouble with her cook, who had charged her twice, in the housekeeping accounts, for a turkey, and when detected, had become abusive. The cook departed and was replaced by another who gave better promise. " The little bodies are quite well, Wa as delightful as ever, and so handsome. For any sake, do not forget to bring each of them some bit thing for they have been very good." She was living very quietly, except for an unwelcome visit from Lady Gifford, at a moment of domestic confusion : " and well she drank of your whiskey ". She had dined out once—" with Mr. Croker and met Theodore Hook and some nameless men, all very dull, but Croker terribly civil, I am sure he wants something from you "—which showed a wholesome cynicism in Sophia.

The year 1828 saw the publication of Lockhart's *Life of Burns* ; a book overshadowed both by his own later masterpiece of biography and by the many subsequent studies of the poet. Such comparative oblivion is undeserved for, within its limits, it is an excellent biography, written with sympathy and balance, with lucidity and grace of style.

Scott praised it warmly, writing to Lockhart (in June 1828) : " It has done you infinite credit. I could give you very good authority where you and I seem to differ, but you have chosen the wiser and better part, and Burns had a right to have his frailties spared, especially *post tantum temporis*. All people applaud it."

It may be questioned whether it were the wiser and better part to spare so much. Certainly it was the kinder way ; for Burns's widow was still alive. The scandals of the poet's youth are admitted and deplored, especially his defiant lack of contrition : " His false pride recoiled from letting his jovial associates guess how little he was able to drown the whispers of the still small voice ; and the tormenting bitterness of a mind ill at ease within itself, escaped (as may be too often traced in the history of satirists) in the shape of angry sarcasms against others."

The love-affair with Highland Mary is presented as immaculate—" this pure love "—" by far the deepest passion that Burns ever knew " ! His forced marriage with

Jean Armour and all that preceded it are treated most reticently and delicately.

Of his wretched last years Lockhart writes with profound compassion :

" The great poet himself whose name is enough to ennoble his children's children, was, to the eternal disgrace of his country, suffered to live and die in penury, and, as far as such a creature could be degraded by any external circumstances, in degradation."

The neglect of so great a genius was, to Lockhart, an infinitely greater sin than the follies and bitterness of the unhappy genius himself.

" It is very noble to despise the accidents of fortune ; but what moral homily concerning these, could have equalled that which Burns's poetry, considered alongside of Burns's history, and the history of his fame, presents ! It is very noble to resist the allurements of pleasure ; but who preaches so effectually against them, as he who sets forth in immortal verse his own intense sympathy with those that yield . . . and the dangers and miseries of yielding." Of Burns's religion he said : " He sometimes doubted with the sorrow, what in the main and above all, in the end, he believed with the fervour of a poet . . . Let us avoid in the name of Religion herself, the fatal error of those who would rashly swell the catalogue of the enemies of religion."

Burns has never had a more steadfast defender or more eloquent apologist. It is a remarkable book coming as it does so soon after the rash and wanton phase of Lockhart's own life. The Scorpion had no part in it. With the general applause of which Scott assured the author there must have been mingled a good deal of surprise—that a work of such compassion and understanding could have come from a pen that could, so often, be a weapon of offence.

In the summer of 1829 Sophia was again in Scotland with the children. They stayed with Anne in Shandwick Place, Edinburgh, until Johnny should be strong enough to travel on to Abbotsford. He was weaker, and had to spend most of his time on a sofa ; so weak that a dress had to be contrived for him " where everything goes on at once and so easily, as it saves him from the fatigue of dressing ".

Walter was a lively and beautiful child. Anne one day promised him a box of soldiers if he would pass a whole day without crying—and he won it, in spite of two or three tumbles, and " though Baby gave great offence by breaking his horse ".

Anne wrote that she found Baby " very like Sophia, and I agree with nurse in thinking she has most engaging manners. Walter leads her a sad life upstairs, but when they are downstairs after dinner, he always calls her his dear little sister, and kisses her in the most affectionate manner."

Walter was, from infancy, an adept in playing to his audience, and could " put across " his very considerable charm in an effective way. One kind and admiring lady even took it into her head that he was treated with harshness ; " he had such sensibility ". Walter undoubtedly knew when to shed, and when to refrain from shedding, tears, and could assume at will that large-eyed look of innocence which is so convincing to anyone outside the family.

Naughty or virtuous he was a delight, and so was Baby ; but Johnnie grew no stronger. He passed disturbed nights, often crying out in his sleep as if in pain, and suffering from heavy sweats. He could not be left alone. But he was heart-breakingly brave ; and his mind was alert and interested. " He is very anxious you should write to him, and tell him if his parrot is gone to Mrs. Wilson's, and how his black Pussy is."

Watt enjoyed the Edinburgh scene, much struck by his first sight of a kilted Highlander, and asking : " Why, the poor man had forgot his breeches " and taking the Newhaven fish-wives for the " Bay and Broom " girls who cried their wares in the London streets.

Johnny was at last able to travel to Abbotsford, lying on cushions in the carriage, with Sophia beside him ; Anne and the other children were in another carriage. Sophia longed to be in her old home, and to see her children " playing about the fountain. Anne is as foolish as yourself about the creatures, and there is no indulgence too great for her not to try to get for them." The little parlour was to be furnished with a sofa for Johnnie, and a new bed for him was put beside his mother's. He settled down contentedly. The weather, perhaps mercifully, was too bad for him to go out, —for " his spirits make him do what he is quite unable for ". Walter and Baby were in wild glee, never to be found when wanted, and Sophia was prepared to lose them twenty times a day, in the grounds, or in the great, rambling house, were it not that " one sure way to find them " was " to ask the dogs with whom they have formed the greatest friendship ". A pointing nose and a wagging tail must often have served as guide towards the hiding-place of lost bairns.

Sir Walter took great pride in his second grandson, " who, to say truth, makes himself most engaging to him ; he climbs up upon his knee, kisses his hand, brings his stick, and now, I have found out, makes him morning visits . . . in his study ".

Lockhart in London was anxious for news, and begged for a letter every other day : " I need not say with what pain I hear your accounts of Johnnie, and with what anxiety I shall expect news . . . I expect not to hear what can be pleasant, but suspense is worse than anything else."

His own letters were entertaining with town-gossip : of a dinner at Lady Gifford's " to see Miss Luttrell's intended, an old, bald, queer-looking but well-informed man—a retired lawyer, a Whig and a saint " (an unusual combination, unless " saint " is " wrote sarcastic "). The odd-looking gentleman was " as loving as 18, however, and so truly was his spinster ". Lockhart went out very little, and Sophia was distressed : " I do not like to hear of your living so lonely, and I had a letter from Lady Gifford in which she said you were looking ill and low. I do expect the last, but for Godsake keep up, we would have been too happy in this world in spite, I feel, of the many, many hard days' work and sleepless nights you have had for me, had it pleased God to have given our dear child good health." She knew that life could not bring perfect happiness. They were paying, in this one grief, for a great measure of joy.

Johnny gained a little strength ; he was able, sometimes, to move from his own little parlour to the drawing-room.

One day he was taken in the " sociable " to Melrose ; sometimes he was drawn about the gardens in his little carriage by kind Will Laidlaw, with Sophia walking beside him, and Walter and Baby riding the pony, Marion. It was Johnny's own pony, but the brave little man did not mind lending her, and was " as happy holding the end of Marion's bridle as if he rode her himself ". Watt and Baby spent all their time out-of-doors : Watt was in danger of dying from a surfeit of " nice pieces of bread and jelly ", having prudently made himself friends everywhere whose friendship was expressed in terms of food. As Johnny became better it was possible for Sophia to leave him occasionally, and one day she went to Chiefswood to visit the Hamiltons and meet their guest, the celebrated Mrs. Hemans : " a vulgar-looking woman with a veil pinned in the mantilla fashion on her head in the morning ", instead of a modest cap. This unfavourable impression of the poetess was deepened by the return visit.

" Mrs. Hemans is a vulgar blue woman ; it will teach Mr. H. to ask unknown friends, he had had merely a correspondence with her, neither of them had seen her, and I do not think they will get rid of her till they leave Chiefswood." (Sophia is never more endearing than when she is caustic.) She must endure further encounters, and drove one day to Yarrow with the Hamiltons and their lingering guest ; on which occasion Anne, left in charge, reported to Lockhart that Johnny was " very happy here. I do not think he suffers much during the day, he is so patient and so easily amused, and takes such great delight in his poney upon which Baby and Walter ride time about while he leads it." He lay on his sofa and read *The Tales of Wonder* and other romances, and was Sir Walter's best listener.

The small Walter continued to divert his relations : " Yesterday when I asked Soph who she thought he was like, Walter answered he thought he was like Tom Purdie. This will not give you a favourable idea of his charm. Baby improves every day. Walter has been teaching her to say Devil which was taught him by Johnny, who says he was taught by Papa " ! ! !

Lockhart was able, in time, to leave London and join his family for a time ; he returned to town in October, taking Johnny with him, as Sophia had fallen ill and could not travel. She was lame in the knee with rheumatism, an ailment that was to prove chronic. The younger children were still with her at Abbotsford to their grandfather's great content :

" I never saw Papa struck so much with any creature as he appears to be with Baby, who now finds him out in his own den ; he says he never saw a child before show so much character," in which The Great Unknown was like nearly all the grandfathers in the human race. He was " highly amused the other morning, seeing Miss Baby march amongst the dogs who were quarreling [sic], with a small stick in her hand, perfectly fearless."

It was now Lockhart's turn to give news of Johnny, on the whole, reassuring. He had stood the journey well, and was now receiving many visitors and enjoying many attentions. Lockhart himself was deep in work with only one night off—when he went to see Fanny Kemble play Juliet : " She is Charles's daughter, 18, and has come on the stage all at once in consequence of his embarrassments. She is more like Mrs. Siddons than anything I ever hoped to see, and I never saw Juliet played before . . . The sensation is wonderful, and even at this dullest season the theatre is crammed to the teeth night after night."

There was again grief at Abbotsford when the faithful Tom Purdie died suddenly, being found by his daughter " sitting quite upright by the fire in his own house . . . I never saw Papa so affected ; he won't go out, and says for the first time in his life he wishes the days were come to take him to Edinburgh . . . I hardly see how Papa is to get over it, for Tom was everything to him "—and to Di his dog, who was in such distress that " they think the creature will die ".

Sir Walter helped to lay his old friend and servant to rest, and the brave shoulders bowed a little more under the weight of loneliness. It was All Saints' Tide, and the nights were " lang and mirk ", with the mists rising from the waters of Tweed, and Abbotsford had too many memories.

Presently Sophia was able to travel ; and there was no longer a small lady of strong character to invade Scott's study in the morning, jump upon his books and papers and when reproved, climb on his knee, with kisses and murmurs of " Dear, dear Grandpa."

The next visit to Abbotsford was shadowed by a fear that could not lessen. Anne wrote to her sister in April of 1831 of their father's grave illness, after a stroke : " On the Monday night he was in great danger for three hours. Dr. Clarkson has since told me that it was to his great surprise that he got through. For myself, I do not think that it is over yet." His face was distorted, his speech blurred, but there was no symptom of paralysis : " Think of his losing his limbs or his mind." That had not yet come ; but the noble mind was never to return to its full power. " He is irritable to a degree that is dreadful, but it is to be hoped that will go off. I continue to feel weary of my existence, and I am sure I have reason to be so."

Chapter 13

ANNE, SOPHIA, LOCKHART :
THE GUARDIANS. 1831–1832

THE light was not wholly dimmed in Anne ; but the fire in her was smoored by this final trial. Fretfulness was apparent in her letters, at times, and was altogether pardonable. She was, much of the time, alone with her father, carrying her burden by herself. Sophia came when she could and was with her as much as possible during the difficult months that followed. Walter too came occasionally, but he had to be with his regiment, and Charles, now in the Foreign Office, was in the Embassy at Naples.

Sophia's letters to Lockhart were full of anxiety. Scott was still very ill and he was a difficult patient. The summer of 1831 dragged on heavily. There was an occasional gleam of fun in Sophia's letters, about the children : " Baby in a fit of anger called Watt a Hound, and Watt desired Anne not to call him a Tailor this morning as it made him feel quite cross." Lockhart joined them in the late summer ; he would have taken his family to Chiefswood, but Anne begged him to stay at Abbotsford ; Sophia added her plea : they could not leave Anne alone. Lockhart, however, held to his plan : they would be better apart : " The cottage would be an object to go out for— and we, when we came to the *château*, would be something like visitors . . . It seems to me it would be a better plan for your papa, and I suspect strongly he really would like it better too . . . I must at any rate have my mornings to my books there, as I must work, and can't now alter my habits and hours of working."

That he did work, regularly and steadily, at the business of *The Quarterly* is shown by the number of letters written that summer, from Chiefswood to Croker and to John Murray, dealing with articles and reviews, with proofs, with many details of editorial business. From his appointment until his reluctant retiral from office, Lockhart lived with his work.

Returned to town he told Sophia of his doings. He had gone to hear Paganini : " It is all as wonderful as the newspapers say and far more delightful than anything I could have conceived of such a concern as a fiddle. He did not strike me as the least horrible—but very like a man of genius, and a gentleman to boot." Paganini was regarded almost as a wizard of slightly sinister genius. " Linley, who is considered the first fiddler here, laughed and wept in delight, all the while he was playing, and says the art, if he dies without telling his secret, will take 1000 years to reach the [height] to which P. has brought it. He makes the fiddle produce all the effects of guitars, pianofortes and even bells and trumpets, and draws from it the sweetest notes of the human voice itself, and he seems perfectly under the pulse of his own inspiration, and is agitated almost to convulsion."

It was decided that Scott must winter abroad, in the sun. Anne and he came to London to stay with the Lockharts and by the end of the year were in Malta. " Everything suited his health on board ship," Anne wrote, " and though Captain Paget lived most comfortably, there was no drinking of wine. I see now more plainly than ever that Papa will never recover as long as he does so." Walter, her brother, accompanied them, to help Anne with her care of their father, though she found him, at times, of little comfort. She dreaded the invitations to dinner that would follow their arrival in Malta. These were postponed for a time, as the travellers were kept in quarantine—for fear of cholera. Anne liked Malta, and would have stayed at least until the end of January ; but Walter chose to move on, and they reached Naples before Christmas. The acerbity was creeping in, and the mutual criticism that comes from strained nerves. Walter was apparently irresponsible : " Out all day long and all night, dining at messes and the swearing at waiters and the like in the morning was too much for one's patience." In one letter she told of the presents she had bought in Malta : " I was, by the way, going to send you Maltese earrings which are the only pretty things here, but I saw what I am sure you will like much better, and Lockhart admire very much, which is tone vases made from the antique, some for balconies, and small vases of all sorts for rooms and to put flowers in." These were to be sent home by a man-of-war. The Navy was an obliging Service, unhampered by overmuch red tape, and Scott's name brought its bearers many privileges.

It was a sad Christmas of 1831 for before the year was out Johnny's frail life came to its close. There had been little or no hope for him of late. Anne's letter to Sophia may strike one at first as being curiously inadequate, for she had dearly loved the little boy she had helped to nurse. But the blow fell on nerves that had borne so much that there was now a certain numbness. " We were prepared for the sad intelligence your letter of yesterday brought, by reading an English paper. Thank God it is now all over, and the dear boy is now at rest from all his suffering. I will not dwell on the subject. I have great comfort in thinking that now there is a considerable time elapsed, and that the blow will by this time be softened to you both." She longed to have Sophia and Lockhart with her.

Naples proved amusing, and Scott found many friends and visitors, two of them being Sir William Gell and Mr. Keppel Craven. " By the bye both of them are old villains "—was Anne's summing-up. " However, Sir William is witty, and Mr. Craven is very accomplished, indeed, and he is so well acquainted with everything here that he is a great advantage in a morning drive."

It was a gay, small and rather trivial society ; Anne was detached and a little satirical : " One thing to be sure of is that there is no one to flirt with, the English being a bad lot, and heaven defend one from an Italian prince, it is only in novels they are handsome, then the Poles and Russians are all ugly."

Anne was beginning to find life easier, and even amusing. She was free from housekeeping cares, for their meals were sent in, and the servants were on board wages. But Papa was sometimes " very cross, and you know how wearing out he is ". She thought, like a good aunt, of the children and the treats they could have in Naples : " Love to Lockhart and the Babes. I wish I could send them a temple as large as a house made of figs, it would strike them with so much admiration."

Charles also wrote, pleasant letters with the undercurrent of humour that was characteristic of him. In March, 1832, he wrote that " The Bart has not made up his mind as to his proceedings "—whether to stay in Naples or go on to Rome. Charles thought the former plan preferable ; travelling did not suit his father's nervous condition. He too gossiped, not without malice : " We have had an inundation of horrid people who, I hope, will be the first victims of the cholera should it visit us." On the other hand, he thought that Anne had " picked up some very decent friends and guardian angels " and was enjoying Naples, which on the whole " were it not for the beastly society, as it is called, is a perfect paradise ".

They did, however, move on to Rome : Scott increasingly ill and melancholy. Then came the slow return to London and, at last, to Tweedside. It is all told in Scott's own *Journal* and in the *Life* ; told with a magic that transforms and lifts up to high pathos the story that in the family letters is almost unbearable. The months dragged on while death forgot to be merciful. Lockhart reached the peak of his genius in describing that return ; the whole chapter holds the music of sadness remembered not yet comforted, but seen " *sub specie aeternitatis* " :

" As we descended the vale of the Gala he began to gaze about him, and by degrees it was obvious that he was recognizing the features of that familiar landscape. Presently he murmured a name or two : ' Gala Water surely— Buckholm—Torwoodlee.' As we rounded the hill at Ladhope, and the outline of the Eildons burst on him, he became greatly excited ; and, when turning himself on the couch, his eye caught at length his own towers at the distance of a mile, he sprang up with a cry of delight." At his own door he was met by faithful Will Laidlaw who helped to carry him to the bed prepared in the dining-room, in the great bay-window that looked on Tweed.

" He sat bewildered for a few moments, and then resting his eye on Laidlaw, said—' Ha ! Willie Laidlaw ! O man, how often have I thought of you ! ' By this time his dogs had assembled about his chair—they began to fawn upon him and lick his hands, and he alternately sobbed and smiled over them, until sleep oppressed him." There is a Virgilian gentleness about these last chapters.

The rest was sadness. Abbotsford became a hermitage for its laird and the devoted group who tended him. Sophia wrote to her brother Walter : " We see nobody, and keep the gates locked, except the Doctor and Mr. Laidlaw, and the servants follow our example as there is not a sound to be heard. We have only been able to get once round the garden since we came. Papa is so enraged if we leave him an instant."

Lockhart wrote about a month later, in August : " The bodily wasting is more apparent and rapid. He can't, I really think, see out another three weeks. Anne has been very ill again, but is to-night calmer. His phrensy has been greatly beyond what you saw, and this has preyed on her spirits."

But it lasted beyond the three weeks ; the shadows were very dark and the way through the valley a long and weary one, before the end of wayfaring, on the 21st of September, 1832, when the last quietude came to that great heart and mind.

" It was a beautiful day—so warm, that every window was wide open—and so perfectly still, that the sound of all others most delicious to his ear, the gentle ripple of the Tweed over its pebbles, was distinctly audible as we knelt around the bed, and his eldest son kissed and closed his eyes."

Lockhart wrote of the mourning, solemn as for a great king, that held the country awed. Sophia's old friend, Miss Clephane wrote to her : " Many that never saw him are grieving for him . . . The world laments its greatest light extinguished."

A century and more after that September day, many more that have seen him in his works and letters, and in Lockhart's pages, think of him as for a friend dearly loved.

In few books—perhaps in no other work of prose—are the tears and mortality of humankind more touching to the mind.

II

Almost at once Lockhart began his task of preparation for writing the *Life*. When he was back in London, in October, his brother-in-law wrote to him, sending a packet of papers found in a cabinet in Scott's dressing-room. They included his own memoir " giving a full account of the family, and his education and pursuits up to the period of his being called to the bar ". There were many letters, too, and poems in manuscript. The memoir was to be most skilfully used in the *Life*.

From Mrs. Scott of Harden came a letter offering anecdotes and reminiscences of Scott's boyhood : " I hope to get some from our minister's wife who was his Kelso school-fellow . . . I think anything which proves he was or was not like another child will be curious." From her Lockhart had the story of the little boy Walter's lying on the hearthrug with a book, and on being asked by an uncle whether he would not rather be playing with the other boys in the Square, replying : " No, uncle ; you cannot think how ignorant these boys are. I am much happier here, reading my book." On another occasion he was found reading *Tristram Shandy*, and when asked whether he understood it replied : " No, and I don't believe the author intended it should be understood."

Mrs. Scott's own first impression of him was of the young advocate of twenty-six, when she was two years younger : " I remember considering him as almost a Boy his appearance and manner were so young and awkward, but flashes of genius then came frequently through the awkward manner."

It has been pointed out by Sir Herbert Grierson that from a letter from a devout lady, at this time, Lockhart took the hint of writing, for edification, one of the most-

quoted passages in the *Life* : that in which he has recorded
Scott's admonition : " My dear, be a good man—be
virtuous—be religious . . . Nothing else will give you any
comfort when you come to lie here."

The letter advised : " When you write anything of the
last very melancholy weeks at Abbotsford, I think it will
be most valuable for you to mention any of the few remarks
he uttered, when his mind was clear, of a religious tendency,
such as I heard he said occasionally : ' Oh, be virtuous.
It is one's only comfort in a dying state '—and anything
of that kind, for there are wicked people who will take a
pleasure in saying that he was not a religious man, and
proving the contrary will do much good."

Scott *may* have spoken the words that Lockhart recorded ;
but in the last weeks of his life he was utterly distraught.
The letters from Anne and Sophia and from Lockhart
himself, tell of long periods of slumber from which he
awakened " wild and violent ", of fits of screaming and,
towards the end, " a constant talking, and very feeble cry ".
He had to be drugged, with henbane and laudanum, to
give him these long sleeps.

Lockhart used, with gratitude and skill, many of the
reminiscences given him ; but they were not always valued.
There was an acrimonious correspondence with Hogg who
wrote to him, in March 1833 : " You must know that . . .
I was applied to from all quarters . . . for something
original about Sir Walter. I refused them all, saying to
everyone of them : ' If I can furnish anything original about
him it must be to my friend Lockhart, his legitimate
biographer.' " But a certain Mr. McCrone presented himself, with an introduction from Cochrane, a London bookseller, giving the strange assurance that Lockhart wished
Hogg to supply McCrone with anecdotes and to take the
credit for all he gave ; Lockhart himself " having found his
material so abundant he hardly knows how to bring in one
half of them ". The adroit Mr. McCrone proceeded to
extract from Hogg much " information " as to Scott's
character, his politics and his religion. He begged also for
" some insight into the family circle such as none but you
can give. Sir Walter in his study was pretty well known.

How was he in the parlour ? " McCrone used the best bait
—the appeal to Hogg's vanity, and caught a lavish supply
of anecdotes and opinions. Hogg, however, insisted that he
had made it a condition that everything should be submitted
to Lockhart to use if he chose. He expected a correspondence to follow, but not, as he plaintively declared, that
Lockhart would have " fallen on and abused me in such a
manner. I am sorry you did, but not angry."

He added in self-defence : " I assure you that if Sir
Walter despised me and held me in the lowest contempt—
his behaviour and his letters to me testified the reverse.
Of that I shall make you sensible when you like. But
though I was to be highly paid, and am paid in part, which
is the worst of it, not for any worldly consideration would I
hurt the feelings of anyone of Sir Walter's family, less your
own than any other's, however deeply you have wounded
mine." He had therefore instructed McCrone to cancel the
proposed volume, but feared the instruction might come
too late, as McCrone had made a copy of the material for
the press : " I do assure you on the word of an honest man
(although a vulgar clown) that there is not one of the
anecdotes which is not literally and positively true." Lockhart had got well under his skin ; it was Lockhart's way
with his adversaries. " I am certain ", Hogg went on,
" that these anecdotes and remarks will be held in more
estimation when I am laid in the dust, than many volumes
that shall be written on the same subject. I am sorry you
have despised even to look at it, else you would perhaps have
formed another estimate of it before the end."

Lockhart replied, by return : " You have been grossly
misinformed as to every point of my conduct and feeling.
The facts are these. Seeing an advertisement that Mr.
McCrone was about to publish a *Life of Sir W. Scott* including
many private letters of the deceased and material furnished
by his friend Hogg, I called at Cochrane's to warn him that
no private letters of Sir W. Scott could be published without
the sanction of his executors." Mr. McCrone was present,
and had asked : " Have we no right to print anecdotes
such as Mr. Hogg's ? " J. G. L. had replied : " That's
another affair. I have no right to prevent Hogg or any

other man from publishing what he pleases on the subject, always excepting letters." He thought he *might* have added that " if we interfered in such a case it was not from any jealousy as to materials that might have been of service to me being given to another person—that our materials were more than abundant ; but as to my conferring confidentially on the subject with either Mr. McCrone or Mr. Cochrane that was out of the question. I know and desire to know nothing of either of them."

J. G. L. on this occasion went up in smoke, and had fuel for the conflagration in the self-centred gossip and idle insinuations provided by Hogg in his *Domestic Manners of Sir Walter Scott.*

The next incident was McCrone's visit to Lockhart in his house, bringing the manuscript. " I was exceedingly hurt and angry—not that you should have sent them such a Ms. but that you should have sent them unseen by me. For I well knew that altho' you always loved and respected Sir W. you could not write so many pages about him without saying things that would give pain to his children." He was convinced that McCrone had made a copy that would be published " after you are gone and after you can suffer nothing from my answer, and perhaps after I and all that could have answered you are gone also. I cast my eye hastily over the Ms. and the first thing I lighted on was your statement about Lady Scott and opium,[1] and then indeed I was wroth and abused you heartily . . . I felt that you had permitted yourself to put before the public a statement which would cause misery to my wife and her sister, and I perceived that there was no remedy—that it would be worse ten years hence than now, and that some day it must come. I hope the scoundrel who has dared to repeat to you the words of my momentary passion, uttered in my private apartment into which he had no right to intrude, has reported them truly . . . I probably said that it would be easy for me if I chose to give the world scraps of letters and diaries which would induce the belief that Sir W. Scott despised James Hogg—and so I could. But did he despise him ?—No.—He condemned some parts of

[1] This does not appear in the printed Memorials by Hogg.

his conduct and smiled at his vanity, but he admired his genius and knew that his heart was in the right place . . . But surely this fool has misunderstood me. I doubt if he is capable of understanding anything. His book, *Waverley Anecdotes*, shows him ignorant of all things human and divine except the art of making a title-page lie, and the outside of a volume swindle."

Lockhart's wrath flamed again when he read the manuscript carefully : " They seem to me very unworthy of the subject and of the writer. And they contain, among other things, several gross misstatements as to matters of fact, one of them what must be a pure dream of yours, and which directly impeaches the personal veracity of Sir W. Scott. You may jocularly talk of leeing—but a man who says that which is not, from malice, is a villain, and from vanity is a slave." The letter ended with a forced expression of regret : " If I said anything seriously derogatory to your character, or implying that I attributed to you any worse fault than that of rashness and indiscretions, I recall the words of hasty and outraged feeling, and assure you that I remain now, as ever, your sincere friend."

But the letter remains as one of the most formidable explosions in the so-called " gentle art ".

Domestic circumstances were not likely to assuage Lockhart's passion of resentment. He was witnessing the further suffering of Anne, who was gradually and not easily slipping out of life. Sophia wrote sadly to Walter that there was little improvement from day to day. " That no immediate danger is apprehended I believe, and that, please God, she may recover, is possible, but it will be very long."

But there was little hope. " I am to get a hospital nurse to-day which is quite necessary, though she is quiet, perfectly so, but much is to be done that cannot be done by any but those accustomed to such scenes. For this and the other necessary expenses I draw upon Anne's funds through Charles, as we both felt Lockhart should not be at any more expense than the extreme misery in the house, and I am sure this would be both the poor invalid's and your own feeling."

Sophia herself was ailing : " I write from my bed, still

confined with my knee, and the worse from anxiety." A
few days later she wrote : " I very much fear the brain has
received too severe a shock to recover wholly or for a very
long time."

Lockhart wrote to Croker on June 24th : " You will be
distressed, I am sure, to hear that Anne Scott's illness has
taken a fatal turn. We have been watching for her last
breathing these 48 hours, yet still she lingers on. My wife
is in sore misery." Next day he wrote again : " Anne
Scott is no more."

Anne's life was like a lamp that had, for a time, shone
brilliantly, and then been dimmed by sorrow. One may
recall the valediction spoken by a Scots Bishop of the
eighteenth century for that valiant old Jacobite laird and
devout churchman, Forbes of Pitsligo :

" What a comfort it is to think that such heaven-lighted
lamps shall never be extinguished ; they are only removed
from the ante-chamber into the inner court of the King
Immortal, where they shine more and more."

Chapter 14

PROFESSIONAL MATTERS :
LOCKHART, CROKER, MURRAY

I

THE correspondence with Croker, begun in the early *Blackwood* days, continued from 1827 to the end of Lockhart's life. Much of it is professional, discussing Croker's own reviews and contributions to *The Quarterly*, Lockhart's plans, proofs, corrections, and such matters. There is a good deal of political gossip, too. But the personal note is rarely absent for long ; Croker must indeed be regarded as J. G. L.'s most intimate correspondent outside his family, and these letters tell some things about him that are told nowhere else.

Croker, at the Admiralty, was in a position of influence, and more than once Lockhart asked his help : once on behalf of his younger brother Archibald, who was going into the Army ; Croker might be able to procure him an ensigncy in the Horse Guards. "He is tall and good-looking, just 18 years of age." Again Croker, as one of the founders of the Athenaeum and a member of committee, was asked to support a candidate for election, Dr. Ferguson "a young physician of very rising character in the world—to whose professional skill and unwearying kindness I owe the (apparently complete) restoration of my poor deformed boy's bodily health." (This apparent recovery was, we know, a sad illusion.)

The 1830's were years of intense excitement in Church and State. The Reform Bill was passed in 1832 ; in the eyes of the Tories, Lockhart among them, this extension of the franchise was a most dangerous measure, a likely prelude to revolution. It was, indeed, a troubled decade. There were recurrent strikes. In one letter Lockhart wrote :

"My tailor called this morning ; all his hands gone. He says the tailors that have struck must be nearly 20,000

. . . and he adds that they are all republican zealots and have ulterior motives." In another he noted "the great alarm of Government about the Trades Associations. The chief Government Contractor at Liverpool came up a few days ago to Spring Rice to tell him they must put down the associations in that town, or allow him *carte blanche* as to time in fulfilling his contracts; and he was allowed time. All because Burton's men struck work lately at Tonbridge Wells, after the visit of a Birmingham deputation. They resumed work soon—but Burton feels they are in hand, and will obey the first summons from headquarters. I had these facts this morning from one of the police magistrates who expresses great alarm at the seeming paralysis of all Government but mob government." The new mastery had begun.

There were, as Disraeli showed in *Sybil*, two nations, not one, in England : on the one side the poor in their dreadful misery, held in serfdom by factory and mining conditions ; on the other the indifferent newly-rich, lacking the traditional kindliness of the squires. Doubtless there were exceptions ; there was the stirring of the social conscience that was to become so active in Victoria's reign. Lockhart's forebodings, expressed in many letters, may at first appear exaggerated, almost fantastic, seen by us across the great space of Victorian and Edwardian security. But taken in regard to their period they were by no means foolish. The wonder is that England came so close to revolution, was so nearly republican without taking the final step.

The Church was respected, by the conservative, as a guardian of morals and dignity and as offering a decent, comfortable way of life. The long torpor of the eighteenth century was only now about to be shaken by the second Reformation of the Oxford Movement, heralded by Keble's Assize Sermon on The National Apostasy. Even in the early years of the Movement, Lockhart was aware of the excitement and its significance. He kept his ear to the ground :

"I fear we shall be thought very much out of our duty in having no article this time expressly on the Church," he wrote, in October 1832. " I wish to God you could excite the Bishop of Exeter on this head. There is no one else capable of writing on that subject as this hour demands."

It is impressive to note, in passing, how much Lockhart was, at this time, carrying on his shoulders. Scott's affairs were in grievous confusion, as he told Croker when he wrote the news of Scott's passing :

" This day it pleased God to terminate the long and hopeless affliction of your old friend, ever most warmly attached to you . . . Sir W. leaves his worldly affairs in a truly wretched state, and this after killing himself to put them right."

He was beginning the *Life*, all profits from which were to help to pay the creditors. His brothers-in-law leaned on him. His seniority, his knowledge of the world of literature, made him the king-pin in their family as he would seem to have been in his own. And he was a professional man of letters, engaged in a career that was at once engrossing and laborious ; editor of one of the most important, most regarded and most criticised periodicals of the day. *The Quarterly* was old enough to be well established, to have formed its policy and principles ; but it was young enough to depend on its new editor for direction and quickening control. He was doing a stupendous amount of work, and carrying a heavy load of anxiety and responsibility ; that he endured it all is proof of a hidden strength and integrity.

To deal fully with the Croker Correspondence would mean a history of the period, social, political, literary and ecclesiastical ; its chief interest for us must be its revelation of Lockhart. He appears most frequently, as the editor, but the letters are rarely impersonal. There are flashes of brilliance, sometimes a gleam of fun, a hint of tenderness, discovered more easily when these letters are read along with those he wrote to his family. His blindness and prejudice are also apparent. The hand that wrote the attack on Keats and The Cockney School could still, occasionally, hold the pen :

" I have read the revised article on Tennyson, and think you have most completely effected your purpose . . . It is wonderful that such folly should pass for poetry with *anybody* . . . *Alfred the Great* will give life to the early part of the No."

He is absolved from being the main criminal in the notorious *Quarterly* attack on Tennyson—in 1833 ; but stands convicted of being accessory. The review was one of the most savage that even Croker ever wrote. It dealt with the *Poems* of the 1832 edition, which it described as " another and brighter star of that galaxy or *milky* way of poetry, of which the lamented Keats was the harbinger ". The tone of the review was one of virulent sarcasm. Having quoted the sonnet : " Mine be the strength of spirit " with the lines :

> And in the middle of the green, salt sea
> Keep his blue waters fresh for many a mile

Croker commented : " A noble wish, beautifully expressed that he may not be confounded with the deluge of ordinary poets, but amidst their discoloured and briny ocean still preserve his own bright tints and sweet savour. He may be at ease on this point—he never can be mistaken for anyone else . . . If a thousand anonymous specimens were presented to us, we should unerringly distinguish his by the total absence of any salt."

" I hope you will murder some other Tennyson," Lockhart wrote to Croker. The Scorpion was not yet scotched.

Sometimes he offered Croker a degree of admiration that almost touched adulation :

" It is a great comfort to me to hear that you mean to render regular assistance to *The Q.R.* Your hand will be the salvation of *The Review,* for not only are your own papers always delightful and valuable, but the feeling that we have your help will strengthen and sustain in a variety of ways both publisher and editor." He apparently found the Croker touch a graceful one : " I have plenty of good solid length papers . . . but nothing of the lighter order to float off these *pièces de résistance.* . . . There are plenty of good, grave articles in hand, but unless you can give them wings, I fear it won't do . . . Perhaps you could give a short, stinging résumé of ministerial blunders, foreign and domestic. But at all events, do favour us with the flagellation of some literary quack." It must be admitted, in favour of Lockhart and Croker, that there was a formidable amount of quackery at this period : poetasters flourished, novelists of unapproachable demerits abounded, memoirs and reminiscences poured forth in streams and there were the *Annuals*, those elegant compilations of insipid verse and prose. But there is no doubt that both enjoyed performing or witnessing the flagellation ; and sometimes, as in the case of Tennyson, the victim was neither quack nor fool.

Lockhart was, however, attaining maturity, and his fundamental sense as a critic, his genuine feeling for literature, his sound scholarship were beginning to produce much good judgement and good writing. His major contributions to *The Quarterly* must be considered separately ; but some *obiter dicta* are worth quoting :

" How many people can *tell* a story vividly and powerfully, for one that can hold the pen without getting cramped into a cold, still, gazette-writing style."

He could himself both tell and write a story vividly and had a talent for pen-sketches ; like that given in one letter, of a French Bishop, known as the Abbé de Colbert, who was by birth a Scotsman, one of the Traills of Castlehill in Caithness. One of his uncles was an officer of high rank in the army of the great Colbert ; and being a kindly Scot desired to use his influence on behalf of his own kith and kin. He requested his elder brother, the laird of Castlehill, to send one of his younger sons to France " to be provided for in the French Church ". A young Presbyterian obediently came over, was converted and received, duly instructed and in time priested. As the Abbé de Colbert he was in high favour at the Court of Louis XVI and Marie Antoinette. He was consecrated Bishop of Rhodes, and so endeared himself to his flock that during the Revolution he was, for a long time, safely hidden. When, at length, obliged to leave his see, he was aided by a lady of frail virtue in Paris, who from the liking she had to the good Bishop, hid him in her lodging and then procured his escape to the Rhine, whence he made his way to Britain carrying nothing with him but a huge wig-block without which he never afterwards travelled ; indeed he honoured it with a title : M. le Chevalier de Rhodez. He came to Scotland, to stay at Bothwell Castle in Lanarkshire, travelling by diligence ; " M. le Chevalier " was somehow forgotten and carried on by coach—and the Bishop could not have his wig properly dressed after the journey. Rather than appear in any way dishevelled as to coiffure, he chose to come down to dinner in his own " venerable grey hair, which being much admired by the ladies, the Bishop never again resumed the wig." On his return to Scotland he found that, owing to the death of his elder brother, he was now " *de iure* Colbert *de* Castlehill ". A younger brother, presuming the Bishop's death, had taken the lairdship, but loyally invited the rightful heir to take his place. The Bishop declined, accepting only a small annuity, on which he lived contentedly until his death in 1810.

Lockhart could have written an excellent volume of historical portraits, especially of little-known characters ; those, for choice, with some touch of eccentricity, or who followed some by-way of a career and were at home in two countries. He had a sense of background, an eye for character, for the traits and touches that make a vivid portrait.

His editorial views and policy were set forth in more than one letter to Croker, when the latter was established as a regular contributor and adviser :

" You have ever been the best-natured as well as the most powerful of our contributors, and I assure you I shall endeavour to bring *The Review* into the shape you describe. But alas, it is most difficult to accomplish such a scheme. The truth is, the man who writes admirable books fails in ten cases out of twelve to make even a tolerable reviewer . . . It is my conviction that *The Q.R.* has two grounds of general support which are not likely wholly to desert us : (1) It is got up with infinitely more care and accuracy of thought and language than any other periodical work ; and (2) It speaks, on the whole, the feeling and opinion and taste of a higher order of society than any other. . . .

We must, I think, consider it as bound up in the interests of the Tory party, and consider how, without absolutely compromising our own personal consistency, it may be possible for us to secure that cause . . . Turning from those who calculate in club-houses on the chances of particular feuds and cliques of politicians, I would then appeal to the good sense of the people at large. . . . There has been a great reaction. Two years ago [this was in 1835], no Tory could dare to show himself, without running the risk of being stoned to death ; now, the Tories are in a large, though not I fear sufficient, proportion of places the popular candidates. Why should this reaction not go on ? It is not the child of delusion and violent reaction—but of sad and sober reflection and repentance."

Early in 1836 he appealed, more urgently than ever, to Croker for regular help :

" The stricter your connection with *The Q.R.* the larger your contributions and the more completely you take on yourself the political department,—the more advantageous will it be for *The Q.R.* in my opinion . . ."

The union was indissoluble. Whether or not Croker's attachment was for the good of *The Quarterly* is beyond the scope of this study. But one negative virtue must be admitted : Croker's political writing released Lockhart for the literary side of the paper. His letters continued to report and discuss political gossip, but it was not his business to treat such matter formally and officially. He became a true man of letters, a leader in literary journalism ; his scholarship, if not his creative instinct, found expression.

II

The correspondence with the Murrays, both John II and John III, began soon after Lockhart's appointment and continued, though never at such length as the Croker letters, throughout Lockhart's career at Albemarle Street. These letters are for the most part business communications, concerned with details of publication. J. G. L.'s personality stamps them; there are occasional items of personal news; but they show, more exclusively than the Croker correspondence, Lockhart in his professional aspect. He was the most industrious and painstaking of editors, devoted to his paper and his House, heedful of details, alert for anything that could affect *The Quarterly*.

He was actively interested in all Murray's ventures; among them being *The Family Library*, that pioneer set of biographies and similar works published at a moderate cost. He encouraged Murray in his plan of popular editions, knowing well that the book-buyers were no longer the wealthy aristocrats building up great libraries in their mansions, but the increasing numbers of the educated middle class, professional men and the clergy: men of taste and education, but of moderate incomes:

" I am sure the scheme of printing in that sort of shape has yet to be introduced to the world at large and that you will do well to think thereof seriously. Why should Fleet St. run away with all this? There are innumerable books which would find their way wide as the winds, were they placed within the reach of the small parsons and so forth."

Proposals for *The Family Library* may be found in a letter to the Rev. Henry Milman, Lockhart's friend from their Oxford days, who was now rapidly rising to eminence in the Church. He had been ordained in 1816 and was now Rector of St. Mary's, Reading. From Reading he came to St. Margaret's, Westminster, with a canonry in Westminster Abbey; and finally was made Dean of St. Paul's, one of the Deans whose names have been familiar to the mass of church and even non-church people. His *History of St. Paul's* made the cathedral better known and his arrangement of services made it better loved. Today he is perhaps best remembered as hymn-writer: he wrote " O help us, Lord; each hour of need " and " When our heads are bowed with woe," and the great Processional for Palm Sunday: " Ride on! ride on in majesty! "

Long before his elevation, while he was still a young and intensely industrious cleric at Reading (in 1828) Lockhart wrote to him of Murray's proposal that " a volume should be issued monthly, beginning with the January of 1829, each volume containing about 350 to 400 pages ". Milman was invited to contribute a volume, the fee offered being 300 guineas, and Lockhart hoped he might also be " not unwilling to give the poor *Quarterly* some assistance ". The history of the Jews was to be Milman's subject : " Surely it might be made more entertaining than any romance and really useful besides."

Lockhart found his hopes fulfilled in " a splendid book " ; though he realised that " some wise folk " might " shake the head at some passages touching miracles ". None the less, he proposed the history of Christianity as Milman's next work.

In the summer of 1829 he wrote to Murray, from Scotland, that *The Family Library* was " only beginning to be heard of hereabout ", but that Blackwood had promised " an article laudatory " and that Scott warmly approved of Milman's volume.

Lockhart was beginning to look on books as possible subjects for an article, which can become almost an occupational disease. His idea of a review was that it should not only (this certainly was essential) give a clear idea of the content of the book, the author's argument, and his style, with abundant quotations, but that it should be a disquisition, by the reviewer, on the subject of the book, whether in support or in contradiction, quotations being used in defence or attack as well as by way of illustration. Even a mediocre volume might have value if it suggested a good article : as would be the case if Milman reviewed the *Life of Bishop Heber* by his widow, which Lockhart found deplorably ill-written. Heber had been a close friend of Milman, as of Lockhart, and much admired by both. The review could well be a tribute to his personality and achievement :

" It is a proud thing for the Church that it always contains men of the same stamp with Heber—gentlemen, and almost universal scholars, sincere patriots, philanthropists and Christians. There is no other Church, certainly no Protestant one, of which all this could be said . . . In your hands I have no sort of doubt that this book might supply abundant materials for a literary, theological, political *mélange* of great popularity."

His opinion of Milman as a poet was considerably qualified, and he wrote to Murray that Milman's poem (probably the *Fall of Jerusalem*) "contains about half a dozen pages of stately and noble versification, but is, as a dramatic work, feeble and poor in the extreme. . . . He never ought to have been a poet, for he becomes, every day, more artificial, and that is a sad symptom at his time of life."

Lockhart's good-will towards his old crony Hogg was shown in one letter among this correspondence—in 1832 ; he had a scheme for publishing Hogg's poem *The Queen's Wake* by subscription, in order to help the impecunious poet. Hogg was in the throes of one of his recurrent crises, this time through the bankruptcy of his booksellers, Messrs. Erskine. Murray and another firm, Duncan in Paternoster Row, were to produce the book with entire profits to the author ; but to ensure this, there must be subscriptions. Lockhart and Murray each gave five guineas. With this in mind, Lockhart's explosion over Hogg's manuscript of reminiscences of Scott is easily condoned.

In these letters Lockhart was often the unofficial critic ; as when he wrote of Washington Irving's new book on Spain :

"I am sorry to say I think the whole affair feeble and vapid. Neither learned enough to be the historian, nor imaginative enough to be the poet of the Rodericks and Julians, he gives matter to us sufficiently familiar, in a middle style which seems to me as in the case of *The Conquest of Granada* devoid of any one characteristic worthy of his reputation."

There is a hint of his ideals of a biographer in one letter, discussing a *Life of Akenside* by Peter Cunningham, brother of Allan Cunningham the poet : "I think it very poor and pert, and him a very small creature, not likely to be serviceable in the *Biographies* for he has the ambition to be a Johnson with hardly the brains to be a Birch. Where shall the workers be found that know how to combine humility with care and zeal ? "

Humility has not been generally regarded as one of Lockhart's virtues : but he saw its nobility, and himself possessed artistic humility, which is essential to good biography. He could stand aside, and present his subject ; and when, as was inevitable in a *Life* so intimate as that of his father-in-law, he must enter the scene in person, he did so with an incomparable modesty and dignity.

There is some proof in these letters, as in the Croker, of the accusation that *Quarterly* articles were rigorously, even unscrupulously " edited ".

" I have read a good deal of Ford's Ms. on Spanish Romances and think a very curious article for *Q.R.* may be chipped out of it—not a very long one, however,—not near so long as he probably supposes." On another occasion he wrote : " I have boldly cut out a prodigious part of Head's paper. Let Clowes [the printer] give us it instantly in the abridged form, and we can then see what H. will say . . . I have also taken out all the offensive things in the article." Head (the traveller), according to report, on that and other occasions " said a mouthful " and much of it offensive.

Lockhart was accused by Harriet Martineau, in an article written long after his death, of doing more than such " editing " articles : of adding to them at his own whim " libels and malicious jokes ". Sophia, according to Miss Martineau, had the task of healing by " her modest dignity and her cheerful kindliness " the wounds thus inflicted. " It was his own callousness which made the sensitiveness of others so highly amusing to him." Miss Martineau's dislike and jealousy of Lockhart intensified her own natural obtuseness. One of the last flaws of which he could be accused was callousness ; he was, on the contrary, over-sensitive, with a kind of intellectual fastidiousness that could easily turn to acerbity of criticism.

Miss Martineau was paying off old scores. Lockhart with his strong religious beliefs and principles, *The Quarterly* with its High Church sympathy, had shown small approval for her Unitarian teaching ; and so she solaced herself with the statement " All the world was always aware of the sins of *The Quarterly* under Lockhart's management."

That there were sins, both of omission and commission, need not be denied. Periodicals are but human in their origin and management, and they reflect the frailty of that humanity. But the sins of the nineteenth-century magazines and reviews were due less to any individual editor or contributor than to the ferocity of contemporary politics and the vigour of contemporary expression. Lockhart's influence was, on the whole, for moderation ; he tried, increasingly as he himself matured, to restrain Croker from excess. The Murrays themselves were men of peace ; Lockhart, in moods of exasperation privately accused John II of weakness and vacillation. But their influence was a restraining one ; it was well for Lockhart to be in harness with them. The Murray temper and influence balanced Croker's. In the latter Lockhart might have seen, had he cared to be analytical and to follow his own excellent powers of perception, his own faults magnified and distorted : read, almost in parody, his own satire and biting contempt.

Miss Martineau, herself a pedantic chatterbox, failed to realise the depth of Lockhart's scholarship, because of its ease and urbanity, and wrote of his gifts, with insufferable condescension :

"Without being a man of genius, a great scholar, or politically or morally eminent, he had sufficient ability and accomplishment to ensure considerable distinction in his own person, and his interesting connexions did the rest. . . . If he had not Gifford's thorough scholarship, he had eminent literary ability,—readiness, industry,—everything but good principles and a good spirit."

There were, and are, other estimates of Lockhart ; there is one of Miss Martineau that could be expressed in a monosyllable, but it would lack dignity, and give pain to dog-lovers.

Chapter 15

CRITIC AND EDITOR :
THE QUARTERLY OF THE THIRTIES

THE third decade of the century was one of development not only for Lockhart himself but for *The Quarterly* and the House of Murray. In these years began the popular series of *Handbooks* which, like so many English achievements, literary and other, came about almost by accident. Young John III went on a tour of the Continent to perfect his languages. Travel in those days was easy in the matter of documents and restrictions, but difficult as to transport. Much of Europe was practically uncharted. There were letters and descriptions of travel in plenty, but none of them intended as guides to the traveller. Young John, having an observant mind and a gift for concise expression, took notes wherever he went— on local history and antiquities, art treasures, churches and castles, about routes and prices, food, customs, inns and climate. He knew from his own experience what questions would be asked, and how to answer them.

His father read these travel-notes, and saw their value both in kudos and in cash. Thus began the Murray *Handbooks* which were to serve generations of tourists. The first was on Holland, Belgium and the Netherlands, the second on South Germany and Switzerland ; then came one on Italy, and so the series flowed steadily on. These three were all by young John who more and more enjoyed his travels. He met Goethe at Weimar, and presented to him the manuscript of Byron's dedication of the poem *Werner.*

Lockhart, coming in age as he did, between the two generations, was able to sympathise with the younger man, and to beg for him paternal encouragement. He knew his own need and appreciation of sympathy : " I have outlived so many misfortunes and disappointments that it is no wonder I should need encouragement and support," he wrote to John II, adding that John III had " of late years given abundant evidence that he is both willing and able to bear a most useful part in our consultation. Pray encourage him to proceed. His youth, his different circle of acquaintances, his own selected pursuits are all new sources on which we may hope to draw largely for spirited suggestions and important advice."

As editor, Lockhart desired the good of *The Quarterly* above all things. He sank himself in his work. Whatever measure of youthful arrogance remained in him was balanced by his self-effacing loyalty. He knew the dangers of the baser kind of publicity :

" I am conscious that when living among the diners of London I am too apt to take their table-talk for my measure of what is telling," he wrote to Murray. " We share their patronage with the meretricious novel and with the smart newspaper and squib, with the scandal of the opera-*loges*, with the tittle-tattle of the Court, with the last of Rogers' sarcasms and Sydney Smith's jokes."

The Englishwoman of the 1830's was far from being the insipid piece of prettiness portrayed by Dickens and Thackeray. It could almost be called a feminist age, and it might not be fantastic to suggest that had they pressed the matter, women might have secured, at that time, the privileges of the franchise and of higher education and entry to the professions for which they had to fight so bitterly at the end of their century and the beginning of our own. Women writers were fluent, popular and successful. They poured out streams of verse—Mrs. Hemans most conspicuously, Letitia Elizabeth Landon a close rival, Mrs. Norton the most fascinating and enigmatic of them all.

There were the Irishwomen too—Maria Edgeworth, solidly established in fame with her Irish sketches, her novels, her stories for children, and the lively Lady Morgan, born Sydney Owenson, whose *Wild Irish Girl* and *The O'Briens and the O'Flahertys* and other novels had considerable vogue. She met the Lockharts in 1835 and recorded, " We were mutually charmed with each other, and have sworn an eternal friendship."

The Quarterly savaged her first books : " Those tomes of absurdity, those puzzles in three volumes," until even Byron protested to Murray about this brutality of criticism. In her later career she found *The Review* in mellower temper. Thomas Moore once suggested to John Murray that she might contribute a volume on The Flemish Artists to his *Family Library*. Mr. Murray had an alternative suggestion ; knowing that Lady Morgan was a good cook, he thought she might edit a new edition of his domestic best-seller, Mrs. Rundell's cookery-book.

But of meretricious novels there was at this time a flood. Exactly how bad they were we can only guess ; perhaps no worse than their modern counterparts. Old-fashioned badness is easily ridiculed, contemporary imbecility is accepted. Many novels were reviewed in *The Quarterly* ; some, now utterly forgotten, receiving serious and even favourable notice. Lockhart took some of them in hand himself. In a notice of *De Vere* by Robert Ward in *The Q.R.* of October 1827, he insisted on the importance of the creative imagination in the novelist : " All the classics of this branch of literature have drawn largely upon their own personal observation and experience in life, but these would have availed them little had they not possessed high faculties of imagination, and been through them enabled to fuse their materials of all kinds into an artist-like unity of form and purpose, blending old things with new so thoroughly as to merit the praise of creation." The irony of it is that Lockhart himself, as a novelist, only just failed to achieve that unity.

In the April issue of 1833 (Vol. 49) he amused himself with a parcel of light stuff : *Recollections of a Chaperon* by Mrs. Sullivan ; *Aims and Ends* and *Oonah Lynch* by Mrs. Thomas Sheridan. " The ladies have always some pretty little manufacture in hand ; twenty years ago they were shoemakers—then came the era of book-binding ; at present authorship is the thing. To have contributed to an *Annual* or a *Court Journal* is no distinction at all. Even a volume of lyrical poems is thought hardly more of than an embroidered cushion or night-cap was in the days of their grand-mothers." A novel was considered the most meritorious form of composition. He satirised the fashionable " silver fork " type of fiction.

JOHN GIBSON LOCKHART
Editor of the *Quarterly Review*.
From a sketch by D. Maclise, R.A., 1830

But he found that even the most indifferent novels might have documentary value as records of a fast-vanishing period of society :

" Believing, as we do, that society in this country is about to undergo some great change, we cannot doubt that these books will be referred to long after the daintiest of their authoresses have stooped to woollen. They will be quoted as evidence that we deserved our fate." They were, these trivial novels, reflections of a trivial and restless life— " town-made or villa-made " that centred in Almack's or in " rich suburbia, the chosen province of the fund-holders and the colonial absentee. It is here that vanity and selfishness, nowhere else leading characteristics of English character and manners, thrive and bloom as in a hot-bed." One has to ask oneself at times whether he is describing the 1830's or the 1930's. " Those of moderate fortune, in place of being country gentlemen, each the pattern of some parish and guardian of some village are apt to spend their whole life-time in the interchange of formal dinners and foppish parody of the manners of the local magnate." He returned to his assertion that the novel was the most influential and expressive form of modern literature : " Now that the novel has come to stand virtually, with regard to the painting of living manners, in the room at once of the Addisonian essay and the genteel comedy, how greatly is it to be regretted that the varied talents displayed in this brand of popular literature should confine themselves to so narrow a world."

He found considerable talent, however, in the works he was reviewing and ended with compliments to both ladies.

" Jane Austin [*sic*] is gone—Miss Edgeworth appears to be determined on silence and Miss Ferrier wisely adheres to Scotland ; the press groans under the burthen of weak and clumsy fantastic trash ; it is therefore no trifle to have to announce the appearance of two new female novelists really capable of tracing with taste and discrimination the more delicate features of English manners."

Miss Edgeworth was not, as it happened, entirely sub-merged in silence ; in the following year, in June 1834, Lockhart had the pleasure of reviewing her *Helen*, praising

187

her for " the admirable but unobtrusive art with which she has contrived to exhibit what we may call the whole gamut of one particular virtue and its opposite vice ", for " the profusion of terse and pungent sayings scattered over its dialogue " and " the deep, piercing pathos of many of its scenes ". He regretted only the absence of the " quaint, humorous oddities that made her Irish tales delightful " for she had chosen to set her tale in London, not in Ireland. He has saved one jewel of criticism for us in quoting Byron's comment : " Miss Edgeworth's Cupid is something of a Presbyterian."

In another issue he wrote of a novel *The Doctor* published anonymously—supposed to be by Hartley Coleridge, but now accepted as Southey's. It would seem to have been a *Tristram Shandy* in dilution, with some excellencies, many faults and a general eccentricity which provoked the truly Lockhartian comment :

" The author says of one of his characters : ' He was born with one of those heads in which the thin partition that divides great wit from folly is wanting.'—The partition in his own head would seem to be a moveable one."

Lockhart was justifying Scott's commendation of his readiness and adaptability of talent ; he was prepared to write and did write on many subjects—from novels to dry rot, from Goethe to deer-stalking, from the campaigns of Washington to Gaelic poetry.

He was mellowing, but the old man in him (to use the Pauline phrase much relished in Scots theology) was vigorous when he dealt with Leigh Hunt's *Lord Byron and Some of His Contemporaries* (in March 1828). Hunt was flagellated for filling " page after page through a long quarto volume with the meanest details of private gossip—dirty scribble about other men's wives and men's mistresses—and men's lackeys and even the mistresses of the lackeys. . . . It is the miserable book of a miserable man ; the little airy fripperies of its manner are like the fantastic trip and convulsive simper of some poor, worn-out wanton struggling between famine and remorse, leering through her tears." Lockhart had, from the first, admired Byron as a poet, and recognised his essential nobility of mind ; he was disgusted by the appearance of the strutting dwarf Leigh Hunt in the presence of so kingly a figure. " As to the more solemn subject of religion, we ought to take shame to ourselves for even for a moment considering Lord Byron and Leigh Hunt as fellow-infidels. The dark doubts which disturbed to its depths the noble intellect of the one had little indeed in common with the coxcombical phantasms which floated and float on the surface of the other's shallowness. . . . Between the hypochrondriac reveries of a poet, and the smug petulance of this Cockney there is about as wide an interval as from the voluptuousness of a Sardanapalus to the geniality of a monkey."

Three years later appeared Thomas Moore's *Life of Byron*, and Lockhart reviewed this (in February 1831) with approval : " A subject of immeasurable interest and attractiveness treated on the whole with masterly candour and manliness. . . . A man of genius is in earnest, and there is nothing either of brutish or of glitter to disturb the interest of the mournful tale." He had high praise for Byron's letters : " Had he lived he would have taken his place in the very first rank of our prose literature. . . . Lord Byron will henceforth be placed in the very first rank of English letter-writers." His judgement of Byron was never pharasaic ; but, himself a man of deep if reticent faith, he deplored the lack of religion. " Lord Byron possessed the temperament of a poet and the accomplishments of a scholar, but religion as a principle for action had no place in his bosom. Self-will was his guide through life." It is the true sentence on Byron, as on many a wayward genius ; and " but for the grace of God " might have been true of Lockhart.

His judgement, mellowed by charity, was pronounced on another somewhat wayward genius—Boswell, when he reviewed a new edition of the *Life of Johnson* prepared by Croker. Without condoning Boswell's frailties, he discerned in him that " most perfect good nature " which drew forth the best in Johnson, and roused " in the sage's feelings towards him a something of paternal gentleness and protection. . . . A curious chapter of the human mind would be that of the friendships of genius ; but perhaps it would bring out few instances in which, after all, something of this kind of paternal feeling did not mingle." He must have thought of his own friendship with Scott and of the great, protective fatherliness he had found there. Lockhart pronounced Boswell's masterpiece to be " about the richest dictionary of wit and wisdom any language can boast ".

His views on the writing of Memoirs were expressed, pungently, in one of his earliest articles—in 1827, in dealing with a bundle of such effusions, all of an imposing mediocrity ; the writers including Frederick Reynolds the actor, Lindley Murray the grammarian, and a military gentleman, Major Cartwright : " The classics of the papier-mâché age of our drama have taken up the salutary belief that England expects every driveller to do his *memorabilia.* Modern primer-makers must needs leave Confessions behind them as if they were so many Rousseaus. . . . It is to be hoped genius will not be altogether silent, merely because dulness lifts up her voice so loudly in Grub Street, and that the virtue and patriotism of the age may be commemorated as effectually, though not quite so voluminously as its imbecility, quackery and vice." He ended : " Few great men—none of the very highest order—have chosen to paint otherwise than indirectly and through the shadows of imaginary forms, the secret workings of their inmost minds ; nor is it likely that genius will ever be found altogether destitute of this proud modesty, unless in the melancholy case of being tinged, as in Rousseau, with insanity." In the phrase " proud modesty " he has sketched not only his subject but himself.

There was friendship behind his interest in Basil Hall's *Travels* appearing in 1831 ; already read by Sophia with some disappointment. Anne had read it in the original Journal which she found much livelier.

Hall was a gifted and lively personality ; a friend of Scott and a frequent visitor to Castle Street and Abbotsford. He entered the navy at the age of fourteen and saw a good deal of service and travel—in North America, in the East Indies, and in China—and he wrote many volumes of travel. It was through his influence that Scott was able to sail to Malta in a frigate.

Lockhart wrote of his " keen, quick eye, voracious curiosity, restless activity ", his " gay temperament, and upright
virtuous mind " ; and of his being—as men of such temperament are " apt to see one side of a thing so vividly as to
forget there is another side at all. . . . His sincerity
cannot always excuse his dogmatism." But his book was
entertaining, and " on the whole the most popular work
of travel in England ".

Lockhart never forgot his Scottish roots : and one of
his articles showed his sympathy with a Scottish region and
tradition remote from his native Lanarkshire and from
Edinburgh. He was reviewing the *Songs and Poems* of the
Gaelic bard, Rob Donn—Robert Mackay, the poet of
Sutherland and Caithness—and made an urgent plea for
the preservation of Gaelic language and literature. He
deplored the lack of a Celtic Chair in any of the Scottish
Universities—or of one in Welsh in Oxford or Cambridge,
or Irish in Dublin.

" There is little time to be lost if the as yet unprinted
literature of this unfortunate people is to be preserved at
all. . . . The short-sighted chieftains who have been
systematically banishing their affectionate kindred for the
sake of increased rentals are already beginning to share
the doom of their victims. . . . Their estates are rapidly
breaking to pieces in their hands ; new men, jobbers and
usurers are, year after year, pushing the haughtiest of them
from their stools."

His prejudices and aversions were still strong ; and were
excited by Heine whose book *De i'Allemagne* he reviewed
in 1835. Heine's bitterness shocked him—though he could
in part understand it, tracing its source to the writer's mixed
blood : child of a German mother and Jewish father, educated in Protestantism but rejecting that faith ; rootless,
bereft of his true tradition :

" He blends a rancorous personal spleen with the frigidity
of the contemptuous metaphysician, and revives . . . the
bitter, sneering malignity of a crucifying Sadducee."

Lockhart saw the danger of Heine's attack on Christianity
and his desire for a revival of the primitive German religion
—the pantheism whose " primitive influence still lives and

breathes at the bottom of the national mind ". It was beyond even his prescience to foresee how strongly it lived and how horribly it was to be revived, a hundred years later ; but there were few at that time or for long after who realized the potential evil in Germany.

But Lockhart, when he chose to praise, could be generous and ungrudging. He ranked Coleridge's *Table Talk* second only to Boswell's *Johnson* ; making the distinction that the latter " presents its talkers in the strictest sense of the word, dramatically "—a quality lacking in Coleridge. None the less—" in every other point of view as unlike Dr. Johnson as one man of great faculties and great virtues can be to another, Mr. Coleridge must be allowed to have been his legitimate successor as the great literary talker of England ".

Goldsmith was praised both for his elegance and his morality ; there was always a moral element in Lockhart's judgements :

" There is no classic of any time whose *opera omnia* may be placed with more confidence in the hands of that sex for whom every author must on all occasions consider himself as writing. In his prose and in his verse *virginibus puerisque* was always the motto of this benevolent and gentle-hearted man. His humour was without coarseness —his merriment without extravagance—his wit without spleen."

He could observe, objectively, the immorality or amorality of a writer of genius, as in Beyle-Stendhal's *Mémoires d'un Touriste* which he enjoyed for its distinction and vivacity ; commenting on its morals : " We have no desire to meddle with M. Beyle's ample assortment of merely gay and festive intrigues and adulteries. The reader appreciates already his profound indifference as to the question of moral and immoral in the affairs of—to use his own phrase—' *L'amour ou ce que lui resemble le plus.*' "

This excellent dryness of rebuke is surpassed by his comment on Beyle-Stendhal's anti-Christian sentiments and his disapproval of the contemporary revival of Christian teaching in France :

" Most strenuous efforts are making to restore the prejudice to which he assigns the date of Constantine the Great—

though we believe it is generally admitted that Christianity was not actually invented by the Council of Nice."

Friendship added warmth and sparkle to literary appreciation when he read a volume of sketches in prose and verse, by the Rev. Charles Townsend, " the peerless parson " of some of his familiar letters ; the vicar of Preston, whose friendship added greatly to the pleasure of Lockhart's visits to Brighton. Along with his book *Winchester* Lockhart reviewed in 1836 the *Rhyming Epistle* of another friend, William Stewart Rose, who had been Scott's friend also ; a scholar, antiquarian and mediaevalist, with a marked talent for verse translation. His *Epistle* was addressed to John Hookham Frere, and its subject was Mr. Townsend, " the peerless parson " himself, and so was doubly commendable in Lockhart's eyes. Rose had travelled much in Italy, and was married to a Venetian lady. His home was in Hampshire, but he spent a good deal of time in Brighton, with the parson.

From the *Rhyming Epistle* one may quote, in order to share Lockhart's pleasure, Rose's description of wines :

> But oft we pass to Epicurean theme,
> Waking from mystic Plato's morning dream,
> And, prosing o'er some Greek or Gascon wine,
> Praise the rich vintage of the Rhone or Rhine . . .
> Or what the Florentine's light flagon fills,
> Cheap but choice product of Etruscan hills,
> Which warmed him with the lyric fire of Flaccus
> That tells the praises of the Tuscan Bacchus.

Brighton must have seen many a symposium between the antiquarian, the cleric and the editor of *The Quarterly*.

Taken as a whole, Lockhart's criticism in his maturity has wisdom even when caustic, and is more often appreciative than destructive. He had his fixed code and standard of literature and of morals ; the two closely interwoven. He had zest, a quality necessary in good critical writing as well as in creative ; and wrote with vigour, never with feeble or jaded irritation. Neither his praise nor his damns were faint.

He mellowed and matured, in the thirties, but the brilliant undergraduate in him was still lively, and found scope—

not quite so madly as in the *Blackwood* days, in a new monthly : *Fraser's*,[1] produced by James Fraser and Lockhart's friend and colleague in *Maga*, Dr. William Maginn, that fantastic Irish genius who was so much larger than life that his portrait in fiction would be deprecated as caricature, his career as extravaganza. He appears as Captain Shandon in *Pendennis*. *Fraser's* had fifty-two years of life, from 1830 till 1882 ; in its early days it included among its contributors, Thackeray, Carlyle, Disraeli, Lockhart, and, most regularly, " Father Prout "—in real life Fr. Francis Mahoney. Daniel Maclise was the staff artist ; he drew a conversation piece of the contributors dining at the round table in " the back parlour " of the office in Regent Street, and he illustrated the *Gallery of Illustrious Characters* that appeared in the early numbers. In this, the pen sketches were mostly by Maginn ; but Lockhart wrote that of Maginn himself.

" The Doctor ", as he was called, and sometimes by his pen-name of Sir Morgan O'Doherty, was born in Cork in 1793 ; he had a dazzling classical career at Trinity, Dublin, where he graduated B.A. in 1811 and LL.D. in 1819. His journalistic career began in *Blackwood's*, where he invented the *Noctes Ambrosianae* if he was only part-author of these extravagancies. His faults were obvious ; he was drunken and extravagant, improvident, and sometimes he was cruel : as in his slandering of Letitia Landon the poetess. But he had great gifts and immeasurable charm.

The portrait of Lockhart, by Maclise, appeared in August 1830, with the description by Maginn :

" There he sits in his Parisian morning-gown, busily smoking his sempiternal cigar." (It is truly one of the most comfortable portraits ever made of a celebrity.) " There is no literary man in all the great republic of letters who is more constantly occupied with puffing." One recalls a reference in the family letters to the number of cigar-boxes at Chiefswood. Maginn mentions that J. G. L. was engaged on his autobiography, which is one of the most tantalising announcements made about him ; from some parts of

[1] *Rebellious Fraser's*. By Miriam M. H. Thrall (Columbia Univ. Press, 1934).

Reginald Dalton, from remembrances in his letters, and from the personal passages in his *Life of Scott* it is plain to see what a masterpiece he could have written in this form. Of Lockhart as critic and editor Maginn has the somewhat surprising opinion that he was too indulgent. " Long may he there [in *The Quarterly*] wield his critical baton, but we must recommend with more truculence."

In the following January J. G. L. portrayed Maginn : " Our artist has caught, with singular felicity, the easy, good-humoured nonchalance of this learned and libellous countenance." After a racy description of " The Doctor's " career he pronounces : " The redoubted O'Doherty has always been, is, and ever will be the jovial, also the simple-hearted, the careless and the benignant." He concludes with the somewhat startling idea that " had the poet Laureate and The Doctor taken Orders, they would have made two admirable bishops ".

Miss Thrall in her scholarly study of *Rebellious Fraser's* suggests that Lockhart may have collaborated with Maginn in his novel, *Whitehall* ; and that he was certainly his partner in the article *Ars Ridendi*, in March 1831, and in the series of verse-satires, after the mode of Juvenal, entitled *Men and Manners* that began in January 1834, with the signature Pierce Pungent.

The tone and flavour of both the prose and the verse is indeed Lockhartian. The exuberant J. G. L. responded to the still more ebullient Irishman. *Ars Ridendi* was a study, chiefly of Thomas Hood and Theodore Hook—the latter one of J. G. L.'s most cherished if not most estimable friends :

" To laugh is the privilege of man. It is beyond comparison, the most valuable right he can boast of. It is, moreover, peculiar to himself . . . We think too little of laughter, and far too little of those who make us laugh . . . Great men and wise men have always loved laughter. The vain, the ignorant, and the uncivilised alone have dreaded and despised it."

Carlyle and Galt were both " Fraserians " ; the friendship between Lockhart and Carlyle may have begun at the round table in the back parlour. *Sartor Resartus* appeared in the magazine in 1834, which says much for the digestive powers of the contemporary readers of periodicals.

In August 1834 Hogg's *Domestic Manners of Sir Walter Scott* was reviewed, and flayed : " It is Hogg all over—coarse, egotistical, vain, regardless of obligation, careless of truth, and ready to take advantage of any opportunities . . . to break through the decencies and privacies of life." This, if not written by J. G. L., must have been read by him with entire approval.

Chapter 16

FAMILY LIFE : NEWS IN LETTERS

I

THE eighteen-thirties cannot, like the early '20's, be called the happy years of Lockhart's life ; they were too full of shadows following hard on the sunny hours, and they brought him his greatest and lasting grief in Sophia's death. But they were his richest and fullest period : he was mature, he achieved distinction in his profession, he wrote his masterpiece, and, for near seven years out of the ten he was profoundly happy in his most intimate life. Sophia and he endured many sorrows : Johnny's death and Scott's and Anne's ; but as long as Sophia lived, happiness flowered from their mutual devotion. There was gaiety too ; Sophia brought a sparkle of fun to everything she wrote or said or did, and the children, Walter and Charlotte, were an increasing delight.

Lockhart's life at this period is well charted by family letters, as by his own professional writing. He was leading a full life ; he was a well-known figure socially. The Lockharts had a wide circle, drawn round them by Sophia's warmth of personality ; they both touched life at many points ; they knew literary London, political London, and were aware of Europe. One has to consider Lockhart in both aspects of his life, the private and the professional, and they are interwoven in his letters, as they were interwoven in fact.

There is, however, a concentration of domesticity in these years, between Scott's death and Sophia's ; a halcyon period much of which is recorded by Sophia herself.

In August of 1833 Lockhart went, with his friend Hay, to Aix-la-Chapelle. Sophia took the children to Rokeby to be deliciously petted and spoiled by the Squire.

" I am almost ashamed of the kindness I receive. I have the best room in the house. Mr. Morritt does not seem to think anything too good for me, and for the children,

if they were spoiled before it is all over with them now.
They were in Mr. Morritt's room long before I was down,
and I found the old gentleman on his knees with them in
the hall, swimming a toy duck for their amusement in a
basin of water, and then the whole servants in a body stuff
them." At the head of the servants was Nicolson, Sir
Walter's butler, who had joined the household of his old
master's friend ; so the link with Abbotsford was strong,
and Walter and Charlotte would still hear the pleasant
Scots of the Borders. Walter was becoming a sportsman :
" There will be no speaking to Watt soon as he thinks
himself quite a man, and is this moment going out with
Nicolson and Mr Morritt's nephew to shoot rabbits."

Nicolson was happy in his new home ; Sophia heard it
from her maid ; the only drawback was that in his position
he must observe a certain dignity and not be so familiar
with the servants' hall as he had been at Abbotsford, and
high dignity can be lonely.

They had brought their dog, Sprig, with them, to visit
various aunts and cousins of the same breed, one of them
also called Sprig, which was confusing, but peace was
tolerably well maintained in the canine family.

Sophia's letters from Rokeby are, like the house itself,
full of children and dogs. It was a placid life : the carriage
in the afternoon, walks by the Greta, long evenings with
books and talk, the Squire often reading aloud to Sophia
and his daughters—Beaumont and Fletcher, or Ben Jonson,
or " our old delight Crabbe ", while they worked at their
embroidery. " If I took a fancy to have the moon, I do
believe some attempt would be made to get it down."

" And now, dearest Lockhart," one letter ended, " it is
real love that makes me say, stay as long as you possibly
can away, do nothing but what is agreeable in the way
of fatigue and let me see you brown, strong and fit for the
winter's work. If you will but be in good case, I feel we
may reasonably look forward with comfort this winter, the
children being so well, to more comfort than has been our
lot for long."

On his side, Lockhart wrote letters full of gossip with a
goodly spice of malice.

Aix-la-Chapelle itself he found dull, stuffed with English and Scots visitors, including an acquaintance Mrs. Calderwood, " looking pretty, still, but very failed and low " and her husband who was " as gouty and ugly as ever ". Lockhart's own companion Hay was taking a cure ; he was addicted to medicine : " The vials of wrath, blue, red and green on his table are already enough to frighten 50 Fergusons out of their wits."

But there were oddities enough in local society to divert J. G. L. " The Wynnes are an agreeable family—he as infirm in body now as he always was in mind, but good-natured and well-informed enough—she lively, managing, gay and worldly of the worldliest, but all the remains of attractiveness, a thorough tender mother thinking of nothing but *parties* (French) for her daughters, and *parties* (English) for herself. Being poor, the home concern is limited to tea and bread and butter, but expeditions to dine at villages where the Privy Councillor is too lame to go, and where the gentlemen who do go pay, are the order, if she can so manage it, of every day in her Aix-la-Chapelle life." This very practical manager entertained him with her gossip.

He also met Lady Morgan with whose latest book Croker had dealt in Crokerian style in *The Quarterly*. Lockhart found her " not so ugly as Croker made one believe, but affected and absurd, and the extremes of vulgar airs and pretensions ".

Except for the occasional stimulus of his humour, Lockhart found little to attract him ; yet it was an experience : " I am not sorry to have seen a little of the very little sort of world that, I believe, constitutes the best of this, as of most other such places—old *habitués*, generals and colonels, Lady Marys dowager and spinster, with labelled bottles of yesterday's Rhine wine,—so free and easy all, and delighted to have got rid of that stiff England. There was a ball one night, and how they did flirt and waltz and gallop with the bearded blackguards in blue and green uniforms who, in plain clothes next morning, seemed not worthy to tie the shoe-strings of their footmen."

The following year began sadly, with the death of Lockhart's mother. He wrote to Sophia from Laurence's manse

at Inchinnan with family news ; his father was now failing
much in mind, which softened the blow for himself but made
a problem for the family. Violet was ill, badly shaken by
this grief, and " had no notion of household management ".
It might be possible for her and her father to join an aunt
and cousins : " But how it is to be brought about with so
many odd tempers and fancies to conciliate God knows."
A further complication was caused by William's affairs.
On the day of the funeral Dr. Lockhart had a letter from
Sir Hugh Palliser, William's brother-in-law, expressing the
surprise and pain he and his sister felt at William's resolution, which was, apparently, to end the unhappy marriage.
J. G. L. dealt with the letter tersely and noncommittally :
" I think the poor booby baronet, even he, might have
had sense enough not to vex the old man at that moment."

This year and the next saw Sophia with the children on
holiday in Boulogne ; they took comfortable lodgings for
a long summer, to be joined by Lockhart when he could
leave London and *The Quarterly*. The children were now
both at school in London : Walter at King's College School,
where Dante Gabriel and Michael Rossetti, and W. K. H.
Boyd were his school-fellows. Charlotte attended a little
private school. Sophia told her cousin Anne Scott about
it, in one of the long letters of family news she wrote in these
last years of her life, which portray so warm and bright
a domestic life :

" I have made a great discovery with regard to Charlotte.
You know I can teach nothing, I would rather die. Now
there is a remarkably nice gentlewoman bought a house in
Hanover Terrace, and keeps a finishing school for nine
young ladies of fourteen and upwards, all the best masters,
French and English governess resident in the house. She
does not condescend to day-boarders but our name did all,
and Charlotte goes there for three hours at present, and
when it is necessary can increase the time. The French
and English governess is all as yet necessary, with a little
dancing in which Cha excels. I am thus spared a governess,
and perhaps though it might be better her being with
children about her own age, still, one can't have everything,
and she will not take harm by being with girls older than

CHARLOTTE LOCKHART, AGED 5
From a portrait by Slater, 1833

herself, unless they have leisure to spoil her and that they have not ; as yet it has answered well, and Charlotte has improved."

The French holidays meant early fluency in French and Charlotte was to prove a most accomplished linguist.

In the spring of 1835 Sophia wrote of the political situation : Peel's government was likely to go out and it made everything uncertain :

"With our usual luck, Lockhart could get, at this moment, a good situation for the asking, but also at the moment, without the crime of murder there is nothing would suit him as he would take nothing that a change of ministers would deprive him of, and while we thus wait for a vacancy the golden opportunity may pass." Charles, too, hoped for a post ; preferably abroad, in a warmer climate, as chargé-d'affaires or consul.

In the autumn she wrote of their safe return from their first French holiday, after a bad passage :

"Before we shot across the pier I was dead, as well as everybody else . . . To add to my misery, a lady had asked me to take care of a diamond necklace and earrings of great value, so I had to keep my horrid desk always under my head, not liking my company. To say truth, in no steamboat did I ever hear such vulgar conversation in the intervals of their malady." But they all came safely to land at last, with the diamonds, and settled down for the winter ; the children returned to school, Walter with reluctance, " after his Boulogne dissipation ". They suffered one of those small but poignant griefs that dog-lovers know. Sprig was lost, during a walk with one of the servants ; "And as she could find her way home from any part of the town, it was certain that she had been stolen." Less fortunate than her famous contemporary Flush, Sprig was never found. " I am ashamed to say how vexed we all are, and poor Ginger looks about the house in such a melancholy way."

They were to spend Christmas 1835 at The Grange, near Winchester, with the Ashburtons (Carlyle's Lady Ashburton) : " Of course there will be a good Tory party ; he was formerly Mr. Baring and very high in Peel's ministry.

I hope ere long he may return to his old place, people do seem to be tired of our present rulers, and I am happy to say I do think they will be out about Easter." (This was Melbourne's government, and it lasted until 1841.) In April 1836 Sophia must still bewail the tenacity of the Whigs, who cannily risked no measure that could throw them out, " but are gradually undermining everything, have great majorities every night, everything like a gentleman avoiding the House in disgust ".

There was a choice piece of gossip about Royalty :

" The *on dit* is that the Princess Victoria is turned Tory and much disgusted with things in general ; whenever she finds her mother making up a dinner she insists on writing an invite to Sir Robert Peel. The other day she found out she was kept far too short of pocket-money, took an opportunity, drove to Bundle and Bridges, bought a service of plate telling them they would be paid one day, but she only wished it to sell the next day and she pocketed the money. A young lady of seventeen with this spirit may do some good yet."

From Royal to domestic gossip the descent was easy for Sophia's pen. Her devoted Strut was leaving to marry a highly respectable and eligible suitor, whose uncle had left him money which he was investing in a brewery. " We both have had many cries over the parting " and sometimes the bride seemed reluctant. Strut had recommended a new maid, named Gammon, and as the Lockharts already had a servant called Dust they would, Sophia rightly thought, " be perfect in surnames ".

As for family news, Lockhart was " hard at work at the *Life*, and will, I think, satisfy expectations from what I heard of it. I only hope his health will stand the labour he takes." Walter was in Ireland, where Jane her sister-in-law was to follow him : " The same dull woman as usual. She was a fortnight in London with Mrs. Jobson who is far more mad than ever, and I was quite worn out with paying attentions to her."

In 1836 Sophia and the children again spent the summer in Boulogne, in lodgings in La Grande Rue : " An excellent house above a jeweller's shop " with dining-room and drawing-room and kitchen on the first floor, bedrooms above, one with a dressing-room that could serve as study, and a *grenier* for their trunks—all for 400 francs a month, " and the indispensable apartment is in the house and as good as the one at home ", which sounds an unusual luxury for a French house. Dinner was sent in at a quarter to five, when Sophia and the children dined, then the maids, and there was enough left over for supper : this at a charge of 12 francs a day. " Our dinner yesterday was an excellent tureen full of vermicelli soup, roast shoulder of lamb, an excellent dish of stewed veal with carrots, potatoes, and for the second course roast chicken, asparagrass [*sic*] and tartlets, all hot, well-dressed and nice—no fire, no trouble of any kind, only in the morning saying for so many and charged a couple of francs per head." It was a housewife's paradise, and for impecunious Britons Boulogne was a haven.

The children were in high spirits, Walter " so excited about everything I have to hold him constantly by the coat to prevent him killing himself with fatigue ". There was a message to Ginger : " Tell Ginger all dogs in muzzles. Will she endure that ? "

Lockhart came over to join his family, and wrote one of his gossip-letters to John Murray ; the core of it being an account of a devoted honeymoon couple who gave great scandal—because the lady was the gentleman's niece.

It was a golden summer. All appeared at last to be going well. When it ended and they came home again Sophia continued her happy letters to Cousin Anne.

The children were settling down again, they were keeping up their French and writing long letters to Monsieur Brunot in Boulogne. Mr. Cadell had been staying with them and had startled the household by tipping the children a sovereign each. But it would have taken more than that to reconcile Sophia to his presence. He had come to discuss the *Life* and the publication of Scott's works, with Lockhart, and he " could think or attend to nothing but his own business, as he hopes to make a mint of money by the *Life* "—having already secured £60,000 by the sale of the novels. But even " hard-hearted Cadell " was pleased with what he had read of Lockhart's work. " I kept my temper beautifully ", Sophia wrote ; and had pleasure in telling a story against Mr. Cadell. Lockhart had taken him to an exhibition of Egyptian antiques : " Everything you could conceive was there—pots and pans, ladies' ornaments " ; but Cadell's sole comment was : " Where's the coin ? I see no money." He had, however, on his return to Scotland sent her a " bread-and-butter " or hostess-gift, of shortbread and a " bun " (*anglice* plum-cake) ; and he had to be endured.

In January they had a Twelfth Night party. Kind Lady Davy had sent a cake, with the lucky beans in it for the King and Queen. It was almost a grown-up party, from seven o'clock till eleven, with " quadrilles to the piano-forte " and other revels.

Sophia wrote, also, to Cousin Walter Scott—Anne's brother, about the children : " Watt is now ten years old, and a very clever, handsome boy, if it please God to spare him, likely to do us credit, but like a true Scotsman thinks as yet of no profession but being a soldier." She told him of Charles, too, safe, if not altogether satisfied in the Foreign Office, and not very sound in health,—" suffering terribly from that curse of our family, rhumatism [*sic*] ".

Of the *Life* she wrote with great pride : " Lockhart is very busy with Papa's *Life* which, I am sure, will do him credit, it is advertised for the 15th of March to come out in monthly volumes till completed. You will find us not richer, but very contented, and I may say have reason to feel much gratified by the constant attention that which is called the world pays."

In this last winter of her life Sophia was happy ; she and her husband had high hopes of their entrancing children. The storms had, it seemed, passed. Charles was at hand, in London, she was in close touch with Walter by letter, and with her cousins ; it was all that would seem secure in family life. And she was probably closer than ever before to Lockhart in mind and sympathy, for her living and loving memory of her father was inspiration to him. She was much loved, and much needed, and for herself the price she had to pay, in her early death, for her happiness, may not have seemed too high. But for her husband and children and all she left, it was indeed costly.

In the spring of 1837 Lockhart wrote to Allan Cunningham : " My wife is, at present, very seriously ill." His letters to Croker told of her decreasing strength : " The Influenza has settled on her stomach and liver, organs hereditarily weak." There was a flicker of hope before the end ; but Sophia was doomed by this hereditary delicacy. Lockhart's diary for May, 1837, has no entries between the 3rd, when Mrs. Thomas Scott arrived to be Sophia's kind nurse, and the 15th, when Walter arrived, summoned by Charles. For the 17th there is the entry :

" At 3 a.m. died Charlotte Sophia Scott, 24 Sussex Place " ; on the 22nd a note of her burial. Milman read the Committal Service.

Lockhart wrote to William, asking him to tell the news to Violet and Laurence, and to assure them that " throughout her long illness her sweetness of temper had never given way . . . But this is a terrible blow, and will derange all my hopes and plans of life." To Violet he wrote, two days later : " Sophia's mind had been, during many weeks, in an unsettled condition, but it pleased God to restore her to full possession of herself for the last fortnight, and though her bodily suffering was occasionally acute, she surveyed her approaching departure with calmness and humble serenity, and at different times signified her farewell feelings and desires to us all in the sweetest manner. I think no one ever lived a more innocent life, and it is my consolation now to reflect that it was perhaps as happy a life as is often granted to human creature."

Charles wrote of her, to Cousin Walter : " She was ever thinking of her friends . . . My dear sister's lively and unaffected manner had endeared her to a numerous circle of acquaintances of all ranks, and her little reunions used to be a source of great pleasure to me. Alas, they are now broken up."

Many besides Charles must have recalled wistfully those happy parties, where many brilliant and famous people gathered, but where the shy and humble were never overlooked by the gentlest and most radiant of hostesses.

" Without any flashy accomplishments or bluestockingism Sophia had more reading and sounder judgement than hundreds of the women who inundate Society here, and without being pretty, it was impossible not to admire the sweetness and animation of her countenance . . . You see I can write and I can talk calmly upon the subject, and Lockhart also remembers his duties to his children, and is cheerful and resigned, but neither he nor I can ever forget our loss."

From the first days of his grief Lockhart thought of his children. Christie's tribute to him—that his love for his children had in it an almost womanly and maternal tenderness, was justified. He was never selfish or self-indulgent in grief ; he had an almost stoical self-control.

" My loss had been for two months anticipated, and now my sense of duty to my little orphans, even without their dear mother's farewell advice and instruction would have been quite sufficient to make me composed and steady in the prospect of my future life," he wrote to Murray. There was the discipline of work and duty. " You may freely send to me everything that you would naturally have sent a year ago, in full reliance of its having my best attention."

He was already practised in sorrow. To Violet he wrote of the children's courage : " They . . . are trying, poor souls, to look like themselves and to be a comfort to me " ; while he for his part was resolved " to make the world continue, as it had begun, to wear a cheerful aspect for them ".

Sophia was buried in " the new cemetery on the Harrow Road "—Kensal Green ; Anne's coffin and Johnny's were brought from the vaults of Marylebone Church to lie in the same dust. Lockhart wrote with gratitude to Croker :

" I was not aware till last night that you had been at my wife's funeral. Accept my thanks for that and all your other kindnesses . . . No man in affliction was more overwhelmed with kindness than I have been."

To their old friend Mrs. Skene of Rubislaw—who had been at their wedding, he wrote from a full heart :

" My present feeling is that my first duty to these two little orphans is to have them, as far as possible, trained in mutual affection, so that in case of my own removal in middle life, they may be supports and comforts in all things to each other." And to this kind old friend he gave a haunting memory—of the laying of Johnny's little coffin on the margin of the grave dug for Sophia : " It had been bleached in its damp vault for five years, and seemed like a cold ghost waiting to receive the comer. Johnny now lies once more on his mother's breast in the dust, and I have no doubt their spirits, both pure and innocent are now happy together among other dear friends that had preceded them, and may we all meet hereafter. Meantime, may God spare your love to Skene and your children."

Of this lasting grief was born, in time, that loveliest of elegiacs, which was to comfort Carlyle and his wife in sorrow, and which alone would keep Lockhart's name living, and in honour :

> When youthful faith hath fled,
>   Of loving take thy leave ;
> Be faithful to the dead,
>   The dead cannot deceive.
>
> Sweet, modest flowers of spring
>   How fleet your balmy day,
> And man's brief year can bring
>   No secondary May,—
>
> No earthly burst again
>   Of gladness out of gloom —
> Fond hope and vision vain,
>   Ungrateful to the tomb.
>
> Yet, 'tis an old belief
>   That on some solemn shore
> Beyond the sphere of grief
>   Dear friends shall meet once more—
>
> Beyond the sphere of Time,
>   And Sin, and Fate's control,
> Serene in changeless prime
>   Of Body and of Soul.
>
> That creed I fain would keep,
>   That hope I'll not forego ;
> Eternal be the sleep
>   Unless to waken so.

It is Catullan in sadness—but with a hope and faith Catullus could not know. In that hope and faith Lockhart lived out his days. There could be no secondary spring for him, though he was still in the prime of manhood. But where his children were concerned he did not hold his heart in fetterlock. It was, judging from contemporary books for children and domestic memoirs, hardly a period of intimacy between parents and children ; the fashion was rather of respect and discipline, though always there were exceptions. But no one was ever more unlike the portrait of a stern Victorian father than Lockhart. Walter and Charlotte had always been much with Sophia, and he continued the happy and easy relationship. There was friendliness as well as affection between them.

They were lively and singularly mature for their age : Walter eleven, Charlotte only eight. Their education had already been arranged, and Lockhart decided at first that Charlotte should board at her school, coming home for week-ends, when Walter joined her. There were many kind friends, Lady Davy, the Fergusons, the Miss Alexanders, neighbours in Sussex Place. He wanted " to keep up somewhat of the domestic education in which the heart is after all more concerned than the head ". Before long, however, he made a change of plan for Charlotte. Miss Watkins came as governess and was to be a capable, devoted and loved guardian to her for the next eight years.

II

The *Life of Scott* appeared in 1837 and 1838 ; Sophia saw only the first number. Lockhart wrote of it, and of himself to Will Laidlaw : of himself as " wiser, at least more sober " than in the old, reckless, but so happy days. " In politics I am a very tranquil and indifferent observer. Perhaps, however, much of this equanimity as to passing affairs has arisen from the call which has been made upon me to live with the past . . . My sole object is to do him

justice, or rather, to let him do himself justice, by so con-
triving it that he shall be, as far as possible, from first to
last his own biographer . . . A stern sense of duty—that
kind of sense of it which is combined with the feeling of
his actual presence in a serene state of elevation above all
petty terrestial and temporary views—will induce me to
touch the few darker points in his life and character as
freely as the others which were so predominant ; and my
chief anxiety on the appearance of the book will be, not
to hear what is said by the world, but what is thought by
you and the few others who can really compare the representation of the whole with the facts of the case."

The book was received with contradictory opinions.
Lord Cockburn entered in his Journal on 2nd May :
" I have finished the second volume of Lockhart's *Life
of Scott*. To those who know the individuals and the locali-
ties, it is a very fair account of the man. Of course, there
are a thousand incidents not told, and a thousand traits
not delineated . . . but nothing is kept back or misrepre-
sented so as to exhibit Scott in a false light."

A year later Cockburn took the last volume with him
on circuit : " A sad, sad volume." He noted that much
blame as well as much praise was being accorded the work,
the blame by " the idolaters " who thought that no flaw
that might exist in their idol should have been exposed,
and by the friends of the Ballantynes and Constable " whom
Lockhart has abused, as they say, unjustly ". With the
latter opinion Cockburn was in sympathy but found that
" the censure of the former is totally groundless. A son-
in-law perhaps ought not to have written the book. But
if he was to do it, it ought to have been done fairly. This
might certainly have been done, however, though a great
deal of the useless and vulgar matter which pervades the
work had been left out . . . All Scott's peculiarities could
have been easily described without the injustice and
offensiveness of expatiating on the exposure of selfish
transactions and paltry thoughts which were probably
immaterial at the time, but are represented in the *Life* as
fixed and essential parts of the man."

Cockburn contrived to deal some heavy thrusts from

under a cloak of commendation. Yet on the whole, he found it a true portrait : " It is Scott to the life ; at least as much so as any man can be exhibited to the public by words." But he feared its effect on Scott's memory. It dispelled the fascination of the remote. Those who had thought of him only as genius, now saw " how much he was a tradesman even in the exercise of his genius . . . and how much less he valued fame and literature than those results of them which enabled him to exercise an intellectual and splendid hospitality ".

But were such flaws a shock to any who had really known Scott ? No man ever made less pose of genius and remoteness, or less pretence of a sublime detachment from worldly and financial success. The idolaters should never read biography or journal or letters.

Cockburn did not love Lockhart, but he had loved Scott, and the features he recalled and set down in affectionate catalogue are those which shine out in Lockhart's portrayal as well as in his own work : " No man was so uniformly gentle." Cockburn found himself seeing and hearing his old friend again, not realising how much of this vision and recollection was given him by the volumes he had just read : " The plain dress, the guttural, burred voice, the lame walk, the thoughtful, heavy face with its mantling smile, the honest, hearty manner, the joyous laugh, the sing-song feeling recitation, the graphic story—they are all before me a hundred times a day."

Lockhart neither concealed nor condoned Scott's extra-ordinary attitude to business or the complexity of his rela-tions with the Ballantynes and Constable, though his exasperation perhaps led him to magnify the faults of those partners and colleagues. Brooding over the tragic tangle of affairs some ten years after the event, he whipped him-self into fury. He could not understand why Scott had so committed himself, he could not discuss it dispassionately ; the pent-up bewilderment turned to rancour, not against Scott but against those others.

Andrew Lang has pointed out, with acumen, that in his *Life of Burns* Lockhart did not think it necessary to write " unsparingly ". He was discreet, even reticent. " Burns he never knew in the flesh, nor loved as a friend. But he would not show Scott—whom he loved and revered,—other than as the whole man he was in his complexity of faults and heroic virtues."

In Lang's view : " Only a good man could have so clearly observed, so affectionately adored, and so excellently recorded these virtues "—and Lockhart, however complex, even perverse at times, was a good man.

Lang does not agree with Saintsbury in ranking the *Life of Scott* next to and very near Boswell's *Johnson*, though he says it was " his breviary since boyhood ". But he saw with sympathetic insight that quality in Lockhart so unexpected in a man whom many thought so proud and who was so shy : " his total lack of self-consciousness "—which was the antithesis of Boswell's diverting egoism. Indeed there could hardly be two men of genius less alike in character, temperament and art, than Boswell and Lockhart.

The most distinguished of living authorities on Scott, Sir Herbert Grierson, finds Lockhart unduly hard on Constable and the Ballantynes, and over-lenient to Cadell ; over-credulous of Cadell's account of the transactions. It was Cadell, not Constable, who induced Scott to borrow £10,000 on Abbotsford. " If Scott ", says Grierson, " turned on Constable somewhat harshly and unjustly, it was because, consciously or unconsciously, he felt in Constable something of his own too-sanguine temperament, a reinforcement of his own enterprising nature. In blaming Constable, he is blaming himself." So Lockhart, in his bitterness against Constable, may be expressing, unconsciously, his hidden disapproval of that one flaw and folly in Scott, his financial ineptitude and obstinacy.

Cadell it was who kept Scott long unaware of the instability of the firm ; as their most valuable asset, he must be left in peace and ignorance to work himself to death. " Our most productive culture is the author of *Waverley*," Cadell wrote to Constable. " Let us stick to him, let us dig on and on at that inestimable quarry—and as sure as I now write to you we shall do well "—which touches the depth of callous cynicism.

Sophia saw clearly Cadell's utter selfishness ; Lockhart

may have been equally aware of it, but thought it diplomatic to be on good terms with him. There was all the more relief, then, in writing of Constable with a pen dipped in vitriol ; a phial of which fluid J. G. L. usually kept at hand, though he used it more and more sparingly, with time. He described his interview with Constable in London, in June 1826 : " It was then I for the first time, saw full swing given to the tyrannical temper of *the Czar*. He looked, spoke and gesticulated like some hoary despot, accustomed to nothing but the complete indulgence of every wish and whim, against whose sovereign authority his most trusted satraps and tributaries had suddenly revolted—open rebellion in twenty provinces—confusion in the capital—treason in the palace." A few pages later, he wrote of Constable's " fluctuating between wild hope and savage despair until, seriously I believe he at last hovered on the brink of insanity ".

Of the Ballantynes he wrote that he believed James " to have been, from first to last, a perfectly upright man " ; of John that he had " many amiable as well as many amusing qualities, and I am far from wishing to charge even him with any deep or deliberate malversation ".

It was humanly impossible for Lockhart to write of the disaster with detachment ; it was still fresh in his mind. Even closer and more vivid and painful was the memory of the last two clouded years of Scott's life, of the collapse of mind and body following utter exhaustion. Even now it is difficult not to be partisan, not to defend Scott against those who fastened on him and drew him down into their catastrophes. Lockhart had seen the tragic results, not only in Scott's own fate but in Anne's, that bright candle-flame quenched in smoke.

He was at once involved in controversy with the families of Constable and the Ballantynes. The latter issued a pamphlet refuting his charges ; Lockhart replied in *The Ballantyne Humbug Handled*. There was a third pamphlet, and a great deal of acrimony. Lockhart still had his enemies who were glad of this stick with which to beat him, glad to see him assailed. Something was added to that " floating dislike " which hung around his name.

Maria Edgeworth, sensible, benevolent, good friend begged him : " Only make a clear, general statement, and let there be an end of all that. Posterity will care nothing about the Ballantynes or Constable or any of them but Scott himself—and let me hear no more of the Ballantyne Humbug—what a vulgar word—unworthy of you ! "

Posterity has truly cared for Scott himself, as Lockhart has given him to us. How honestly and vividly he wrote is best realised by comparing this *Life* with a host of Victorian biographies ; the solemn two-volume memorials and monuments of piety, tributes to some eminent personage departed, in whom there would have appeared to be no fault, and no vitality. Lockhart presented Scott, both directly and indirectly, in full reality, whether in recollection and description or in Scott's own words. It is as if he introduced him and left him to talk to us ; sometimes taking part in the conversation, with an adroit comment or question, never obtruding himself, always drawing us— his guests—together, stimulating Scott to speak at his best, and us to receive him with the utmost sympathy. We live with Scott as we do with Johnson ; Edinburgh and Abbotsford have a solid reality so that we walk the streets or the country ways with him, sit with him in his study or diningroom, meet his family and his friends. That biography can be as creative as poetry or drama or fiction is amply proved by these two masterpieces.

Whatever its faults of omission or commission, its proved flaws and negligencies such as the deliberate and unexplained telescoping of letters, the *Life of Scott* is one of the great creative works of literature, its author one of the supreme artists. Lockhart had, before he wrote it, shown flashes of genius : in a few passages of *Adam Blair* and of *Peter's Letters*, in phrases of poetry, in subtleties of criticism. Now he reached his full achievement. His two most excellent works are in singular contrast as to length and scope ; for one is this many-volumed biography, and the other the brief, haunting poem : *When Youthful Faith has Fled* ; but they are both of the same fine stuff. Both proceed from the inmost places of the heart.

Chapter 17

LOCKHART AND HIS CHILDREN

LOCKHART kept his resolve, to live for his children in the utmost cheerfulness his courage could summon, and the children helped, by their own endearing qualities, to bring him out of the shadows. " Walter is now a tall and very handsome boy of near eleven years," he wrote to Laidlaw (in January of 1837) " and Charlotte a very winsome gipsy of eight, both intelligent in the extreme, and both notwithstanding all possible spoiling, as simple, natural and unselfish as if they had been bred on a hill-side and in a family of twelve."

He was never a remote parent, leaving them in the care of even a devoted governess. He saw very carefully to their education and to their physical well-being ; they were very seldom out of his thoughts. When they were from home, staying at Rokeby with the beloved Squire Morritt, or in Scotland with Aunt Violet or Uncle William, or in Brighton where Miss Watkins was bidden to take them after a London winter of fogs and chills, he wrote to them constantly, enjoined and enjoyed frequent letters from them, especially from Charlotte, who was a regular and devoted little correspondent.

At home he resumed his social life ; his diaries record again many dinner engagements. He met and entertained people of distinction ; and though Charlotte was still in the schoolroom and probably did not often come down to the drawing-room for evening parties, she lived in an atmosphere of intellectual brilliance, and in private, was much with her father. Both children were quick of mind ; but Charlotte was unusually mature even in childhood ; and her dignity of mind and character as she grew up were to strike many people, including her future husband. But she was not a solemn child ; a father of so much teasing humour as Lockhart possessed would not have permitted his clever and good little daughter to degenerate into a prig or resemble the heroine of one of the Victorian moral tales that were, in his lifetime, to multiply.

There were many kind friends to help him in his willing task of making " the world continue, as it had begun, to wear a cheerful aspect for them " : his own family, especially William, who would appear to have been one of those benign, indulgent and slightly comic uncles essential to complete family life ; Lady Davy ; Dr. and Mrs. Ferguson ; the Misses Alexander—who were also a little comic, and again of a type often found in a happy circle ; Miss Yates at Tunbridge Wells, whose house, Fairlawn, was a port of call, very often, between Brighton and London, or after any absence from London if J. G. L. was not ready to receive the children at Sussex Place.

That the stern Victorian father did exist is proved by memoirs and biography as well as by fiction ; but he was not universal. If he was a rule, there were exceptions. And chief of these must be Lockhart. His relations with his children, from the first, showed both tenderness and comradeship. He cared for them, thought of their welfare, cherished them with almost maternal solicitude ; he talked and wrote to them as to comrades and equals, shared jests with them, had, if not a secret language, at least that *lingua franca* of allusion and shared interests that is part of the most agreeable domesticity.

The Victorian governess, like the Victorian parent, lives in fiction and sometimes in memoirs, as a type : expert in education of the " prunes and prisms " order, but no more. Doubtless this type did exist, and there were schoolrooms in which girls were instructed in long lists of Kings and Queens of England, geographical names, plants and minerals and other such catalogues ; in mechanical questions and answers ; in a little French, music and drawing and in a vast amount of needlework and " fancy-work ". But there were governesses who possessed and imparted sound culture. The best sort of schoolroom training developed the memory ; it taught girls to read seriously, with concentration and discipline ; it drilled them in arithmetic, history, geography, in music and in drawing, gave them a good elementary knowledge of botany, and made them at

home in, at least French, often in Italian and German.
Miss Watkins must have been of the best type ; Charlotte
was an apt pupil. She learned French very young, aided
greatly by those holidays in Boulogne ; and by the age of
eleven she was acquiring Italian and German, begging
papa to find her a Bible in each of these languages.

She used to write in French to J. G. L., much to his
pleasure. When they were at Brighton, on their first visit
after their mother's death, Walter reported that Mr.
Townsend, J. G. L.'s friend, " the peerless parson ", was
trying to find him a tutor ; if unsuccessful, he would teach
him himself—probably Latin and Greek and mathematics
which might be beyond Miss Watkins' scope.

" I also told him your message," added Walter, " and
he says that you are the funniest person he knows."

Lockhart wrote announcing his own probable arrival
at the week-end, with Mr. Hay, and bidding the children
" step over to the New Steyne Hotel on Friday morning,
and bespeak for Hay and me the rooms Morritt and I had
last time ". He added that Uncle Charles was in Scotland,
and that Ginger and Pepper were very well. These two
pets were well established in Sussex Place. Lacking exact
information, we may assume that they were of the true
Border breed of terrier made famous by Sir Walter ; Lockhart rarely failed to report on their welfare. His letters
were full of social news : a whitebait dinner at Greenwich,
given by Christie, being one of the events. " Little Sophy
has quite got better of the bad foot "—Sophy being Christie's
daughter and Sophia's goddaughter and name-sake. " Go
and tell Mr. Rose [the poet, and friend of Townsend now
with him at Brighton] I will write him a rhyming epistle
one day soon."

The epistle was, in due course, written :

> Dear Rose, I know you did not brood with wrath
> On my not answering your kind lines from Bath. . . .
>
> I hope, whatever aids your deglutation,
> To see you soon in bumperly condition,
> And crack a quart (by leave of Dr Todd)
> With you and Shoreham's fat round man of God.

(I think 'tis Shoreham has for recreation
Townsend's hebdominal expectoration,
But if I'm wrong, put in the proper ' ham '
Our Curate has been Rector'd to undamn.) . . .

My children wait upon you with this note,
They both have got some weakness in the throat
Whereby their glands swell out when health so-so,
And they turn deaf as you or Martineau :
But this, the only malady they bear,
Will vanish soon in Brighton's bracing air.
Once more I'll see you and our oily priest, or
(My name's not Lockhart) the week after Easter,
Whereof in witness I've my mark affixed,
This Tuesday morning, March the twenty-sixth,
This second year of Miss Victoria's reign,
When sugar's scarce in Kingston, wine in Spain,
And many other things are in the dark
Besides the obstetric skill of Sir James Clarke.

The children went to Brighton again in the spring of
1839 ; they had rooms in Devonshire Place. Later, in
the summer, Lockhart thought Charlotte should go to Aunt
Violet at Dunoon, to continue the benefit of sea-air.
Dunoon was only then beginning to be a resort for Glasgow
and West of Scotland folk ; a tiny village on the Firth of
Clyde, on the borders of the Highlands, where visitors came
to stay for two or three months at a time. Among other
family news J. G. L. announced that Uncle Walter, with
his regiment at Chatham, would be coming to town for the
Queen's levée and would be dining at Sussex Place, soon
after the children's return home. As regards that return
he consulted them on the important matter of dinner,
suggesting the following menu—to be considered between
them, " in conclave " :

1 dozen oysters ; 2 soles fried ; 1 fowl roast with egg
sauce ; 1 pudding ; toasted cheese.

" If this programme is approved, we shall proceed to
action."

Charlotte went to Dunoon, as suggested, in the following
June, and a little later Walter was " set adrift in the world
for the first time solo "—on the journey to Scotland by
water. " Sorry though he was to leave me in solitary
state here, he was evidently great in the feeling of his

217

independence—an oiled cap on his head—a well-corded
trunk and carpet-bag containing, among other necessaries, a
stone bottle of ginger-wine, and £5 in his purse." He was
to share a cabin with " a dignitary of about his own standing,
emancipated from Eton, bound for the territories of some
Laird of Castle Fraser ". Cadell was to meet the traveller
at Newhaven and convey him to friends in Edinburgh ; and
after a few days in the capital, he would be packed " into
the coach for Garrion Bridge where Uncle William will be
waiting for the illustrious traveller and his traps in the
Irish car . . . which he is destined to drive habitually
between Milton and Carluke Kirk during the season ".
Lockhart meanwhile consoled himself with the thought of
his own holiday and the prospect of going to Scotland " to
collect and escort back my two chickens who meantime are
sure of warm *cosies*, a word that Aunt Vie will expound if
you need an interpreter ". Although Charlotte was so
young, and the younger of the two, he spoke to her of
Walter as to an elder, much more mature sister : " I
thought that . . . the little adventure I was trusting him
to might help his education in a department even as important as the scanning of Horace." Charlotte herself was
making fast progress in languages : " Many thanks for the
French bit of diary which I thought very creditable to
Madame Morritt, and if she turns Signora next time, so
much the better—the Fräulein will follow in due course."
Three languages, even in the rudiments, at twelve make
no small acquisition. " Madame Morritt " was a family
joke—Squire Morritt having proclaimed Charlotte his
sweetheart. Ginger and Pepper were in high fettle but
were well-mannered, having learned " from a mere exhibition of the whip to conduct themselves more quietly
in the garden, which must be a great relief to the ears of the
King of Onde and my other neighbours ". A meeting with
His Majesty of Onde had been reported in a previous letter :
" He talks goodish English and is up to trap—and can flirt
like a Christian, so he is in high favour with the spinsterhood
of the Row." Since Charlotte's departure, five puppies
had gone (it is hoped merely to other earthly homes) :
" all save one little gentleman who has broken a leg in an

attempt to mount the area steps, but his bones being only gristle, the damage will soon be got rid of." " The personal dog " (to use E. Œ. Somerville's phrase) or dogs counted for much in the lives of Scott's grandchildren.

Lockhart himself arrived in Scotland in August, staying with William at Milton Lockhart, which was still in process of being completed or improved and a cause of much absorption to its owner. The two brothers were to visit Laurence at Inchinnan and then J. G. L. would come to Dunoon ; " but William does not come with me from Inchinnan : 1mo : because he is always expecting a visit from his architect to settle about the gate-way at the bridge ; 2do : because the roof of the drawing-room is new gilding ; 3tio : because he does not choose ". There is usually a hint of affectionate laughter in allusions to William.

Brighton continued to be a habitual resort in the spring, Charlotte under the schoolroom regimen with Miss Watkins, Walter reading with Mr. Townsend. In one letter there is a hint of paternal authority :

" You are not to go into any boating excursions whatever unless in company with Mr. Townsend or some other friend of mine as to whom I shall have been previously consulted. Mr. Maynard is a mere fool, and I would not willingly trust him with the care of a donkey that I took any interest in . . . nor do I know, at present, of anyone in Brighton whom I could place such reliance upon as Townsend. I say this once for all. I indulge you as much as I can, for your own good, permit myself to do, and in return I have a right to insist upon complete obedience whenever I choose to give a distinct command. In all cases whatever you will understand that Miss Watkins has, while I am absent, my full authority over you, and I expect that you will consider this as your sole law on all future questions, whether about boating or excursions of any other class."

Characteristically, he passed quickly from admonition to gossip, and told of the distress of Lady Stepney who had dedicated her new novel to the Duke of Wellington as " The Hero of England ", only to find it misprinted as " The Nero of England ".

A letter to Charlotte was full of local and family news :
Walter's school report was satisfactory ; the Miss Alexanders had been tempted by the spring sunshine to walk
in the Park ; but " I found it in vain to preach Brighton.
They are the ' Immovables', tho' no longer, I hope, the
Incurables." Perhaps like Dr. Johnson the good ladies
held it folly to quit London where all reasonable pleasures
and amenities were to be found. Uncle William was safe
at home at Milton, " with all his cocks and hens in perfect
preservation, and he says they have been and are much
admired. His letter is chiefly about them—the rest about
you and Walter, which is fair, for they are the children
and you but the nephew and niece . . . Ginger and
Pepper are well too, the latter hairless for the nonce like a
fine lady, but she will soon recover what Rowland calls ' the
chief charm of the fair sex '." From dogs to royalty was no
great step for J. G. L. and he reported : " Victoria and
Albert as usual enlivened our Park yesterday—he bowing
and smiling, she glum and cross-looking, also as usual."
The young Queen Victoria was not always a glamorous
figure.

The summer of 1840 saw Charlotte, with Miss Watkins,
in Calais, staying with Madame Chely in the Rue de la
Douane, while Walter went to Scotland to enjoy country
life with ponies and other attractions, doubtless including
the famous cocks and hens.

Uncle Charles had gone to Scotland " in a blue neckcloth
and tartan waistcoat and rough gaiters " ; Uncle Walter
and his lady were in India, at Bangalore ; and Aunt Violet
had taken a house in Lanarkshire, between Milton and
Glasgow, where Uncle Bob lived with her. There were to
be agreeable new neighbours in Sussex Place : Sir Francis
Grant, the artist, and his wife had taken Sussex Villa, with
a separate studio. " They will be a very pleasant addition
to our little society here, and will be fine fun for you to see
his pictures while in progress, and also very instructive
should either you or Walter turn out to have a turn for the
arts. But what a critic he will have at his door in Miss
Margaret—beg pardon, Miss Alexander." These ladies
would appear to have been somewhat formidable. It is

evident that London was still small enough to be neigh-
bourly ; Regent's Park formed a community, like that of a
country town. Further reference to the Grants gave the
romantic news that " she " had fallen in love with " him "—
" for his beauty, as he was carried, seemingly dead, from a
fox chase, past her window on a hurdle ".

To Walter, papa made complaint that he was not being
generously used as regards letters " Cha, is more dutiful . . .
I miss your voices and your feet and all your plague sadly."

Walter did, as a rule, achieve a weekly letter, but " he
does not treat me to either such long or such entertaining
letters as you do ", Papa told Charlotte. He missed her
face and voice at breakfast ; " I . . . lament your little
interruptions " (we seem to catch an echo from those far-off
invasions of the study at Abbotsford) " and our cosy little
dinners on Sunday."

He sent Charlotte the English papers, including Theodore
Hook's *John Bull*, which she passed on to the English
clergyman : " You are quite right . . . I hope he will
edify you more than my friend Theodore is likely to edify
him."

By the beginning of August he was able to join Charlotte
in Calais, and wrote an account of it to Walter. He found
Charlotte looking well, grown a head taller, and took her
and Miss Watkins out to dinner, with champagne to drink :
" I thought I had afforded them a treat, but of that I was
disabused next day at 2, by the capital, *magnifique, superbe*
spread which old Mad. Chely gave me and which I was
assured was not better than usual except that the ancient
dame produced a bottle of excellent champagne, another of
still more excellent white burgundy in honour of a guest of
the masculine gender." Madame was " a fine, gay chatty
motherly body " who at eighty was " as lively as a bird in a
cherry-tree ". Her daughter, Madame Sarazin, lived with
her, " very gay too, clever and well-informed ". There
were other pupil-boarders, pretty girls, with " a couple of
dumb governesses "—and it seems as if he anticipated the
American use of the word " dumb ". But with the lively
Mesdames " we had a most jovial doing, and after dinner
I got another carriage, and took as many as it would hold

(including the prettiest of the *élèves*) a drive for 5 or 6 miles into the country ". Charlotte's papa must have been a popular and well-remembered visitor, held up as example to other parents. They drove to the estate of an old Baron, once a Colonel in the Imperial Guards, and his superb rose-garden : " He said he had 840 species . . . This fine old lad was dressed very much like a peasant, save and except 2 or 3 ribbons at his button hole." He was devoted to the memory of Napoleon, but had attached himself to Charles X at the Restoration ; and retired from the army at the Revolution of 1830. Now he had " bowed the knee to Baal or Louis Philippe, and accepted the office of Mayor of the neighbouring town. There was at this time threat of war between Britain and France. The old Baron was confident that Louis Philippe ' *arrangera tout cela* ' ; but his son and son-in-law " were keen for a row, especially in the hope " *voir un peu Regent Street* "—to make up for the British visit to Paris. Discussion grew warm, but was calmed by J. G. L.'s tactful offer of a billet at Sussex Place. " So they gave us another flask of champagne, and we parted kindly and gaily ' *au revoir* '."

It does not sound like a typical outing for a Victorian " *jeune fille* ". One would like to read the letters from the other girls, describing this enchanted visit.

Lockhart was happy about his daughter. It was no frigid *pensionnat*, but a kind home for her. She and Miss Watkins had a pleasant room in the big house built round the courtyard ; it was near the ramparts which gave them " a fine breezy walk ". Charlotte's French was already fluent, and she was sufficiently *au fait* with French politics to be asked by her father, after his return to London, for news of Louis Napoleon, who was then very active. " I have met him occasionally in society, and he always appeared to me a stupid and vulgar corporal with nothing Imperial about him but a breast-pin of diamonds in the shape of an eagle."

In August (1840) he wrote about her homecoming, enjoining her to bring " a little treasure of real French receipts for soups and vegetables to enrich cook with ".

There were bits of family gossip : " Uncle Charles has

come back, and his wise head is calm and comfortable on
this occasion. I half thought he had gone to Scotland on
a matrimonial expedition . . . but behold, he has only
been fishing . . . He continues calm and immalleable.
But I had a capital rise (in angling phrase) out of the
spinsters here for I had set them quite agog with my sober
predictions that he would bring back a lady to his lodgings,
and I believe they had been ransacking their brains for a
fortnight about nothing else." Charles made some amends
for his own " immalleable " condition by bringing news
" of Uncle Bob's being awfully in love with a beautiful
Ellinor Ferrier, niece of the novelist, my old friend. He
says the poor youth is really quite sad, sentimental, and, as
Walter used to say, ' off his feed '." As for Ginger and
Pepper, they continued to be " very good and attentive
to their papa ". Polly the parrot was " shining with several
new accomplishments "—though not so many as adorned
the parrot belonging to the Jew at No. 19—" which really
must be a devil. How it barks and laughs ! . . . Its
bark sets Pepper mad."

Charles was sent out to Persia ; a fatal mission for him.
The climate defeated his imperfect constitution ; he had,
like all Scott's children, no enduring strength of body.
Lockhart's diary for that year, 1841, has as one of its last
entries : " This year died Charles Scott. October 29th."
In this diary too is written in full the poem already quoted :
" When youthful faith has fled."

Another had joined the undeceiving dead.

The news did not reach London until December. Maria
Edgeworth heard it, and wrote to Lockhart in deep sadness :
" Another Scott gone ! Of all we saw so well, so happy, so
prosperous, so kind at Abbotsford, but a few years ago.
Only Sir Walter his son left now upon this earth—and you—
you who have at least the satisfaction, in this deep sorrow,
of knowing all you have done for the character, the everlasting memory of your beloved father—all you have done,
while yet they lived, to make his children as happy as
possible. Happy as she was amiable, and that is saying all
that can be, your wife ever appeared to me when I had the
happiness to see her in her home, with you and her children.

A more loving and beloved creature I never saw. I
earnestly hope that her sweet daughter who is so like her,
may some time, tho' I can never live to see it, be as happy
in marriage as her mother was, and may in the meantime
continue to be your consolation, pride and joy. . . . You
did all you could for Anne Scott. That is another soothing
recollection for you. . . . I believe you had as much of
poor Charles Scott as you could have while he lived in
London, and have no doubt you added to his happiness. . . .
I am glad there is a new edition of Sir Walter's *Memoirs*
compressed into cheap form. If it have the spirit preserved
in it, as preserved and heightened the spirit of *The Life of
Napoleon* in your powerful compression of Sir Walter Scott's
Memoir of Bonaparte, I shall delight in seeing the work.
But if any profane, vulgar hand has been daring to touch
and thinking only of abridging, may I never see it. I have
taken up your *Life* of Sir Walter at different times, and
was never able to lay it down without reading on, on, on
with insatiable interest and admiration." The abridged
Life was by Lockhart himself.

In return she had a long, kind letter :

" I am very grateful for all your kind thoughts and
recollections. Charles has only joined a company who are
and ever will be present to me while memory remains, as if
they still were partaking in what we call Life. It is, however, a very serious calamity to me—for we had very much
in common, and it was to him I had always looked, in case
of my own death, for protection to my children during their
tender years, or rather, I should say, for giving them that
cast of mind and sentiment which I would fain have them
inherit from their mother." For all his resolute cheerfulness
and his absorption in work, Lockhart dwelt much with
memories, and in awareness of the departed.

In 1842 William Maginn died, of tuberculosis, deeply
in debt. His widow and children were left penniless, and
Lockhart and other friends were generous. R. P. Gillies
in his *Memoirs of a Literary Man* recalls going with Maginn
to visit the Lockharts at Wimbledon, in those early days of
their life in London, when Johnny was the adored and
enchanting child of the house. " One of the bonds between

Lockhart and his friend may well have been the devotion which each of these caustic natures had to children." They found the best in each other.

So, when he died, Lockhart took out the mock-epitaph he had written for him, to read some ten years ago at one of those merry dinners in *Fraser's* back parlour :

Here, early to bed lies kind William Maginn,
Who with genius, wit, learning, life's trophies to win
Had neither great lord nor rich cit of his kin,
Nor discretion to set himself up as to tin ;
So, his portion soon spent, like the poor heir of Lynn,
He turned author while yet was no beard to his chin ;
And whoever was out or whoever was in,
For the Tories his fine Irish brains he would spin,
Who received prose and verse with a promising grin :
" Go ahead, you queer fish, and more power to your fin ; "
But to save from starvation stirred never a pin.
Light for long was his heart, though his breeches were thin,
Else his acting for certain was equal to Quin.

It had been truth in jest ; and now in truth the kind and witty friend had gone early and weary to bed, broken by life : Lockhart, with characteristic tenderness and wit commingled, added his valediction :

But at last he was beat, and sought help from the bin,
(All the same to the Doctor from claret to gin),
Which led swiftly to goal with consumption therein ;
It was much when the bones rattled loose in his skin,
He got leave to die here out of Babylon's din.
Barring drink and the girls I ne'er heard of a sin—
Many worse, better few than bright, broken Maginn.

(He had been imprisoned for debt ; and was released, only to die—at Walton-on-Thames.)

But the young life in his household was active. There was about this time an idea of sending Walter to Eton ; which would mean a sacrifice on his father's part, and a loss of companionship to Charlotte ; but it might be the best thing for Walter. It did not, however, take shape.

Walter, on holiday in Scotland, was exhorted to read Greek :

" Now mind *Medea*. It is the first Greek play I ever

read and I can still say every chorus of it by heart, so you may expect a strict examination." Charlotte was in Boulogne, this summer. " I am afraid there was some very unpleasant occurrence at Calais—but I have no doubt Miss Watkins had good and sufficient reason for the change."

Lockhart sent a morsel of spicy gossip : " The Tories are likely to take the government with every prospect of success. Their only difficulty will be with the young lady. They say Leopold has been called for to appease a quarrel between her and Albert. He had invited some Germans to dinner at the Palace, Victoria said they had never been presented and could not come—so Albert ordered dinner at the Clarendon, and there spent a joyous evening with his friends—but this was only the last of a long series of tyrannies." The royal pair had not yet reached a state of unalloyed mutual devotion.

He went that summer (1842) to Milton, to help William to celebrate his election as M.P. with a dinner-party ; then to visit his father who was in failing health of mind and body ; and finally to Rokeby, whence he wrote good reports of himself to Charlotte, again in France. His own health had improved, thanks to fresh air and riding. " I am glad you are to have a little dancing, singing, etc., and also to jabber with the French–Irish widow. But above all, walk, bathe and be strong." Walter was leading a bookless life, acting groom to the Squire, page to Mrs. William Morritt, and " flirt in ordinary to 2 or 3 hoyden lassies of the neighbouring squirearchy ". Charlotte had, it seemed, written to Squire Morritt in French : " But I suppose it is very tender, for he has not had the face to show it to me."

Walter, on their return to London, gave his sister news about the alterations in Regent's Park—the fields opposite Hanover Terrace being thrown open to the public, about the Miss Alexanders' " row about their servants ", and about the welfare of Ginger. (Pepper would seem to have departed.) Lockhart added details about Ginger : " She had drooped during my absence, but the moment they began to lay down carpets in the dining-room she said to herself an advent must be at hand, and remained on the *qui vive* until our arrival which she welcomed with more genuine enthusiasm than I can muster even for the accession of the Tories."

The holiday letters of the early 1840's recapture much of Lockhart's youthful humour and gaiety of spirit. He led a full life and told Charlotte of many breakfasts and dinners, and tea with the Alexanders where he had " plenty of scandal. Lots of marriages announced but I can't remember whose." There was a full account of one marriage, a Miss Fanny Harvey's, which had been on a grand scale, with " lots of Generals, K.C.B.s and East India Directors . . . a breakfast at noon, alias a tiffin, alias a splendid cold dinner, and thereafter regular speeches and three-cheering and champagne and *parfait amour* in floods." On one occasion he had a Brahmin as guest, and announced that " the rice must be nicely done and the coffee pure as amber. . . . I wish you had been here to receive him, but petticoats being scarce, I have invited two Bishops to sport their aprons instead."

In the autumn of 1843 Charlotte and Miss Watkins were again established in Calais " chez Mad. Sarrazin " ; and Lockhart took Walter on a tour of the Continent ; from the end of August until the end of October. Mr. Hay was with them. They sailed to Ostend, and travelled through Aix-la-Chapelle, Heidelberg and Strasbourg to Lucerne and the Italian Lakes, then south to Milan, Genoa and Naples ; on to Rome, Florence, Venice and Verona, then back to Germany and Belgium. Walter kept a travel journal, which is preserved among the family papers at Abbotsford ; a very good-boy production, written, one imagines, by paternal injunction and submitted to papa's inspection. Walter took notes and recorded impressions industriously, but one could wish for a little more boyish vivacity ; there is an occasional glimmer, as in his admiration for some of the exhibits at Pompeii, notably an egg-pan " with 30 separate places to place the eggs, thereby saving all chance of breaking ".

Lockhart himself wrote at length ; describing the long journey from Milan to Genoa as " 21 hours of real horror in a diligence " through splendid scenery but " in some fear of robbery " by a gang of escaped galley-slaves. He had wanted to come to Italy, thinking the chances of any future visit to be remote ; wanted specially to see Pompeii. But it was by no means a good time of year. " Should I ever be rich I shall try to have your company for a winter in Rome . . . if not, I shall not henceforth look beyond the accessible and civilised borders of the Rhine."

Rome and Italy, however, amused him, even when he looked on the scene with a sardonic eye. The peasant women he thought beautiful in their classic dignity ; but the men " by far the rudest animals of their kind in Europe—fierce, violent passions written on every face. . . . I am satisfied they are only endurable when there are Germans to rule over them." The middle and upper classes, however, he found " civil and intelligent ". The priests and monks seemed " refined and accomplished—at least as much so as the corresponding Puseyites at home ".

The Oxford Movement was still a matter for passionate interest and discussion, and the name " Puseyite " was in frequent use. In Rome he found " Puseyites of every shape and shade " (using the term to signify clerics). " Most picturesque old fellows in white gowns and beards worthy of the apostles occur now and then, but you are quite jostled among the browns and blacks." He was not impressed by High Mass in St. Peter's : " very poor—nothing could be more careless than the appearance of either performers or audience, and the band was not much—but this is not the season for any class of theatricals here ".

At the beginning of the following year (1844) Walter was sent to a tutor, the Reverend Henry Holden, at Rumford in Essex, to be coached, it was hoped, for Oxford. His father made him write weekly letters in Latin, which were severely criticised, and keep a journal of his readings. Walter was not as much of a scholar as his father hoped ; quick of mind, he was showing signs of a lack of stability. There was a slight undertone of reproof and disappointment at times, in J. G. L.'s letters ; though the racy, affectionate gossip continued too. In one letter there was an account of Miss Watkins being " tift " or piqued about some imaginary slight. The particular reason was a visit from Miss Rigby (later Lady Eastlake), the distinguished woman-traveller and author, who was one of J. G. L.'s most valued contributors. Miss Watkins considered that too much attention was paid to the guest, too little to herself : a point of view with which the master of the house had no sympathy at all. He would not permit even the most trusted and valued governess to step out of her place. The trouble blew over ; but it may have had something to do with a decision he was soon to take.

One of his reproofs to Walter was delivered in a way that reveals a certain amount of amusement ; the disapproval being assumed on principle. " It was wrong to make any joke about the Puseyite Calendar to Mr. Holden. Consider these gentlemen think the fate of the world hangs on their nonsense—laugh at it in your sleeve as nonsense, but respect the sincerity, and at all events be polite."

About this time Mrs. Thomas Scott wrote to her son about the young Lockharts, his cousins :

" I have some fears for dear Walter. He is a charming and gentlemanly boy, but I fear is not fond of hard study . . . I only hope his father will recollect his own boyhood and have patience with him, poor fellow. I had a letter from dear Charlotte lately, telling me that she was arrived at the grave age of sixteen. She is a delightful girl, an extraordinary likeness of both mother and poor Anne, but with the extreme gentleness of Sophia. There has been great care bestowed on her education, and with much success, indeed Mr. Lockhart has been one of the best of fathers."

" The best of fathers ", indeed, and the most imaginative and amusing ; witness a letter to Charlotte written as by the beloved and gifted Ginger :

" Dear Miss,

" I was very disconsolate Saturday and Sunday, fearing you were all gone for good, but yesterday morning Papa came back and dined at home with me, no other company, and he gave me my bones then, and my milk this morning as usual, and to-day I have not stirred from his fireside, nor have the least intention of doing so, it being a cold, windy day. I shall endeavour to keep up my spirits as well as I can. I heard Papa say he was to dine with Miss Edgeworth, but that he would not leave me any other evening soon. Your letter was the only one by this morning's post. Yesterday there was one from Walter, for I know the postmarks perfectly.

"Give my compliments to Miss Watkins, and if she has not forgotten me, to Miss Yates. By Papa's looks when reading your letter I conclude you are all pretty well and comfortable. It is very cold—yet I had my turn before breakfast, and barked at two newsboys and one baker, and also at the hodman on the Jew's premises.

"Yours respectfully, Ginger (her mark). [The mark being a neatly drawn bone.] "

Young Walter thought, for a moment, of the bar, but was not encouraged by his father who was sceptical about his powers of concentration and drudgery. Besides, he must first find out if he had any gift for public speaking. "The last I never had—and it was the great error in my early days that I nevertheless selected the bar . . . But I had to make my selection at a very early age—19 ; and I had no relations capable of understanding the case, or of advising me judiciously."

He had missed the advantage of the debating societies at Oxford, established since his time. The period at home in Glasgow, following Oxford, must have been difficult ; there may have been some family urgency about his finding a profession, perhaps some disappointment on Dr. Lockhart's part when he did not elect to enter the ministry of the Kirk ; and Lockhart's choice of the law would seem to have been made somewhat as a *faute de mieux*.

Walter did not follow his father to Oxford. He was sent instead to Cambridge ; and was hardly settled there before he showed a marked preference for soldiering over any other career. There was a little solace, of a wry flavour, in the realisation that he would never make a scholar ; but Lockhart had hoped he might enter diplomacy.

Charlotte was growing up. He wrote to Walter of her confirmation : " She looked very pretty in her cap and frock, poor body." She was unusually mature in mind, through so much companionship with her father, and was an increasing comfort to him. Probably she had gone far ahead of Miss Watkins by this time ; and perhaps that good lady had begun to take too much upon herself—we have already had a hint of that ; perhaps too (though this surmise is merely a feminine and feline suggestion) she was betraying too warm an interest in her employer. Whatever the reason, Lockhart found it advisable to end the relationship. In August 1844 he wrote to Charlotte—who was again in Calais with Miss Watkins :

" I know you will be greatly distressed when I tell you that I have written to Miss Watkins stating that I consider it better that she and you should not again spend the winter in your present relationship under this roof. I know she and you have a very warm affection for each other—a most tender one—but on the whole I feel that what I have done could not have been deferred without involving us all in increasing difficulties and discomforts."

It was all to be arranged with every possible deference to Miss Watkins, and Lockhart would procure introductions for her, if she wished another post as governess : " She is well entitled to the very highest situation of that class. . . . I am sure Mad. Sarrazin will give you her best advice and assistance in case you need it, and it is some comfort to me that Miss W. is with so kind a friend at a moment which I fear may be one of some trouble and anxiety to her. But I would fain hope that there may be no scenes, and that hereafter you are often to have your early friend with you, under circumstances of a different description." In a second letter he added :

" Miss W. will feel, on a few days' reflection, that my proceeding was no unnatural consequence of a conversation she herself held with me some time ago. After such things have been said, the sooner the whole thing is brought to an end the better for all parties . . . Miss W. writes as if she thought I meant to entrust you to some other lady's care— I fancied I had written so as to prevent that notion being entertained. I never for a moment dreamt of such a scheme."

Walter spent part of his vacation with William at Milton,

and Charlotte was to go there in October. Walter was making a very good impression. William thought his manners prepossessing, and likely to fit him for diplomacy ; but Walter was set on an Army career still.

Ginger was in excellent health : " Her hair is as black as ever upon her back. She ought to write a note for her oil-merchant's advertisements."

The young people were leaving the enchanted years of childhood. The difficult years were opening for them. In regard to Walter the difficulty was to become a tragic estrangement. Charlotte was to come closer than ever to her father. But by 1844 the Indian summer of Lockhart's life was ending.

Chapter 18

WORK AND FRIENDSHIP

I. LETTERS TO CROKER

THE letters to Croker in the years from Sophia's death until the end of Lockhart's own life, grow more and more intimate. They vary between professional communications and personal confidences that supplement the story told in the letters to Charlotte and Walter.

In 1838 Lockhart had been reading a memoir of William Wilberforce by his sons. He thought it badly edited, disliking " the repetition of set phrases and feeble *enfantillages* in the Diary and letters ", and he came to the conclusion that " no man so very good and endowed with more than common talents was ever further from greatness ". Yet it was impressive in one way : " I could not but feel very strongly the beautiful composing and sustaining effect of religion in Wilberforce, and wishing with all my heart that Sir Walter had had more of that element mixed in him." (This would support the case against the death-bed story : " Be good, my dear, be religious." Did Lockhart give Scott the words he wanted him to say ?) He dwelt on this lack : " Surely the decision and vivacity of our friend's nature would have been gloriously embellished by that capacity of looking on worldly things from a serene point of view which no mere philosophy can ever give us."

Scott had his share of philosophy ; witness his reflections on parting with the Lockharts : " Of all schools, commend me to the Stoick " ; his fortitude and dignity in disaster ; his sorrow, controlled and not without hope, at his wife's death. Lockhart himself, at the conclusion of the *Life*, wrote of the " sober, serene, and elevated frame of mind in which he habitually contemplated man's relations with his Maker . . . his humble reliance on the wisdom and mercy of God ".

It may be that Scott was too Stoic, with a fortitude of the mind rather than of the soul ; and that when the mind gave way, there was no inner refuge. It may be that Lockhart remembered, with anguished clarity, only the torment of these last months when the clouds veiled so much that was truly Scott himself—his serenity, his magnanimity, his patience ; he could not see beyond these clouds. Indeed, few people can ; what is thus veiled, but still endures in the inner heart and soul of the sufferer, is known only to God. Lockhart, when he read that Memoir of Wilberforce and wrote his letter, was himself struggling towards the serenity of faith.

In 1839 came the first of a series of references to the religious reform that dominated English thought and life for a decade and more—that of the Oxford Movement : the awakening through the teaching of the Oxford Apostles, the Tractarians, Puseyites—call them what you will—of the semi-somnolent Church of England to a sense of her Catholic heritage and her responsibility. The Movement is usually dated from Keble's Assize Sermon in 1833 on *The National Apostasy*, though it was the name of Keble's friend and colleague, Pusey, that was bestowed, not always with respect, on their followers. (It is strange that they were not known as Newmanites from the name of their greatest genius and most alluring leader.) The controversy was lively ; it could hardly have been more lively in Scotland, that home of theological argument. There had not been so much religious discussion since the Reformation, and now it was safe to argue, even in public. Controversy, however acrimonious, no longer led to the Tower, the scaffold or the stake.

The Tractarians observed the Gospel caution against setting a light under a bushel. They set theirs high, lit innumerable candles in tall, branching candlesticks, to light the household of the Church, until one of their critics (Croker in *The Quarterly*) accused them of trying to set the church on fire. They preached dogmatic sermons, they wrote tracts, edited the works of the Fathers and of the early Anglican divines ; they revived usages and ceremonies ; their arguments were made audible, visible and readable. Lockhart, with his native interest in theology, added to his staunch Churchmanship, was alert to the Movement ; as editor of the High Church *Quarterly* he realised the need for some official pronouncement. He wrote to Croker in January 1839 :

" I am going . . . to Oxford (Balliol), and on Saturday to Pusey (Philip Pusey's house near Faringdon) . . . My chief object is to enquire, but not speak otherwise than enquiries touching the state of the Oxford Tract Controversy which Mr. Gladstone's book [on Church and State] has drawn out of the academic bowers, and to which, as you lately hinted, *The Q.R.* must turn its attention. I have read a few of the Tracts, and yesterday went through Froude's *Remains*, and hitherto I feel adverse to the whole system as I comprehend it, though I daresay it may end in acting as a salutary counterpoise to equally baleful errors previously in fashion." In the following month—February—he wrote : " I left Oxford with strong hopes that Newman's party might be stopped from going further . . . The agitators meanwhile have done some signal services. They have stirred a new zeal for theological research, they have turned the printing of Oxford to a very useful course—producing beautiful editions of the Ante-Nicene Fathers . . . they have excited feelings among the young men which attest their value in a very extraordinary improvement of manners and habits. Thus far, well ;—the point is to keep them from going beyond the principles of our own Reformation, and I hope *The Quarterly* may contribute to this by dealing with their literary history and productions in a gentle and candid vein, avoiding for the present anything like a keen controversy as to the doubtful points."

In March there was such a contribution in *The Quarterly* : a review of several Oxford publications, including : *Tracts for the Times* (1833–37) ; the first volume in *The Library of the Fathers* ; sermons by the Tractarians, one of Keble's, one of Pusey's, and Newman's *Parochial Sermons* and his *Lectures on the Parochial Offices of the Church* ; Pusey's *Letter to the Bishop of Oxford* refuting the charge of Romanism ; and Hurrell Froude's *Remains*,—the notes, journals and letters of that " pard-like spirit " who was, almost incredibly, the brother of that stout Protestant, James Anthony Froude.

The writer of the article was the Rev. William Sewell,

almost, at that moment, a Tractarian himself; an Oxford worthy who deserves remembrance in more than one aspect of the scholar's life. He was born in the Isle of Wight in 1804 ; was a Wykehamist, and came up to Merton in 1823. In 1827 he was elected a Fellow of Exeter. He was one of the founders of St. Columba's College near Dublin (intended to be the Irish Eton) and of Radley, the Church school near Oxford. There is a pleasant story of him, as tutor, devoting an hour intended for reading of the *Georgics*, to a discussion of Newman's *Theory of Development of Christian Doctrine*, which may have appeared to him a natural enough transition from Virgil, that " *anima naturaliter Christiana* ".

In 1839 he wrote with approval of the Tractarians, seeing them, as did Lockhart, as defenders of the Faith against both dissent and Rome. " Neglect of the daily services, desecration of festivals, the Eucharist scantily administered . . . drive people to Methodism . . . or Rome."

He dealt with most of the publications in " a gentle and candid vein " with, indeed, more of praise than of blame ; commending Newman's phrase : " True faith is what may be called colourless like air or water : it is but the medium through which the soul sees Christ " ; commending also the tracts in general for counteracting " the popular religion-ism of the day ", that is, the subjective and emotional type of Evangelicals within the Church as well as of the sectarians. Froude, however, startled him ; for Froude was the *enfant terrible* of the Movement. The Church will always have a few of this type, as well as the usual saints, sinners, and the congregation here present : infants not without guile, delighting in paradox and provocative exaggerations. His *Remains* had not been intended for publication and were somewhat too indiscreet for contemporary liking. But even Froude was defended by Sewell, and still more were the leaders and teachers of the Movement : " Men are called Papists who are writing against Popery . . . traitors to the Church of England when their time, talents and money are devoted to support it, violators of the Rubric when they are enforcing its authority . . . We think the publication of the *Oxford Tracts* a very seasonable contri-bution to the cause both of the Church and the State . . .

And as long as the authors continue in adherence to their original declared principles . . . abandoning all thought of self and looking only to God's Glory in all things—so long we trust and believe they will find a blessing resting on their labours—and all who love their country and their Church will heartily wish them God-speed."

Lockhart approved. He was perturbed, at this time, by the influence of Strauss' *Leben Jesu* which he found " most wearisome ", and which he advised Croker not to touch in a review. It could be dealt with only in a series of controversial articles. " I incline very strongly to believe that until Strauss or some other German of this school shall have been formally and effectively answered in a separate Treatise it would be rash for an unprofessional Journal to meddle directly in the spreading of the odious debate."

There was more danger from Germany than from Rome, but there must be vigilance on every side ; so he accepted and approved a further contribution from Sewell—who by now was perturbed by the developments of the Oxford Movement—its tendency, as he thought, towards Romanism. His review of a new edition of Bishop Andrewes' *Sermons* was made the vehicle of some reproof :

"He seems to have, without one word of severity, demolished the leanings of the Pusey party as to influence with those who really mean to stand by the fathers of the Church of England . . . I think this will be one of the most remarkable papers *The Q.R.* ever had in point of interest, and I have very strong hopes of its success practically in arresting the movement towards popery, without at all weakening the impulse that has been given to High Church principles such as they were in the best days of the Church."
—Thus Lockhart wrote to Croker, and reported letters of commendation from the Archbishop of Canterbury and the Bishop of London.

From a modern Anglo-Catholic, or even from a moderately High Church standpoint, Sewell's article would seem to have more than one word of severity. His praise of the great Anglican divines of the seventeenth century implies frequent criticism of their successors. In emphasising the courage and steadfastness of those earlier defenders of the

Church he overlooked the no less gallant zeal of the Tractarians in fighting against indifference and lethargy : the
heritage of the eighteenth-century worldliness that had
invaded the Church and crept up to the very altars where
the Holy Sacrifice was too seldom offered. Sewell found
them too tolerant of Rome, too courteous in controversy,
lacking in realism. He warned them against cherishing
the " all imaginary hope of effecting an impossible reconciliation " and against accepting, as typical of Rome, the
sympathetic Gallican Church in France, " least Popish of
all Popish communions ", which then, as now, showed a
friendly disposition towards the High Anglican Church.

In other directions *The Quarterly* was active in comment.
Croker was writing, in addition to political contributions,
articles on Shakespeare, and on Fanny Burney, whose
Journal, Lockhart thought, gave " in spite of its very pleasing
portraiture of George III and his Queen, especially the
Queen, such a horrid notion of Court life and the whole
interior of Royalty, that it is sure to be laid hold of by those
who hate the Monarchy and all its belongings. Yet I think
a great deal—almost the whole of Miss B's misery came
from her own vulgarity, her silly cowardice in not telling
what she wanted and expected, tho' the Queen and Princesses were evidently most willing to listen to her on all
occasions, and most anxious for her comfort."

J. G. L. himself, though officially and no doubt sincerely
a loyal monarchist, looked with mildly sardonic eye upon
contemporary Royalty.

" I observe with wonder the progress that most unfortunate of Ladies is making in alienating from herself the
only real friends of her crown," he wrote in 1841, referring
to the young Queen Victoria's anti-Tory feelings too plainly
shown. " This monarchy seems destined to a suicidal end.
But I hope it is not true she has not invited the Duke to
her wedding." (The Duke was Wellington.)

As always, his *obiter dicta* in these letters, whether of
literary criticism or of gossip, are enticing. Taking up
a reference to Cicero he wrote : " Cicero himself is surely
—with the one exception of H. Walpole—the best letter-
writer in the world . . . I would rather part with any

other set of his writings than with them . . . The rapidity and clearness of his narrative the brilliant conciseness of his descriptions of men and places, together with the eternal amusement of his self-portraying vanity make the whole collection to me the most pleasing Latin book in the world except Horace."

It was not merely a reading age ; it was one of an easy, classical scholarship that lasted long beyond college days. For Lockhart, and he was far from unique in this, the Greek and Latin classics were books to be enjoyed equally with the great French and English works of the past and present.

He could himself gossip almost as racily as Horace Walpole. In one letter he referred to " a very ugly story " about Jeffrey—his old rival of *The Edinburgh Review*. Lockhart was shocked, but, one might guess, not altogether unpleasantly, by the rumour, which a letter from Scotland presently declared to be " a gross fabrication, at least a very malicious exaggeration of mere imprudence "—and not the case of adultery that was believed at first. Had the tale been true, it would have ruined " the little judge ". The mere hint of it must " call his septuagenarian mind to a sense of the folly of flirtation, with pretty young wives especially ". The lady concerned had a reputation for piety—which added a flavour to the scandal. " The gossips alleged that she had begun with a zealous ambition of converting F. J." The gambit is not unknown.

One of the personal matters revealed in this correspondence is Lockhart's hankering after a Government post, not altogether a sinecure but one that would mean security of income with considerable leisure for literature. In 1841 he consulted Croker about the chances of his being appointed one of the Commissioners of Lunacy : " Such a place would make me easy and contented and infer healthful travelling. But I fear my pretensions would be found unworthy of so valuable a post." He added that he was an English as well as a Scots barrister, thus qualified in both forms of national law. He was in one of his moods of dissatisfaction with his post as editor, irritated by what he considered the weakness and vacillation of John Murray. The mood became more intense and in January 1842 there was almost a breach : " I would be disposed to put up with various things if Murray be alone concerned, out of pity for the shattered condition he has reduced his nerves to ; which things I could not consent to tolerate if it appeared that they might proceed not from his weak caprices but from the calculations of stupid strangers. I have no longer the motives for submitting to certain annoyances that were all powerful in former years, and have for some time been contemplating very seriously a retirement from the anxious situation of *The Q.R.*—the more seriously because I have sometimes suspected that I was used by M. as I should not otherwise have been, in consequence of his fancying I was tied by necessity to the post."

This storm, like others, blew over. Ten years were to pass before he loosened the ties with *The Quarterly*, and then reluctantly and because of his failing health. Only two months later he was writing, very much the editor, to Croker, about Sewell's handling of the Tractarian question, and expounding his own views about the parties in the Church ; and in January 1843 he was permitting himself an editorial grumble, by no means ill-humoured, about lack of space and lack of funds. An extra number was being contemplated : " Of course I had erred in accepting too many papers— but the authors too had erred in making their papers longer than was understood or expected. But it is needless to write an article on the accumulation of articles." *The Quarterly* paid well, and most of its contributors were " persons to whom a £50 note or even a £20 one is of real consequence ".

The Tractarian controversy was still lively. Sewell, however, was somewhat out of favour : " It seems to me that now I have let Sewell preach long enough ", Lockhart wrote, " and that the time is now come when the intervention of a new hand—such a hand as did the Liturgy paper might really be of the most essential service " ; and the hand was the heavy one of Croker. But there was also a new hand— that of Archdeacon Manning ; still a loyal and influential Anglican, who had offered an article on the question of suppressing the Welsh sees. Lockhart hesitated about accepting it ; he was " fearful of being overlaid with Church papers ". The article was accepted but held over. It finally appeared in the same number as Croker's review of liturgical works which had also been delayed in publication. Of Manning, Lockhart said : " He has taken pains and produced a paper which would, I think, be very popular with the clergy and give offence to none of your friends." Croker continued to cause doubts and qualms. However much Lockhart might deprecate " Romanizing ", he recognised the fundamental kinship between the Roman and the Anglican Churches in their essential Catholic teaching :

" You seem to me ", he wrote to Croker, " not to give any weight to one great fact—to wit, that our Church recognises the orders of Rome, but not those of either Geneva or Scotland or the Lutheran Churches even. Surely this is *prima facie* evidence that the English Church acknowledges a nearer kinship with the Roman Church than with the most orthodox of the non-episcopal persuasions." Croker's first draft had, apparently, been ultra-Protestant, beyond even the tone of contemporary episcopal admonitions : " You would hardly, I believe, have one Bishop of English authority with you, except Whately who is no more an Anglican than a Mohametan. I know there has been and probably still is a prevailing flavour of Puritanism in the Church of Ireland," and Croker, though of Devon stock, was by birth and upbringing Irish.

Lockhart was increasingly aware of the danger of the new German agnosticism and paganism ; he was one of the few intellectuals of his time who saw the peril to mind and spirit of that teaching. Croker had stressed the infidelity of Revolutionary France ; Lockhart commended the Oxford men for perceiving and exposing " the utter infidelity of the German literature—all Protestant ". The failure of all religious authority in Germany had produced " the school of the Rationalists and Pantheists which includes the vast majority of the educated classes, wherever German literature prevails, and has, I fear, gained not a few adherents here, since that literature was brought into vogue among us by the imitators of Carlyle, etc."

Croker's article (ostensibly a review of a number of books

241

and pamphlets, including the Bishop of London's *Charge to His Clergy*, and treatises on *The Thirty-nine Articles* and on *Recent Changes of Ceremonial*) began calmly enough with a reference to " the visible and, we trust, substantial increase of religious feeling among the members of the Established Church especially in the higher and middle classes ". (Religion was being allowed to influence even a gentleman's private life !) Young people especially, and most of the clergy, were turning against the prevailing secularism, and ready to be inspired.

" All these the Tractarians found ready to kindle at a touch, and the zeal of the writers grew hotter and hotter at the flame they excited, till at last, growing blind at the blaze, they have burned their own fingers and very nearly, if not actually, set fire to the Church."

More, far more than Sewell, Croker was shocked by the revival of ceremonies and Catholic observances : Confession, vestments, altar-lights, the use of a crucifix (carried by a clergyman on his way to give the Last Sacrament to a dying man) were all packed into a catalogue of commination. Of the leaders of the Movement whom, unlike Sewell, he regarded as perverts, traitors and hidden Romanists, he wrote :

" Open defection, even when we suspect it to be the work of an irregular intellect and morbid vanity, is less deplorable and infinitely less dangerous than the masquerade orthodoxy whose heart is already reconciled to Rome, though its hands are still willing to carry the bag and take the sop, and to participate in the Communion of the Anglican Church, as Judas did at the Last Supper." There are comparisons that, once made, put the maker beyond forgiveness. On a lower plane of criticism it may be suggested that Croker must have been deserted by whatever sense of humour he ever possessed. When that sense is lacking there is room for many devils.

He would appear to have hoped for new opportunities of attack, but Lockhart wrote to him in July 1843 : " Murray . . . is much and seriously alarmed about the probable effects of a vigorous anti-Puseyite paper in the next No. The last, it seems, has been generally ascribed to you, and he continues to receive letters in which painful liberties are taken with your name, and vengeance threatened on the sale of *The Q.R.* But he seems to be still more troubled by the coldness with which the article has been received by clergymen from whom he expected warm approbation." The tide was turning towards the new reforms.

In his private life Lockhart was, this year, gratified by being given the post of Auditor of the Duchy of Lancaster. It was unexpected : " I had long given up all my dreams of Government patronage in any shape—therefore this small affair (£400 a year, but nearly, I believe, a sinecure) is not only a comfortable but a totally unexpected addition to my small means, and will be very serviceable to me when I send my boy to Oxford next year." The post was offered him by Lord Grenville Somerset with the approval of the Queen. It brought him relief—not only in the possible expenses of Walter's Oxford life, but in the provision of a larger insurance for his children. Walter would probably be heir to William, as well as to his maternal uncle, Sir Walter Scott ; but Abbotsford was an encumbered inheritance. There were legacies due to both children ; but Lockhart's fear was that he might die before these fell to them and that Charlotte and Walter might be left dependent on his relatives. He was, for a time, obsessed by financial problems and by the future of his children.

" If I were to obtain any addition of income I should be lightened in spirit and enabled to provide for them more liberally in the insurance way. Otherwise, I am now verging on 50, have long since lost all that made life pleasant enough to be much worth caring for." Then came the confession of his lost dreams :

" Time was when I sighed and prayed for the means of release from the eternal worry and small negotiations and explanations inseparable from the management of *The Quarterly*. I used to dream of being at liberty to choose my literary tasks ; then tasks no longer, for myself. I had fond dreams of doing something permanently worthy in letters. But with less idle dreams these too have flown. I am persuaded very thoroughly that I am no longer fit for anything better than the course of drudging which has fallen hitherto to my share, and which is probably less disagreeable to me than would have been the pursuing of my profession at the bar."

Maurice Baring quotes, more than once, Balzac's phrase : " enchanted cigarettes " for the books that every author dreams of writing : masterpieces of imagination beyond anything ever achieved. Lockhart smoked many such cigarettes ; he was, to the end, unfulfilled, except in what he undertook in filial piety—the *Life of Scott*, and in that one perfect and poignant lyric that he wrote out of his remembered grief; that key with which he unlocked his heart.

" And now I have said more to you than I ever did before to anybody, of my worldly and personal condition and views ", and it is one of the most vivid flashes of self-revelation he has left. Not the least fascinating of the problems in Lockhart's life and character and work, is this sudden, recurring revelation of his secret life to the man who often exasperated him and whose acerbities complicated his work as editor. There was, from first to last, a strange, strong bond between the two men ; Croker had a mysterious power of evoking confidences from one well schooled in reserve, and protected by irony of temper. Whatever we may think of Croker himself, as a personality and as a critic, and of his influence on *The Quarterly*, we must be thankful for him as the correspondent and confident of Lockhart the enigma.

II. LETTERS TO MURRAY :
AND CONTRIBUTIONS TO *THE QUARTERLY*

The three men, Lockhart, Croker, and Murray were so closely, almost indivisibly, bound together as to make mutual exasperation and criticism inevitable. The mutual confidences of Croker and Murray about J. G. L. would, no doubt, make lively reading. Lockhart, as we have seen, released a good deal of his pent-up feelings about Murray in letters to Croker ; and could then write about that worthy with a caustic pen to their principal : " He is incapable of seeing anything but faults in any work of any living writer except himself and his own immediate connections."

The letters to John II though briefer and more strictly professional than those to Croker have gleams of intimacy also. Lockhart could not for long restrain his individuality ; his critical mind flashed out in comments by the way : " To suppose that Shakespeare didn't understand French and Italian is just as absurd as to suppose that Sir W. Scott did not, and I believe the one was at least as good a classical scholar as the other. How should Shakespeare, living when there was so little worth reading in English, have wanted the curiosity to make himself master of the other languages ? But the great argument is . . . the enormous richness of his phraseology . . . No man has inlaid our Saxon speech with such boundless profusion of Latin."—Intimacy with Scott is no bad preparation for an understanding of Shakespeare.

Lockhart's ideals for *The Quarterly* were expressed in a letter to John Murray in 1838, that in which he begged John II to encourage the progress of young John III. *The Q.R.* cannot hope to rival journals of more frequent appearance as a " herald of mere novelties " to London readers. It must look for audience to the clergy and country gentry, who read and reflected on their reading, and who chose to read articles of depth and substance. Their approval would depend " on the belief that *The Q.R.*, is written and edited not by recluses but by men of the world " aware of " the tone of thought and feeling in the highest and best society of London on subjects of all classes—light as well as grave." The editor and his contributors must have " unlimited sympathy with society, and no motto could be better than your ' *Quicquid agunt homines* ' . . . I should like it to be a running panorama of English life and thought and manners."

Lockhart had a clear picture in his mind of the cultivated section of English society—which included aristocracy and gentry, the clergy and the professional classes : " It is in early life, chiefly at the University, that the gentlemen of England form and fix their tastes as well as their creeds. They are then eager readers, and what they there accustom them to respect and like, they are apt to adhere to through life with the constancy of the national temper." There was still a tradition of intellectual aristocracy ; certainly one of intellectual gentility (using the word without its insipid modern meaning) : of a culture solidly founded upon the classics, of learning early acquired and taken for granted, of a *lingua franca* of common knowledge of literature and history. Its weakness might lie in its conservatism ; it might not seek to add new riches to this heritage. But there was a sense of quality, a standard of judgement which the new literature must satisfy. *The Quarterly* must itself have quality and balance.

" No one number, nor even two numbers should be allowed to determine our judgement on any one part of the general scheme." This caution was apparent later when he restrained Croker from further incursions into theology and ritualism.

" No one can be more painfully aware than I am that we have never done what we ought to have done, and might do. Yet I think the right course has been in the main adhered to." *The Review* had gained and held new ground. " I am prepared, next winter, to make a most ardent effort to give my individual attention to *The Review* . . . to do all I can for regulating and quickening the exertions of our allies."

This was written in the year (1838) after Sophia's death ; the time of his deepest desolation, but of his strong resolve to live for his children and his work. The loss of Sophia was an incalculable one, at that period of his maturity when he needed a companionship at once emotionally and intellectually satisfying. His friend Gleig wrote, afterwards, of Sophia that she was " the beau ideal of a poet's daughter and a poet's wife, proud of her father, more proud perhaps of her husband. She was frank, open, playful, affectionate, possessing the tact and talent which made sunshine in the house ". Lockhart, with his reserve, needed such a confidant ; and these first years of bereavement must have been, at times, almost intolerable. He may well have driven himself too hard ; spent over-much nervous energy in his work.

Being himself ambitious for *The Review*, he thought

Murray at times over-cautious. "You must allow me to say once more what I have often said," he wrote in 1839, "that The Q.R. would lose its place among those whose suffrage ultimately commands that of the multitude if it were to adopt the rule of meddling with nothing until its notoriety had gone beyond the select circle. This is, I think, one of the few points on which you and I hold a fixed difference of opinion." (The immediate cause of argument was Strauss's *Leben Jesu*, which, Lockhart thought, must be considered with care and discussed with authority.) In the same letter he exclaimed : "O ! if we had but a first-rate man of science who could write clearly and briefly—a Playfair or a Davy . . . any hand that could command attention and give pleasure and instruction however imperfect. Our Whewells, Brewsters, Lyells, etc., are all heavy clumsy performers—all mere professors—hot about little, detached controversies, incapable of carrying the world with them at large." *The Voyage of the Beagle* had just been published, in five volumes—which had to be compressed into a review of thirty-two pages.

A letter of 1841 is one of the recurrent expressions of his *apologia pro vita sua* as editor :

"I have, and can have, no object but to get the materials of *The Review* into the best possible shape on all occasions. I have no personal vanity in the least involved. I know very well that the Editor gets no credit at all. Surely I must be an ass if 15 years had not cleared my head of that dream. I am only anxious that your book should be in repute and that the honour given to contributors should be reflected on it to its best advantage."

Yet the dream had been a cherished one and died painfully. These years of work and self-discipline had been stern.

He carried his interest abroad with him. On that tour of Italy with young Walter he noted and reported, with pleasure, the success of Murray's *Handbooks*, especially Palgrave's, " which stands its ground capitally, throughout, except that he praises as good sundry indifferent enough inns,—among others that where I now write "—in Leghorn. The landlord was a Scot, " a grand specimen of the Scotsman *à la* Smollett—a rigid Presbyterian who has not been in his native country these 50 years ".

He was called north in 1842 by the death of his father : " I have heard to-day of the death of my aged father, who had for many years been in a state of complete oblivion," he wrote to Murray ; and to Croker that it was " an easy death ", the end of years of paralysis and torpor. " He had not recognised me for ten years past." The bond with his family and with Scotland was in no way loosened ; between J. G. L. and William it grew stronger with the years and Milton Lockhart was second home.

Sometimes the correspondence is interwoven with his own contributions to *The Quarterly* ; as on the publication of *The Life of Sir David Wilkie*, the artist, by Allan Cunningham, with the artist's own diary :

" I don't know if you have read much of the *Life of Wilkie* ", he commented to Murray (in February 1843) ; " all Cunningham's part seems to me wretched." Wilkie's diary of his early life he found dull, but his travel-diaries excellent, and his art-criticism stimulating and sound. On the whole, he was not captivated : " I can see little to admire or like . . . some good, homely Scots kindness for kith and kin . . . but generally the character seems not to rise above the dull prudentialities of a decent man in awe of the world and the great, and awfully careful about No. 1 . . . a fellow that you can't suppose ever to have been drunk or in love,—many a mile too much a Presbyterian elder for either you or me." He was in some doubt as to whom to pass the book for review ; and finally did it himself, with more zest than might have been expected from his unofficial comments. He extracted one plum of a story.

Wilkie was, like J. G. L. himself, a son of the manse, his father having been parish minister of Cults, and so the background and atmosphere of his boyhood were familiar. He had, from earliest childhood, a passion for drawing— like that of *Jan of the Windmill* in Mrs. Ewing's story ; and used to draw in church during the sermon, using the fly-leaf of a Bible or a psalter. " While his reverend parent preached his best ", the graceless son would be " catching the features of some devout Mause Headrigg or critical

Andrew Fairservice in the congregation ". Once he was inspired to caricature the minister himself, in soft charcoal, on the bald head of the miller who sat in front of him, deep in slumber " before the sermon reached its nineteenthly ". What penalty followed this double—or triple—sacrilege is not stated. Had Lockhart ever himself been guilty of such unedifying behaviour in the College Kirk in Glasgow while the Doctor was prosing? He quoted the proverb that " Manse bairns are seldom menseful " (i.e. discreet or " wyse ") and may have applied it to himself.

Murray published a new edition of the *Spanish Ballads* in 1842 ; Lockhart wrote to John III about it, the elder John being ill : " I should think you might sell as many as would do a little more than save you—if not now, when Xmas comes round again." It is a handsome edition in crimson morocco richly tooled, and with illustrations from drawings by William Allan, David Roberts, William Simson, Henry Warren, C. E. Aubrey and William Harvey ; the pages with wide margins, bordered in colour and decorated with vignettes and tail-pieces.

The 1840's—like the 1830's—were a period of considerable feminine achievement. Lockhart had sympathy with the intellectual woman, and he valued such contributors as Miss Rigby (familiarly known as " Lofty Lucy " from her height, which approached six feet). Her *Letters from the Baltic* had been published by Murray.

Most brilliant among the women of the period, with something of legendary charm and sadness, almost of fatality about her, was Mrs. Norton, born Caroline Sheridan, granddaughter of Richard Sheridan.

In September 1840 the work of a group of poetesses was reviewed in *The Quarterly* ; the article has been ascribed to Lockhart (and also to Hartley Coleridge). The books noticed included two by Mrs. Norton, *The Dream*, and *The Undying One* ; a volume of poems, *The Seraphim*, by Elizabeth Barrett and her translation of *Prometheus Bound* ; and others by Lady Emmeline Stuart Wortley and by Mrs. Southey.

The tone is distinctly favourable to the work of women as a whole, and it is made clear that they had a large public, and earned very substantial royalties. " We wish

Milton had as many readers." Mrs. Norton is praised as "the Byron of our modern poetesses", with the same "intense personal passion by which Byron's poetry is distinguished from the larger grasp and deeper communion with man and nature of Wordsworth", and with Byron's "beautiful intervals of tenderness, his strong practical thought and his forceful expression".

Miss Barrett was not so highly favoured. Her poetry lacked the discipline of art, and "her success has not been in proportion to her daring"—in translating from the Greek. Her version was "a remarkable performance for a young lady, but . . . not a good performance in and by itself". Mrs. Southey was called "the Cowper of our modern poetesses". In the absence of proof one can only hope these assertions were not by Lockhart; if they were,—they must be admitted to do credit to his kind heart.

A later review (which *was* by Lockhart) discussed what is perhaps Mrs. Norton's best-known poem, and her most effective : *The Child of the Island*. It was a plea for the childworkers in the factories of England; those pitiful waifs held in slavery and worse than drudgery, before the first of the Factory Acts was passed to relieve them a little. The "Child" of the title was the small Prince of Wales.

Lockhart while deprecating the didactic tendency of much modern poetry—"We object to buying a song which turns out a sermon"—praised Mrs. Norton both for her intention and her achievement. Her judgement that "the grand universal rule of Christian practice" was being "most flagrantly violated in England" was supported by her vivid pictures of the sufferings of these poor children. Lockhart agreed with her, and conceded the art of her description ; poems and novels should not be directly and obviously didactic, but should "reflect life, and teach as well-observed life teaches". Mrs. Norton taught in that way. In an unusually florid conclusion he pronounced her book to be "the fairest wreath as yet woven in the service of the graver muses for the name of Sheridan".

To refer to Lockhart's ladies might be misleading to the mind hoping for light scandals. There was no whiff of impropriety in his life or about his reputation ; he was not even given to epistolary flirtation. But he enjoyed feminine company, appreciated women of character and intelligence —like Mrs. Norton and Miss Rigby ; and had a warm and faithful affection for those old friends who had known Scott and known Sophia : Maria Edgeworth and Lady Davy. Fanny Kemble was, with her sister, Mrs. Sartoris, to be a most valued and understanding companion for him in his last visit to Rome.

A redoubtable lady of the past who came under his criticism was Mrs. Calderwood of Polton, whose travel journal formed part of *The Coltness Collection* of family papers, published in 1842 and reviewed by J. G. L. The old family of Coltness in Lanarkshire and in Dr. Lockhart's former parish of Cambusnethan, were Steuarts, of the old legal gentry. The last of these lairds had died at Cheltenham " a landless man ", his fortune having been spent " between the constant hospitality of a great country house, and the usual results of a gentleman farming on a large scale ". Lockhart reviewed the *Papers* with zest and intimacy and a certain nostalgic wistfulness ; recalling too " the elegant hospitality of recent times " at Coltness, which his father most probably enjoyed,—the minister dining with the laird ; and J. G. L. himself may have known, for the last Sir James Steuart lived till 1830 and Coltness was within visiting distance of Milton Lockhart.

An earlier laird, Mrs. Calderwood's brother (she was born a Steuart), had been sufficiently Jacobite in sympathy to be obliged to spend many years abroad, after the Forty-Five, and the main reason for the lady's tour of the Continent was to visit him in Spa, in Belgium. Lockhart regarded her with a mixture of amusement and wonder " that a remarkably clever woman, bred up in a distinguished crown-lawyer's family, and always accustomed to the first society of Scotland, should have been, in 1756 but forty years of age, so thoroughly penetrated with all the prejudices of her province—so calmly and completely satisfied with the vast superiority of Scotland and the Scotch over England and the English ". He enjoyed—as we still must enjoy— " the easy promptitude of her self-complacent conclusions from every comparison " and found that it was " in the perpetual intertissue of shrewdness, sarcasm, ignorance and obstinate blindness that the charm of the performance consists ". Mrs. Calderwood was a vindication of the truth of Smollett's portraits against the charge of caricature : one has indeed only to read some eighteenth-century journals and memoirs to realise the accuracy of portraiture in Scott and Galt and Smollett. Lockhart noted—being himself a good Anglican with a clear memory of his own Presbyterian boyhood and of Presbyterian prejudices—that although her brother the laird had " easily cast aside the hereditary attachments " to the Kirk, she was so held by them as to look with contempt on both Episcopacy and Popery. (It must be pointed out, however, that like many undeviating Presbyterians abroad, the good lady was fascinated by Catholic practices, was on excellent terms with many priests, and visited various convents with a lively curiosity about the details of difference in their respective Rules.)

Lockhart might well have written some memorable character-studies of Scots " leddies " of the older, vigorous and entirely native generation. The heroines of his four novels are conventional figures ; the only female portraits that linger in the mind are those of Mrs. Sempill in *Adam Blair* and old Mammy Baird in *Matthew Wald*. Had his dream been fulfilled—of more leisure for private writing, for creative work—he might have brought to life many of the types of Scottish society he had known in his youth. Among the lost or unwritten masterpieces of literature lie Lockhart's novels of Glasgow and Edinburgh society in the late eighteenth or early nineteenth century, and of Scots provincial life in manse and mansion.

He could write admirably as a detached critic, with judgements firmly based on his classical training and strengthened by wide reading. But some of his most attractive work—even in periodicals—is, like his master-piece, coloured and warmed by personal feeling ; it is indeed " emotion recollected in tranquillity ". His genius for biography was apparent in brief sketches as well as in a full-length portrait.

One of his best sketches was his review of a posthumous

volume, *Peregrine Bench*, by his old friend Theodore Hook.
He did not find the book itself particularly meritorious ;
but made it the starting-point of a brief memoir of Theodore
and his somewhat turbulent career. Lockhart credited
him with a response that has been ascribed to more than
one, including Jowett ; when asked, on matriculating,
whether he were ready to subscribe the Thirty-nine Articles,
he replied : " Oh yes, sir—forty if you please."

Theodore had, for a time, a social success in London :
" The delicate and fastidious but, on the whole, very dull
world of fashion never wants more than a decent pretext to
receive with alacrity a recruit possessing any considerable
faculty of entertainment, not overbalanced by gross un-
towardness of aspect, manner or temper "—and Theodore
was an expert entertainer, if over-addicted to hoaxes. (He
once caused a major traffic-block by sending out a thousand
letters of invitation to eminent personages and of orders to
tradesmen, in the name of a quiet householder—which
Lockhart appeared to find an amusing escapade ; the undergraduate in him being not yet dead.) He was a superb
raconteur who " could not tell any story without making
it his own by his ever-varying, inexhaustible invention of
the details and aspects, and above all by the tact that never
failed to connect it with the persons, the interests and the
topics of the evening. Nothing was with him a patch "—
a phrase which by implication states an aesthetic truth—
that creative art is known by its organic unity.

Hook held for some years a comfortable appointment as
Treasurer to the Governor of Mauritius, but was accused of
malpractices, sent back to England under arrest and sub-
jected to a long enquiry. He was finally cleared of criminal
charges but held for civil debt ; lodged in a spunging house
where, as recorded in an early letter, J. G. L. dined with
him very cheerfully ; then in the King's Bench prison.
Scott's influence helped him to the editorship of *John Bull*—
which J. G. L. used to send to Sophia and later to Charlotte.
He was a member of the Athenaeum, which is not generally
regarded as one of the more raffish clubs, and was a fairly
copious author.

Lockhart never wrote anything more warm and generous

than this memoir : Theodore was one of his odd friends—
but he was loyal to his oddities, and therein was the more
lovable himself.

In an earlier issue of that year he reviewed one of Murray's
Handbooks : Richard Ford's on Spain. He found it not
altogether satisfactory as a handbook, being deficient in
some useful details ; but altogether excellent as a " first-
rate library book ", to be enjoyed for its disquisitions and
reflection of the author's mind. Ford was, " as may be
expected of a Devonshire gentleman, a High Churchman,
a staunch Anglo-Catholic, nay one might almost suspect
him from incidental expressions of a leaning to the doctrine
of the Oxford Tracts "—a pronouncement which itself
reflects the contemporary interest in Church matters. Is
this one of the earliest uses of the term Anglo-Catholic ?

Lockhart was never pedantic ; he would probably not
have claimed for himself the title of scholar. His criticism
always brought literature into relation with life. But he
took pleasure in a work of scholarship, in the classics and
classical research. A book that pleased him was *A Critical
History of the Language and Literature of Ancient Greece* by
William Mure of Caldwell, in Renfrewshire. Mure had
travelled in Greece, and was a scholar of the humaner kind.
Lockhart praised his book for its knowledge of men and
affairs as well as of literature. The Homeric question was
then much discussed—whether the *Iliad* and *Odyssey* had
been written by Homer himself, or by another man with
the same name, or by a committee ; J. G. L. " guyed " this
last theory with gusto : " Such is the art of extracting
sunbeams from cucumbers . . . So divine a system can
never die." He suggested that critics of a future century
might dismiss Byron as a myth, and ascribe *Don Juan* to
" a licentious humorist named Southey—who had the
impudence to dedicate it to himself by way of blind " ;
and might also doubt the existence of Scott. " Were Hogg
and Scott dialectical forms of the same name ? Was
Shepherd Gaelic for Sheriff ? "—Lockhart on the Bacon
controversy would have been pungent.

Mr. Gilbert Macbeth has pointed out in his *Critical Study*
of Lockhart that he was influenced by his early studies of

German literature, especially of Herder and Schlegel, and by their teaching that literature must be the reflection of life, and that each age has its own tone and *ethos* ; that the literature of one period thus cannot be made the standard for another ; and that in both life and literature there was a law of change and evolution, an ebb and flow. Whatever the origin of Lockhart's theory of literature and literary criticism, his realism and humanity are more and more apparent as he matures. Indeed the arrogance and acerbity of his youthful criticism, in the *Blackwood* period, are only an exaggeration, it may be distortion, of this spirit. He was, in the 1820's, aggressively moral in judgement as well as arrogantly intellectual, a true Scot in his desire to guide and reform mankind. But he learned of life, and applied his learning.

Chapter 19

THE CHANGING YEARS

T HE last decade of Lockhart's life began with a faint
hope of a " secondary May " in his " brief year ".
He considered, or accepted the suggestion, of a
second marriage. The story is told in two or three letters
to Croker, and in brief entries in his diary, which themselves would be hardly explicable without the letters.
Until the Croker correspondence was discovered, there was
no hint of the matter, although there were rumours from
time to time of possible matrimony : Miss Rigby was one
of the ladies suggested. But J. G. L. would seem to have
taken such rumours lightly ; only this one affair touched
him.

It would appear to have been Croker's idea : " I have
been thinking a good deal of the kind advice you gave
me ", Lockhart wrote, on 2nd August 1844, " and tho' I
am very much afraid you have miscalculated my chances,
I feel disposed to try it. I think the most respectable way
would be to offer myself for a day's visit next week."

The lady was Letitia Mildmay, daughter of Sir Henry
Paulet St. John Mildmay of Dogmersfield Park, Hampshire, the third Baronet, who had died in 1808 and been
succeeded by his eldest son, another Sir Henry. The second
son Paulet was an actor in the brief drama of Lockhart's
wooing. Another was married to the widow of John
Morrit of Rokeby, which made a link with the Lockharts,
through the old Squire of Rokeby. The families had
friends in common, Croker and Dr. Ferguson, who shared
Croker's view as to Lockhart's " chance ".

Lockhart duly arrived at Dogmersfield on the 9th of
August, in time, as he wrote to Croker, to walk with the
ladies in the garden, before dinner ; and presently alone
" with L. M. to whom I told my story, as she said, ' in
a way she liked '. When I hinted that perhaps I should
have spoken to Lady M. she said : ' Better leave me to
speak to Mamma.' We parted very kindly, she agreeing

'to think of it'. I considered I had been not only gracefully but graciously received." And then, an incurable editor, he went on to discuss the business of *The Quarterly* ! Later he continued the tale of that evening. Letitia did not appear at dinner, pleading a headache ; and Lady Mildmay was distinctly cold and stiff in manner. At bedtime, Paulet, who was host, took Lockhart into the library for a difficult interview, announcing that " his sister had been entirely taken by surprize, all flattered, etc. etc., but she could not at present listen to any proposals at all, or even speak to her mother on any such subject. There had been much to distress both the ladies . . . He seemed greatly confused and agitated." Lockhart replied with dignity that he would do anything his host wished and suggested leaving early next morning ; a proposal which Paulet accepted with relief. " He was very civil, and used language far too lofty about my doing them honour, and so on." Later, he brought a note to Lockhart in his room, lighting a candle for him to read it, and this note J. G. L. enclosed to Croker ; but it has, unfortunately been lost. Next morning he left the house, in company with another brother who appeared to have heard nothing of the matter : Lockhart himself feeling bewildered and not a little hurt.

" Had it not been for Letitia's own words to me during my explanation and Paulet's afterwards, I should have thought from the appearance and manner of L. M. that I was expected to tell the tale I told, and that she led me into a wild part of the garden purposely—but this only shows how we may be mistaken when we ourselves are interested."

It was made more difficult for him by the fact of his hardly knowing Paulet. It would have been easier to discuss matters with one of the younger brothers, George or Humphrey, whom he knew well. He tried to talk or write himself out of his bewilderment :

" I am, when under any excitement, calmer than usual in all outward things, but men so constituted suffer afterwards for what they suppress, and I had a sleepless night, and am still in some trouble of nerves . . . I would have come to you this morning, but felt I needed the quiet of my own cell, which in time to come I think I shall not allow to be disturbed by visions of the matrimonial order." But he remained perplexed—and a little disturbed—by the memory of Letitia's sweetness to him in the garden.

" All Letitia's bearing and language to me in our half-hour's interview was eminently unaffected and elegant, and certainly no two people could have parted after such a scene in a manner more confidential—I may say and more tenderly so. Her note is very pretty."

A week later he heard from friends that Letitia was ill : " I hope and trust my rashness was not, in any important degree, the cause of this additional evil . . . *Talia peccanti nunc mihi finis erit.*"

Three days later there was a brief note : " I think it right to let you, who have been so very kind to me, see the terms in which P. M. has communicated to me the tragical conclusion—which, of course, you heard of as soon as I."

This tragical, brief tale appears in his diary thus :

" Sunday, 28th July : Croker gave me some advice about M. M. [Miss Mildmay] on Friday 26th.
Sat. 3rd August : Wrote to Croker about M. M.
Monday, August 5th : Croker answers : Yes, decidedly.
Thursday, August 8th : To dinner at Dogmersfield. Paulet M. and wife, etc.
Friday, August 9th : Home by one p.m. R.I. [Re infecta ?]
Sunday, August 18th : This day died Letitia Mildmay."

What happened that evening—between Letitia and her mother, then between Lady Mildmay and Paulet, and what was written in that " pretty " note which J. G. L. read by candle-light late that night ? He was not easily attracted and he was not a vain man ; if he was drawn by Letitia's charm, and found her gracious, it is probable that she was both charming and gracious to a marked degree. If he were not a brilliant match, he was far from being ineligible : well-born and gently bred, with a notable name in his profession, at home in both the literary and the social world ; of great distinction in looks and of that reserve of manner that can be more fascinating than facile geniality. It would have been no act of condescension had Letitia accepted him. Her death, so pitifully soon, suggests almost with certainty, a deep-rooted delicacy ; perhaps tuberculosis. Her family, realising how slight was her hold upon life, may have been startled by Lockhart's proposal. They may have regarded her illness as something to be concealed —in the Victorian manner—a reason that they would not admit. Lady Mildmay's stiffness like Paulet's embarrassment may have held fear and shock, and been in a way protective—both self-defensive and protective of Letitia. If marriage had been tacitly recognised as impossible for Letitia, if Lady Mildmay had known the gravity of her condition, Lockhart's proposal and Letitia's declared liking for him must have shaken her mother's fortitude.

That Lockhart felt the double blow deeply can be realised from his very reticence. His pride as well as his heart was hurt by his dismissal, and he was left bewildered. The news of Letitia's death must have given him a sense of fatality : a stern reminder that for him there could be " no secondary May ". So he put aside such dreams, and went stoically upon his way again.

Mercifully, the days were full of events, and *The Quarterly* exacted a concentration of effort that left little space for brooding. His own family matters needed his care. He took Walter up to Cambridge in October, feeling a little easier in mind about the boy ; and alert for any signs of the religious fervour that for the past decade had moved Oxford :

" I think the Tractarian Movement has reached Cambridge only for good," he told Croker. " There is a great increase of Church feeling and religious zeal—but as far as I could judge . . . no symptoms of the Romanizing propensity in any quarter possessing the smallest authority or influence." He gave a slight rap over the knuckles to Mr. Croker ; having heard much criticism of his recent Liturgical article, chiefly in regard to what clerical readers thought " injudicious phrases, not at all in the scope of your argument. I fancy the real offence was that a layman had ventured to invade a subject which they considered their own property."

The religious question of the moment was, however, not so much that of Oxford as that of Ireland. The Government's proposal to endow Maynooth was being bitterly opposed by the Nonconformists in England and the Presbyterians in Scotland, and by some of the English Bishops. *The Quarterly* was not unfavourable to the project ; and even the cautious Mr. Murray agreed that the matter must be discussed. Lockhart's own interest was keen, and in one of his letters he gave, for Croker's benefit, a summary of Scott's changing attitude towards Roman Catholicism. In 1807 he had deplored the pro-Catholic tone of *The Edinburgh Review* ; but in 1821 he considered, without animosity, the possible passing of the Catholic Relief Bill. His visit to Ireland warmed this tolerance into sympathy. As for his private beliefs : " He thought the English Church the best in the world—but in truth he would rather have been a Roman Catholic any day than a Presbyterian ; and he often remarked that the Anglican Church in Ireland had leaned too much to the Puritan side." Among his close friends, Morritt, Rose and Joanna Baillie were pro-Catholic.

The Quarterly itself had been pro-Catholic in its early days ; Southey had tried to turn it in an anti-Catholic direction, and Southey found Lockhart too sympathetic with Catholicism.

Young Walter's career at Cambridge was brief. " The lad has got the red fever," Lockhart reported. " A disease of which experience is the only, and, I believe the unfailing cure." It was decided not to send him back to college " where, in truth, he has done little but row on the Cam " (but at least he rowed for his College), but to a Military Academy near Liége. It was a disappointment for Lockhart, who would have chosen to see his boy follow one of the learned professions, or enter the Diplomatic Service ; still, soldiering was in the family on both sides, and the new discipline might work him no ill.

Meanwhile, there was comfort in Charlotte's companionship. She had grown up to be a charming, intelligent and sympathetic girl with, as her grand-aunt noted, much of her mother's gentleness with Anne's vivid looks. Ruskin fell in love with her, and wrote in his *Praeterita* of Lock-hart's " little, harebell-like daintiness of a daughter ". On one occasion, when dining at 24 Sussex Place, he made directly for his young hostess on entering the drawing-room. " I made every effort to ingratiate myself with the little dark-eyed, high-foreheaded Charlotte, and was very sorry—but I don't think the child was—when she was sent to bed." (The parenthesis somewhat endears Mr. Ruskin to us.) If the child Charlotte captivated him, the girl proved even more enchanting. After their next meeting he wrote that she " had by this time become a Scottish fairy, White Lady, and witch of the fatallest sort, looking as if she had just arisen out of the stream in Rymer's Glen, and could only be seen by favouring glance of moonlight over the Eildons ". It was better for Ruskin, and for Charlotte, that he should continue to see her in such " glamourie ". He did see her also, however, " by the dim lamplight of this world "—at one of Lady Davy's parties, when he tried to achieve a more human friendship. But the Scottish fairy had her own elfin elusiveness. " I never could contrive to come to serious speech with her ; and at last, with my usual wisdom in such matters, went away into Cumberland, to recommend myself to her by writing a *Q. Review* "—which Charlotte's papa accepted but which he " cut ", thereby infuriating his potential son-in-law. " I returned to town in a temper "—and met with no sympathy from Charlotte. Their last meeting was at one of Lady Davy's dinner-parties where he took her down to dinner, and where " Mr. Hope Scott took the foot of the table ". (Actually he was then merely Mr. Hope.) " I found she didn't care for a word I said." One can hardly blame Charlotte, for (apart from her interest in Mr. Hope—of which more, much more, later) she had on her other hand Mr. Gladstone. Ruskin and Gladstone may have been two of the loftiest minds incarnate during Vic-toria's reign, but they were not amusing table-companions. They talked across poor Charlotte, about Neapolitan prisons. " He couldn't see, as I did, that the real prisoners were the people outside." We must wish for Charlotte's own account, or Lockhart's, of that conversation.

The dream-love lingered in Ruskin's heart. Many years later, in 1867—when Charlotte was dead and her daughter was heiress to Abbotsford—he visited Melrose and went to look at Chiefswood, " where Miss Lockhart was born " ; permitting himself, no doubt, many fond imaginings, forgetful or ignorant of the fact that she had been born in London.

Charlotte wisely evaded Ruskin ; but she was not so much of faerie as to escape an unsatisfactory first love. A letter to J. G. L. from Wordsworth, in November 1846, ends : " Our congratulations to your daughter, and our best wishes for her health and happiness through a long life. The connection, as you represent it to be is one which I feel would have been highly gratifying to her grandfather, Sir Walter, had he survived to see her settled so favourably in his own country and yours."

The story is told in a few entries in J. G. L.'s diary and in letters to Croker and Traill and Miss Edgeworth. On 20th October, 1846, while staying at Milton Lockhart, he noted a visit from Mr. Nisbet of Cairnhill—a Lanarkshire estate. Next day : " Nisbet goes home. *Hodie* J. N. *mihi os aperuit."* On the 22nd, "William and I go to Cairnhill—at dinner, met the Houldsworths " [the new lairds of Coltness]. On the 5th of November he took Charlotte and Walter to Cairnhill, and later wrote to his old college friend Traill :

" My daughter is to be married (I think probably at Easter) to a worthy young friend of ours who is just taking possession of an estate of some £10,000 a year in this shire, John Nisbet of Cairnhill. You may remember his excellent father and also his mother . . . all good people, and all the friends on both sides are delighted. This was going on quite unknown to me while I was near you in September."

To Croker he wrote in much the same way : " The affair was not suspected by me when I saw you in town, but I found it nearly settled on my return to this place. I have reason to be well pleased with my child's choice— the son of an old friend—the heir of a respectable family in this county, just entering in the possession of a large

estate with a very handsome residence about 15 miles off
. . . He is an amiable youth with a very sufficient rental "
—a sentence that would have delighted Jane Austen.

It was all very suitable and everyone was pleased. There
was need of some happy prospect, for the news from India,
about the second Sir Walter, now the only survivor of
Scott's children, was grievous ; his doctors had pronounced
him beyond hope, and Lockhart expected daily the news
of his death. He lived, as it happened, until April of the
following year, when he died on his way home. Like his
brother and sisters, he died in his prime ; the only one of
the four to pass forty. He left no children and the heir to
his name and to Abbotsford was his nephew and namesake,
young Walter Lockhart, who took the name of Lockhart
Scott.

His affairs were complicated. Lockhart, after much
labour, disentangled them : there was a debt on Abbotsford
of £8,500, one to Cadell of £16,000, and one of sundries,
of £1,000. This last Lockhart took upon himself, and told
Croker : " Cadell obliterates the £24,500 on consideration
of getting the whole remaining copyright of Scott's Works.
In a year or so, thus, my son gets Abbotsford burthened
only with his aunt's jointure "—the estate bringing in, probably, an income of £400. Young Walter was now in India
with his regiment.

Meanwhile, since that happy announcement in October,
Charlotte's engagement had run its brief course. On
January 11th, 1847, Lockhart noted in his diary : " *Epistola
ab J. N. recepta unde sequitur aliquid haud levis momenti* " : and
two days later recorded another letter, in which the matter
of no small moment was becoming worse. Whether Charlotte was changing her mind, whether there had been a
quarrel, or a timely discovery of incompatibility he does
not confide even to his diary and even under the cloak of
Latinity ; but the sequel came on the 25th and 26th. On the
25th Mr. Nisbet called at noon " and exit 3 p.m. Letter
from J. M. N. at night " ; next day " J. N. *iterum cum anulo*".
So the engagement was broken and Charlotte returned
her ring, and—exit Mr. Nisbet. There was broken also
another possible link between Tweedside and Lanarkshire.

There is no further mention of the matter. Doubtless J. G. L. told Croker about it ; but they were probably meeting frequently in town, and not exchanging intimate notes. To Miss Edgeworth Lockhart wrote some months later : " Charlotte is still *my* Charlotte. I think she made an escape in acting as she did as to her affair last autumn, for it was better to discover an incompatibility of temper before than after the irretrievable step. She is with some kind relations in Surrey till I reclaim my housekeeper and constant companion and comfort." He wrote this letter from Abbotsford where he had escorted the widowed Lady Scott. He was in a mood of deep sadness. For him Abbotsford now was full of ghosts :

" You, my dear friend, can imagine with what a heart I have re-entered this house which I had not seen since the morning after your old friend's funeral in September 1832. Everything in perfect order, and every chair and table where it was then left, and I alone to walk a ghost in a sepulchre, amidst the scenes of all that once made life worth the name for me."

Scott's children had none of them his genius ; and neither of his sons was, in any degree a man of letters, though Charles had a quiet wit, a humorous turn of mind, an endearing kind of cleverness that his intimates relished. But all of them did honour to their paternity in character. Sir Walter the second was very much the soldier ; direct, possibly limited in outlook and interests, perhaps a little dull ; but a man of integrity and kindliness. He was a good officer, caring very much for the welfare of his men. His marriage, though made as one *de convenance*, was a happy one. To Lockhart he had always been a much-loved brother, and he was mourned sincerely by that affectionate and loyal heart.

Lockhart's inner life was devoted more and more to the past, to things and loves remembered ; but there were still the emotions stirred by his children, the life he shared with them. The old happy unity of three—the father with his two children—was broken by Walter's absence, and still more by his waywardness. Charlotte was not for long to be " my Charlotte " first and entirely ; but her going

264

brought a new comfort and strength, for her marriage gave to Lockhart a true-hearted son.

In the summer of 1847 he noted frequent visits by Mr. James Hope ; then Charlotte went to dine with Mr. Hope's mother, Lady Hope. Finally Mr. Hope paid a formal call at 24 Sussex Place, and thereafter " *Puella rem certam narrat patri* ". The certain matter was, no doubt, the state of Mr. Hope's affections and her own ; and it was a good matter even if it meant the loss of Charlotte as housekeeper and companion.

The course of this new and true love ran smoothly and swiftly to its consummation in a happy marriage. These visits took place in July. Lady Hope came to dinner with her son at Sussex Place ; Lockhart took Charlotte to join the Hopes at the Opera, where they heard Jenny Lind. And on the 19th of August, 1847, Charlotte Harriet Lockhart was married to James Robert Hope, by the Rev. Lord Henry Kerr, brother-in-law of the bridegroom. " Be it known to you ", Lockhart wrote to his sister Violet, " that Cha's wedding and the breakfast after (in her absence and her youth's) went off very prettily. She conducted herself well, and with very tolerable firmness and they were at the altar, a very handsome pair indeed. They retired cunningly to Richmond, and left me to do the honours of chicken, cutlets, all cold, tea and coffee and plenty of champagne . . . Sophia Christie and Isabella Grant (the painter's daughter) were among her bridesmaids."

The bride and bridegroom, after three days at Richmond, (where J. G. L. came to dine with them one evening) went to Gloucester, whence the " dutiful son-in-law " (as he signed himself) wrote to Papa : " We have both felt a sort of revival from the change of air—Richmond with all its merits was oppressive. I see a marked improvement in Charlotte since she was ventilated by purer and sharper air. She felt her final separation from you not a little— but she is not of a temper to show all she feels."

" I know Charlotte's temper well," Lockhart answered, " and quite understand the feelings you alluded to. It is my greatest comfort now in this world to feel and know that you and she are as likely as any two people could be—to comprehend and appreciate each other,—and I am satisfied that in whatever regards her welfare, you and I will always sympathise entirely. How easy, how happy I should be if I could but think that Walter had acquired for himself such guidance in the conduct of life as his sister had when much younger—as she has now, more than doubled, in her present acquisition."

Charlotte's husband, James Robert Hope, was the third son of General the Hon. Sir Alexander Hope of Rankeillour and Luffness, and a grandson of the second Earl of Hopetoun ;—the family is now that of Linlithgow, the seventh Earl having been raised to the rank of Marquess. He was born in 1812, being thus nearly sixteen years older than Charlotte : was educated at Eton and Oxford, where he entered Christ Church in 1829. One of his contemporaries at both school and college was Gladstone, and they were to become lifelong friends. He was a sound scholar, rather a serious youth, and for a time seemed likely to yield to his mother's desire that he should take Holy Orders. His own preference was for the law. After taking his degree he was elected a Fellow of Merton ; and in 1835 he began his law studies at Lincoln's Inn. He proved a brilliant lawyer ; was called to the bar in 1838 when he also proceeded B.C.L. at Oxford. His career was chiefly as a Parliamentary barrister, and in that he was well and solidly established by the time he met Charlotte. His inner life was then increasingly devout ; he was a devoted Anglican deeply influenced, like his friends Gladstone and Archdeacon Manning, by the Tractarians ; profoundly interested in liturgy and theology. He told Gladstone once that he thought of his professional work as his kitchen-garden, his work for his old college and his church as his flower-garden ; and both were carefully cultivated. It was a type not uncommon in that generation : there is a sketch of such a one in Charles, the hero of Newman's novel *Loss and Gain.* In every way, in his background, his cast of mind, his personality, he was exactly suited to the mature and thoughtful girl who was Lockhart's daughter and Scott's granddaughter.

Mr. Hope wrote to his sister, Lady Henry Kerr, on

July 23, 1847, about his marriage and about Charlotte :
" I have for a long time considered the possibility of
marriage, and had resolved that, all things considered, it
might, under God's blessing, be the best course which I
could pursue. It was not, however, till I had made
acquaintance with Charlotte Lockhart that I was satisfied
I should find a person who in all respects would suit me . . .
She is not yet twenty, but has lived much alone ; much
also with people older than herself, and people of high
mental cultivation. She has also had the discipline of
depending on those habits of her father which are inseparable from a literary and, in some degree, secluded life. In
short, she has had much to form her, and with great sim-
plicity of character, and unbounded cheerfulness, she com-
bines far more thought than is usual at her age. Having
no mother and few connections she is the more likely to
become entirely one of us . . . I have said more to you
about her than I have written to any one else, for I distrust
marriage puffs, and desire that people may judge for
themselves."

He was not, it would appear, likely to have fallen in
love without good judgement ; and with another type of
girl—one more exuberant and frivolous or one accustomed
to the lively companionship of sisters and brothers and
young friends—his marriage might, at least in the first
year, have been difficult. But Charlotte and he seemed,
in the old-fashioned phrase, made for each other ; and he
was, from the first, the son that Lockhart needed.

His biographer (Robert Ornsby) describes Charlotte at
this time as " a very attractive person, with a graceful
figure, a sweet and expressive face, brown eyes of great
brilliance, and a beautifully shaped head : the chin, indeed,
was heavy, but this added to the interest of the face by its
striking resemblance to the same feature in her great
ancestor, Sir Walter Scott."

The Hopes continued their wedding-journey to Scotland ;
first to Milton Lockhart, then to Rankeillour where they
spent the autumn, returning to London for the winter.
In the following year, they rented Abbotsford from young
Walter, and made it their principal residence.

267

Walter joined his sister and brother-in-law at Abbotsford
for the Christmas of 1847, much to J. G. L.'s pleasure.
His own work kept him in town : " I am very weary and
the daylight waxes dim apace, and so I must merely wish
all that is good for you and Hope and Walter," he wrote
to Charlotte, " and say how it gratifies me that he is with
you at this season, and how sincerely I hope that you three
may spend many happy Christmases together." He was
sending Charlotte Croker's new edition of Boswell, and he
also mentioned a new novel which she might like to read :
Jane Eyre : " I think it more cleverly written than any
very recent one, and it has a strong interest but hitherto
a very disagreeable one. It must be—if not by a man,
by a very coarse woman."

Jane Eyre was reviewed in *The Quarterly* (in December
1848) by Miss Rigby, who also admitted its power, but
deplored, more, much more than Lockhart, that element
which contemporary readers found coarse and violent and
altogether shocking. She considered that if it were not by
a man (which she thought probable) it must be by a woman
who " for some sufficient reason has long forfeited the companionship of her sex ". One minor point made by Miss
Rigby in favour of masculine authorship, was that Jane
Eyre's dress-sense was so bad, and she quoted the execrable
instance of Miss Ingram's morning-dress in a country-
house-party—the famous " sky-blue crape ".

Lockhart himself would have been more indulgent : " I
have finished the Adventure of Miss Jane Eyre," he wrote
in another letter, " and think her far the cleverest that has
written since Austen and Edgeworth were in their prime,
worth 50 Trollopes and Martineaus rolled into one counter-
pane [he meant Frances Trollope] with 50 Dickens and
Bulwers to keep them company, but rather a brazen Miss.
The two heroines exemplify the duty of taking the initiative,
and illustrate it under the opposite cases as to worldly goods
of all sorts except wit. One is a vast heiress and beautiful
as angels are everywhere but in modern paintings. She
asks a handsome curate who will none of her, being resolved
on a missionary life in the far East. The other is a thin,
little, unpretty slip of a governess who falls in love with

268

a plain stoutish Mr. Burnand aged 20 years above herself. Sits on his knee, lights his cigar for him, asks him flat one evening, and after a concealed mad wife is dead, at last fills that awful lady's place."

Charlotte's absence meant a renewal of letters, full of the characteristic mixture of news and gossip, personal and literary. Lockhart wrote of his visit to a Catholic country-house that he had been " not a little impressed with . . . a most gorgeous chapel all over popery and heraldry " where he heard Vespers " with very fair chaunting from the villagers "—the butler playing the organ. There was a good deal of religious " shop ". Church gossip, Roman or Anglican or both together, has its own flavour and one much relished by J. G. L. There was local gossip also : of " the suicide of a certain magnate of my row, a fat old glove-and-india-rubberman by name Keane. Margaret Alexander came to sit with me yesterday, and behold, she had always considered this person to be no other than H.R.H. of Cambridge, & had settled that the lady who rode about with him so conjugally was a left-hand colleague of the royal duchess established in this moral vicinity. This will speak volumes for the presence and port of the man, and for the charity of spinsters."

Hope was thinking of buying the portrait of Scott by Knight ; Lockhart was dubious : " At the time I disliked it as a representation of Sir Walter. I should like to see it again before you buy it."

Hope wrote, too, of his own plans and career :

" I certainly do not propose to continue long at the Parliamentary Bar. I look on it only as a means of getting a certain amount of money ingloriously enough—but neither can I resolve to plunge into the general business of the profession. House of Lords Appeals and Privy Council business would suit me best, and might enable me to push up from one to two thousand per an. which with my savings would put me quite at ease, and yet leave me much time at my own disposal. For politics I have at present no taste, and indeed my ambition, generally speaking, is nearly exhausted." In the same letter he announced " the prob-ability that Charlotte will be confined in June or July "—

of the following year, 1848. " The tokens are pretty certain to my mother, but as we may be mistaken, say nothing to others."

This expectation was not fulfilled ; Charlotte was to find motherhood difficult, and like her own mother, have disappointments. But apart from that anxiety the marriage brought increasing happiness both to her and her husband, and to Lockhart. It was his only comfort when his unhappiness about Walter grew more and more intense. Walter was now with his regiment ; military life, though congenial to him, was perhaps the worst he could have chosen as regards discipline. He was by nature extravagant, something of a *bon viveur* or would-be-so ; he had great charm but with it much vanity, and he lacked stability. Vanity was the root cause of his troubles ; he probably tried to " keep up with " his fellow-officers, though some of them were, no doubt, men of wealth, and he had only his allowance from his father ; and Lockhart, though a successful man of letters, able to live in comfort and with dignity, was not a rich man. Walter ran into debt ; was involved with moneylenders and in all the muddle of bills and promissory notes. Lockhart wrote to Croker on 1st September that he was detained in town by most unpleasant business : " some very painful disclosures in *Times* of Saturday last [26 August, 1848]. The report—of a trial at Bristol, was not seen by me until a friend called my attention to it, and I am in great alarm, as when you read it you will well believe . . . I have not yet heard from the poor lad himself, nor have I seen him for months, tho' this trial shows him to have been in town among Jews and thieves."

In the report of the trial Walter appeared under the name of Scott : the suit was *Scott* v. *Ferris* and the charge was that of bill-stealing. Plaintiff's counsel stated that : " There existed in the metropolis an organised gang who . . . obtained bills from the unwary by the fraudulent pretence of getting them discounted, and for which the parties who gave the bills never received a shilling." Walter's vanity and stupidity had brought him into evil company, and entangled his affairs almost beyond straightening. There was still the bridge of pity between his father and him ; he was still " My boy " and " The poor lad ". But this was shaken, if not destroyed, by Walter's writing " in a most impudent, disgusting manner ". Lockhart's generosity would have responded to any appeal ; but his pride and rectitude flared up at any touch of insolence or defiance. " I am in such great perplexity and distress about my son that I can't write to you properly ", he told Croker.

Walter's regiment was stationed at Norwich, where he presently fell dangerously ill. Lockhart and Hope went to him at once, and Charlotte came down from Scotland : " Walter is in a brain fever, and in a very alarming state " was the report to Croker. His affairs were in an even worse state than had been supposed. But Charlotte's presence, her sympathy and tranquillity seemed to be bringing her brother back from the darkness in which he wandered. Lockhart was, presently, able to return to London, " relieved from the horrid anticipation . . . of seeing a young creature cut off—in the fever of self-invited insanity ; but every hour darkens our horizon as to pecuniary claims, and indeed the whole retrospect seems to indicate such a degradation of tastes and habits that I am in the lowest water altogether ". Then Lockhart's stoicism re-vived : " But are these things necessities ? Then let us bear them like necessities."

He stayed on in London, mercifully involved in work, and miserably involved in Walter's affairs. Walter him-self, as soon as he could travel, was taken to Abbotsford. It seemed better that father and son should not meet, for a time. Abbotsford proved healing. His recovery was speedier than his family had dared to expect, and Lock-hart began to hope that with restored health of body there might come some amendment of mind ; that Walter might " so think and feel and act as to merit a return of tender-ness ". But the penitence must first be apparent. " Espe-cially he must be assured that as base and selfish vanity has been the mainspring of evil in him, so I will do nothing to shelter the vain part of him. That must be pierced to the core and bruised to the ground before I shall hold him to have any claim on me." It was sternly spoken. One recalls the description of him in his Oxford days—that none need go to him for solace for any wound to vanity— he would only mock at such wounds. That trait is the very cause of the tragic estrangement that now began. Lockhart himself lacked this ignoble form of pride ; but consciously or subconsciously, he knew it as the caricature and perversion in his weak son of his own pride. Vanity was his potential sin ; and he had small mercy on the sinner who erred through that weakness. Walter had indeed gone into a far country, and lived as a swineherd. " That horrid den of filth and folly has poisoned my imagination ", Lockhart wrote, on discovering the depths of his degradation.

Lockhart was in Paris with Christie, at the end of that year (1848) of revolution and turmoil in Europe. " This L. N. B. [Louis Napoleon Buonaparte] concern must come to an end very soon. The bets are within three months." He had attended a sitting of the Assembly, " a horrid row indeed—in a place as big as our Opera house but made chiefly of paste-board . . . Nothing like argument can be even attempted when there are from 1000 to 1500 French people, male and female, all crammed together and all jabbering." He had seen two plays " very cleverly acted and very amusing—on the state of public affairs . . . the usual scornful derision of this and all revolutions, and with what gusto the audience gulp it ! " Like a true Scot he had indulged in " sermon-tasting ", going to hear " the great Protestant preacher Coqueril, who is, I think, the best preacher I ever heard "—though a melancholy one, full of foreboding for the new year. Paris the travellers found " quite a camp " with soldiers in every part of the town, detachments passing through the streets and drums beating every five minutes, the forts full of artillery, the Tuilleries and Place de Carousel bristling with cannon. " I did not meet with one person—French or English, German or Russian . . . who did not abuse the Republic and laugh at Louis N. B. " ; no one expected that adroit pretender to be in France by 1850 otherwise than as a prisoner, or, possibly as a showpiece without power : " he may have a chance to retain his palace and pomp and get drunk ".

As for family matters, there was no letter from Walter, now with his regiment again. " This is very sad indeed. Be sure I shall never break your injunctions "—which were, no doubt, that he should be patient and gentle.

A long letter to Croker after his return to London, gives a similar, but more highly-spiced account of French affairs and the derision in which the Buonaparte family were held.

Croker at this moment was eager to undertake the massacre of Macaulay, and Lockhart's reply is interesting both as expressing his own opinion of Macaulay and of his editorial and critical standards. Croker was, he admitted, well qualified to deal with the new *History* ; but he feared a too-evident animosity towards the author :

" Now I don't think such a feeling should animate *The Q.R.* . . . I know that he has been most unjust and insolent to you—but still he is one of the most vigorous writers of his time, and I think any disparagement of his intellectual powers would only tell against the review." There follows what may almost be read as Lockhart's confession and apologia : " It is, however, very difficult— no one knows it better from experience than I do—for a man with a pen in his hand to forget rules and regulations, that he approves ever so much in his own mind—not to indulge any rooted feeling of hostility, however he may previously have resolved to keep that for a more proper place."

An unprejudiced review could be severe enough ; for Macaulay, for all his brilliance, was " not over honest in scope and management " ; and some of his arguments and handling of material could be exposed so as to " confound him a good deal, and check his breeze from El Dorado ". His hatred of the Church of England was blatant—" the only very strong feeling in the book " ; his sketches of the seventeenth-century clergy " but a symptom " of this bitterness. " I can hardly fancy a better opportunity for asserting the true principles of *The Quarterly* "—and so all the less need for animosity. " Violence nowadays does not answer so well as it did 30 years ago ; few respond

to it." Lockhart was no longer the reckless critic he had
been thirty years before ; he had learned his lesson—at
least in part ; one that Croker never learned. Croker
belonged to the prize-fighting era of criticism. Lockhart's
final summing-up of Macaulay is more pungent than any
abuse, and is one of the most adroit left-handed compliments ever paid by critic : " I doubt if Macaulay's book
will go down as a standard addition to our historical
library—tho' it must always keep a high place among the
specimens of English rhetoric."

Charlotte had a miscarriage in January 1849. " My
dearest," her father wrote to her, " You are so right to
keep a cheerful heart. This is the true and wise submission. Such deep disappointments well endured prepare
the soil for fuller happiness hereafter, and you will have
your reward in good time."

A letter, on the same day, to Hope, was full of Church
gossip of a high-Anglican flavour which is usually the
spiciest :

" Taffy Williams, Archdeacon of Cardigan, is here,
consorting with Sawny Sinclair, ditto of Middlesex, and
settling their respective mitres." The former, Lockhart's old
friend of Balliol days, favoured, naturally enough, Welsh
Bishops in Wales and " prophesies that in 20 years Bishops
will be the only Lords in the land ? His grog however
will have settled St. Taffy ere that day."—He lived and
died un-mitred. " He is publishing now the *magnum opus*
of his life, or rather of our age—*The Life of Julius Caesar*
to wit—so Macaulay had as well enjoy the breeze while
it lasts." Taffy also brought gossip of " a grand row
between my dear Diocesan and Bennett of Belgravia "—
one of the " ritualists " who in the decades immediately
following the Oxford Movement suffered (or possibly in
some cases enjoyed) episcopal censure. Father Bennett had
" counselled some Italy-bound sinners of that region to
confess them, in case they found no Philo Bennett, to a
Roman priest rather than an Evangelical ", and then had
confessed this counsel to his Bishop. " If this be true,"
added J. G. L., " I suppose he will soon follow the *usum
Dalkeithensem* "—referring to the reception, into the Roman

Church, of the Countess of Dalkeith, later Duchess of Buccleuch. There is more irony in this than J. G. L. intended—for the following of the " *usum Dalkeithensem* " was to affect him most intimately in a few years' time.

He was still anxious about Walter, in spite of a recent letter from him ; and anxious about Violet, his much-loved sister, who was slipping out of life. She had for many years been an invalid, and death when it came was merciful. But he mourned for the gay and pretty sister of his youth, and for her lost and frustrated gaiety and youthfulness.

" She was in youth very beautiful, and had cleverness and taste, sang charmingly, and was a favourite with all who knew her ; but she was a scornful maid and let the market-day pass, and then her spirits failed, and lastly her physical power, so that she is now released from a painful existence and enjoys I think, the reward of her innocent and pious disposition." The youngest of the Lockhart family, Violet was " turned of 40 " but looked nearer sixty ; a lamp unlit, or with a pale light that had flickered out. Did he recall Anne Scott who also had died unwed, unfulfilled, wearied ? He had loved Violet dearly and her passing added to his sense of " the long littleness of life ".

But it was a gentle sorrow. The bitter grief of estrangement from his son was to be added to his burden. Walter no longer answered letters. " Can he have made up his mind to permanently severating himself from me ? If not, what can account for this conduct but insanity—however produced ? . . . Perhaps Hope will try one more epistle to the Barracks, but I have scarce heart to ask more of such painful work at his hands."

But even in his desolation of spirit, J. G. L. retained, incurably, his taste for gossip about people and about books. He sent Charlotte the successive numbers of *Pendennis* as they came out and he read them ; and also news of a marriage in high life. " Lord Devon made a 4-hour journey in a mail coach with a penniless spinster of 40 and on reaching the Dublin terminus asked, and was accepted out of hand." On a nearer level the Misses Alexander had, at last, found a footman after rejecting

275

the brother of Lockhart's man Paul as "too short for Joanna, and by £2 too dear for Margaret" and a man recommended by William Lockhart because they thought him insufficiently good-looking. The successful applicant, one Ludwig, proved satisfactory, and after a period of probation was put into livery. Presently he implored his ladies to allow him to wear trousers, because the maids scoffed at his calf-less legs in breeches. But the ladies refused ; their late mamma had held that for footmen plush breeches were the only wear, so the unhappy Ludwig must endure mockery and remain in a state of armed truce with the flippant maids.

Other plums to be picked from his letters at this time include an explosive reference to the historian of *The Queens of England* : "D—— take Miss Agnes Strickland and all she-historians . . . I think I once met her many years ago. She called on Sir Walter, and my remembrance is of a rather handsome virago with the air of a Greenwich booth tragedy Queen, but this may have been the sister . . . Is Agnes a Papist ? . . . I should like to know on account of her *Life of Mary of Modena*—the best of these in the series that I have happened to read."

There was more church gossip : the see of Llandaff was to be filled, and the deanery of St. Paul's. "Taffy" Williams had hopes of Llandaff but was disappointed ; Milman's expectation of the deanery was fulfilled. There was a caustic reference to Croker : "Croker departed on Saturday to my inexpressible relief—he is very deaf and never was less dumb."

To Croker himself he was still writing, somewhat anxiously, about the review of Macaulay :

"I trust you don't pass over the most admired chapter . . . his conspectus of manners . . . Here most clearly comes out his settled antipathy to the landed gentry and the English clergy, and the boldness with which he draws on comic dramas and the like in the production of his caricatures is really astounding . . . The attempt to degrade the clergy as to birth . . . might be triumphantly repelled. Certainly his drawing such a line between the accomplished clergy of the city and the ignorant brother

of the country is absurd, for the city was then, as now,
supplied by parsons primarily located in the village, and
the great works of the Anglican theological library of every
age have been produced in the country parsonage, not
either in the city or in the college."

His social life was full and amusing enough to provide
some distraction of thought. There were dinners : one at
Lord Mahon's to meet " Sam of Oxford and Mr. Vanity
Fair Thackeray " where there were " many enquiries and
kindnesses for you " ; and one at Lady Davy's where Lord
Brougham " was full of fun and stories, not always over-
proper, to which listened, among others, Gladstone and
the young orator Pal [Palmerston] who sat by me and
seemed really a most agreeable and intelligent young man
with manners such as would vastly have improved the
general popularity of his papa ". This dinner was followed
by a " drum " or reception, " a very hot drum " the heat
of which drove Lockhart early away ; and he walked for
an hour in Grosvenor Square with Brougham, hearing
news of Paris. He came home one evening to find Paul
his man with a black eye " fearful to contemplate. He
said he had struck against his bed "—an explanation received with the incredulity it deserved. " I fear, I fear
there has been a return of unapostolical proceedings."

More grand than any dinner and hardly less amusing
was the Queen's State Ball where J. G. L. " saw lots of
friends and flirted as usual, vastly—chiefly I think with
the Duchesses of Buccleuch and Northumberland, Lady B.
Balfour, Mrs. G. Hope and Miss Angela Coutts. *On revient
toujours a ses riches amours*—no, most of all with Lady Jane
Charteris who made her responses most affectuously."
The Queen was in good spirits, " danced every dance, and
very elegantly as well as cordially—her partners foreigners ".
Lady Davy had also, one gathers, honoured Her Majesty
with her presence : " Whom should I see but Jinny ? I
thought these two queens were never to be contemplated
together, but there she was, in all her diamonds, of course,
and in white . . . from top to toe, even the roses all white
above her jet-black wig, so that the rouge blazed gloriously
. . . I was told later she did not approve the scene—said

the company was so low, etc. I guess the little V. had not been duly reverential."

Behind these letters lies the world of Trollope's political novels, and his London novels of young men heedless, foolish and erring. Walter Lockhart might have been the hero of such a tale, but it would have been a pitiful story with no happy ending. He stayed with his father for a few days, but suddenly left the house and went to his club, and thence to Ipswich, on pretence of military duties. " I know not whether he was willing to avoid another evening with my dulness—of lectures he had tasted nothing ; but so it is." There had been some improvement in him— but Lockhart was " vexed and mortified " by Walter's ignorance and perhaps he showed his vexation too plainly. He could never suffer fools gladly—and there was much folly in his son.

There was always the " Lockhart *du monde* " delighting in gossip—and the " Lockhart *du foyer* " ; never an angel in one sphere or devil in the other ; but in the world, brilliant and witty, with caustic edge to his wit ; in private, ill, old beyond his fifty-five years, and perplexed by helpless grief for his son. This year, 1849, ended sadly for him.

Chapter 20

THE YEARS RUN OUT

HIS children and his work had been (under God), since Sophia's death, the reasons for his fortitude, the means of life for him. In the last four years left to him, Lockhart was to know through one of these children the bitterest grief of all ; Charlotte was to be his sure comfort always ; but his work became a weariness as his bodily strength failed. He wrote, sometimes, of his longing for leisure ; but whether contentment would have lasted through a long retirement is a doubtful matter.

Early in 1850 he was writing, to Charlotte, in great anxiety about Walter, who was supposed to be somewhere in or near Boulogne : his address unknown. His father proposed to write to him through the English consul : " saying that if he now at last will see me, in sorrow, not in anger, I will go over immediately to wherever he is, and tho' I fear any attempt to meddle with his debts here would be vain, am ready to make any sacrifice to detach him from the woman who is with him and afford him an opportunity of reflection ". The burden of anxiety was almost beyond endurance now. But, as always, he could find some escape in humour of his own dry, caustic type : " Gladstone's speech was the most wonderful see-saw or cork-screw affair that ever Jesuitism produced "—is a typical bit of criticism. Typical too, both of narrator and of subject, was his story of the Misses Alexander having bought " a whole lot of magnificent Doges and Chancellors from Venice for an old song ", and having found among the pictures " a most exquisitely indecent Venus late the property of a parson "— which seemed hardly decorous in a chaste spinsters' establishment. He had dined out to meet the Eastlakes, Lady Dufferin, now " terribly altered and aged ", Thackeray, " who is a rude, vulgar person quite destroyed by success of late " and Edwin Landseer " who sang charmingly ".

The topic most often recurring in his letters at this time (apart from that of Walter) was one that absorbed the interest of many reflective people : the question of the doctrine and authority of the Church of England. The Anglican waters, once so calm, were still rippling from the splash of the stones cast in by the Tractarians ; and now other pebbles were being cast in showers by their successors, the Ritualists and Anglo-Catholic clergy. The Gorham Case shook many Anglican minds. Bishop Philpotts of Exeter, a sound High Churchman, refused to institute to a charge in his diocese a clergyman, Mr. Gorham, whose views on Baptismal Regeneration were heterodox, being Calvinistic in tendency, and, in the Bishop's view, enough to disqualify their holder from the privileges of the Anglican priesthood. Gorham appealed, without success, to the Arches Court of Canterbury ; then to the Privy Council whose judgement was given in his favour. This decision, clean against episcopal authority and given by a lay body, caused dismay, and was a reason, or excuse, for many conversions to Rome ; it influenced Manning's change of allegiance. There is, nearly always, during an epidemic of Roman fever, one such event to precipitate the crisis. Lockhart reported to Hope that the Bishop of London, with other two Bishops, was defending Gorham, and that the Queen had expressed pleasure at this attitude. " This is bad news—very. I apprehend very serious results." The Queen made no pretence of impartiality ; she was, indeed, one of the most determined opponents of the Catholic revival in the Church. Her own innate Protestantism was fostered by the Prince Consort's Lutheran—or liberal-German-intellectual mode of belief. Her visits to Scotland developed, with little difficulty, her liking for Presbyterian austerity of worship, and it might not be improper to see in her a resemblance to Lockhart's grandmother, who, years before, had stated, with reference to little Johnny's Episcopal baptism, that Episcopalians with their crosses and abominations were little better than Papists.

In the summer of 1850 Manning sent a letter of protest to his Diocesan, the Bishop of Chichester ; " and must, I think," wrote Lockhart, " cut our Establishment at last ". He told Croker of meeting the Bishop of Oxford (Wilberforce) at dinner and finding him reticent and " very shy " about the Gorham question, but admitting that Manning's letter would demand an answer. " If Manning be at all consistent, he can't stay in the Church, which of course S. O. [Samuel Oxon.] has no intention of leaving."

The part Queen Victoria played in the drama of church reform during her reign has never been fully discussed, but is too large a subject for development here. A homelier and more amiable aspect of her is revealed in a little batch of letters, from Lockhart to Charlotte, which might be called " The Story of the Queen's Dogs ".

This began with Her Majesty's reading the *Life of Scott*, and being filled with a desire to possess a Border Terrier or Dandie Dinmont, like Scott's own Peppers and Mustards. Sir Edwin Landseer consulted Lockhart on the matter ; Lockhart himself cherished a terrier : " a very desirable little creature ", devoted to her master and compelling him to take healthy exercise. He investigated possible puppies. There was one at Huntly Burn—but not quite up to standard. Lady Scott offered to give up her pet—" but as it has silky hair, it can't be of the true breed ". It was not until the following February (1851) that he could report to Charlotte that Francis Scott had come to stay with him, bringing " a pair of most charming pepper pups four months old of clear descent from the Abbotsford race ". They were collected by Landseer who conveyed them to Windsor ; and his report, to Lockhart, of that final episode, was passed on to Charlotte.

" Sir Edwin Landseer . . . had taken the doggies to Windsor . . . and on being introduced told the Queen that they were in their basket in the corridor. She instantly ran out and began to open the hamper. He said, ' Take care, Madam, they have been dressed with a little oil and brimstone.' ' Pooh,' said she. ' What signifies that ? ' and so she took out one, and said : ' Oh ! a dog I see,' then the other, ' Oh ! a girl.' She then caressed both so skilfully that they began to run about after her and she went for the children who joined in enjoyment of the new plaything, as did Albert when he came in, by and bye, for luncheon. After that, the Queen said she knew not which to choose, they were both so charming, and L. said it was designed to place both at her feet. She said it was too much—but she would give Mr. F. Scott on return a couple of pups of whatever kind he chose from her own stock. I was asked by L. to write this to Frank, and did so. So ends the little play of Pepper and Mustard "—and one of the most endearing anecdotes of that somewhat but not always formidable Majesty of England. " We gave them before delivery the names of Master Ettrick and Miss Yarrow." A complete chronicle of Sir Walter Scott and his dogs would not end at Abbotsford, but continue, through his granddaughter's much-loved Ginger and Lockhart's pet and companion, to the small lady and gentleman who found so illustrious a home and mistress at Windsor.

Walter's tangled affairs were now in the hands of an agent, Holt, with whom Lockhart was in close touch for the next three years. Charlotte went abroad, to Germany, with her husband, to regain strength. Lockhart wrote to her frequently : sometimes the briefest of notes : " I write merely that you may have no excuse for not writing, for I have no news " ; he must talk and be talked to, even if only on paper. More often, there was a bagful of news. There was criticism of the conversation-group of Scott and his friends by Thomas Faed, whom Lockhart liked : " He . . . is a modest youngster, and I think his work pleasing as a composition . . . but the whole carries no air of reality to one who knew all the characters." The proportions were out of scale : " Old Mackenzie seems a bigger man than Sir Walter who could almost have put him in his pocket ", James Ballantyne " a little, stumpy citizen " appeared " a lanky, lathy Werter ". But to later observers " I daresay the scene will be as correct as the one of Johnson and his cronies at Sir J. Reynolds' dinner-table ".

Church-gossip continued to be lively : a rumour of Henry Wilberforce's having gone over to Rome, of Manning's being " on the eve of the same step ", and that " the Pope might entertain fair hopes of the Bishop of Brechin (Forbes) ". This was the much-loved Alexander Penrose Forbes, one of the greatest of nineteenth-century Scots bishops, who was deeply influenced by Tractarian teaching. His *Charge to his Clergy on Eucharistic Doctrine* was

censured by his fellow-bishops, who decreed that it must
not be accepted as the official teaching of the Church in
Scotland. But Forbes spoke truth and the truth has endured
in that Church's worship.

"Tell me what you are at liberty to say of these matters—
if indeed you know anything," Lockhart added. Charlotte
and her husband were of the High Church party, and
Manning was a close friend. Hope especially had his ear
to the ground about all those affairs.

By way of light relief he had a good story of a shooting-
party at Balmoral, concerning a guest, Sir J. Russell, who
was far from expert with a rifle. "The ranger took him,
without any fatigue, within 25 yards of 14 very fine harts
. . . and the result was no harm to one"; on which the
ranger commented : "What could make the Queen choose
sae wauf a bit body? If you could tie up a stag by the head,
and let him come and fire away for a fortnight, maybe he
might kill it at last."

There was also an art-story, told him by Chantrey, about
a Colonel's widow "who came, all tears and no hair, to
order a statue" of her late husband ; came again, without
the cap, to suggest a bust instead ; then came a third time,
"escorted by a Captain", to say that "a tablet with a
profile would suit her better". *Sunt lacrymae rerum*—but
not always unquenchable.

It was a difficult period in the Anglican Church ; many
were alienated by official coldness, and there was a stream
of converts to Rome. Lockhart thought one of Murray's
sisters would follow Manning when he went over. Popular
anti-Popish feeling was roused by the restoration of the
Roman hierarchy in England ; in Protestant eyes, an act of
aggression, and, in the view of some Catholics, inopportune.
Lockhart reported a friend's account of a visit to Arundel,
where the Duke of Norfolk's chaplain and many of his
guests had been openly anti-Wiseman, deploring Pius IX's
weakness in granting to "Wiseman's personal ambition
and vanity what the old English Catholics by no means
wished for" and the result of which might "be to throw
them back for 50 years".

There was a rumour—it came from Murray, that Richard

Doyle of *Punch* (" the man of most originality on the line—
witness : *Manners and Customs of the English* ") had been
threatened with excommunication, by Wiseman, if he continued to work for " the anti-papal Punch ". A meeting
of shareholders voted " for war to the knife ", and Doyle
" was forced to resign "—which meant " a great loss to
Punch and Judy and to us ". A little later, in 1851, Lockhart commented : " It strikes me as odd that no one has
ever alluded to the fact that we had no trouble with Rome
till we lost Hanover." This occurred on the accession of
the Queen—who could not succeed to the throne of Hanover
because of the Salic Law. " Till then, the King of Hanover's
minister at Rome was, in fact, our minister also." Now,
there was only an attaché to Florence " attached *sub rosa*
to Rome " and so " an end of the relations that subsisted
between George IV and the Papal power when they ex-
changed pictures and other courtesies, and we see the fruit ".

Croker, that most ardent of anti-Catholics, was at work
on another liturgical article, which appeared in July, and
was extremely Crokerish : " Neither the clergy nor the
people at large would tolerate these superstitious practices "
of ritual and devotion, now that " all the most eminent and
distinguished among the first practitioners and partisans of
these innovations have thrown off the mask . . . by passing
over into the Roman camp ". He talked of " Jesuistical
dealing " and " accommodating faith ", demanding a
return to " the decent seriousness and sober splendour of
the Anglican Church ". He, and others, ignored the fact
that two of the greatest of the original Tractarians and of
English Churchmen, Pusey and Keble, remained faithful to
the Church of their baptism, and cultivated always " that
decent seriousness and sober splendour ".

Newman's secession was the first and heaviest blow to
the Anglo-Catholics ; another came this year, in 1851 when,
on Passion Sunday, Manning was received into the Roman
Communion, at the Jesuit Church in Farm Street. With
him went his friend James Hope. In the following Whit-
suntide Charlotte followed her husband. Lockhart had
long foreseen the probability of this step. It hurt him
deeply, as it must always hurt those of Anglican loyalty

when others renounce that allegiance ; but he wrote to them both wisely and tenderly :

" My dear Hope, I thank you sincerely for your kind letter. I had clung to the hope that you would not finally quit the Church of England, but am not so presumptuous as to say a word more on that step, as respects yourself who have not, certainly, assumed so heavy a responsibility without much study and reflection. As concerns others I am thoroughly aware that they may count upon any mitigation which the purest intentions—the most generous of tender feeling on your part can bring. I trust that this, the only part of your conduct that has ever given me pain, need not, now or ever, disturb the confidence in which it has been of late a painful consolation to live with my son-in-law." Charlotte's decision affected him still more, but it brought an end of anxiety, and meant there could be no need for " mitigation ". He wrote to her : " I shall say nothing more but that I hope and pray what you have done may prove beneficial to your comfort and happiness. That is my only concern. It can in no way affect my feelings to Hope, nor, most surely, towards you."

His diary for Sunday, 6th April, recorded : " At night, letter from Hope. He and Manning have this day been received into the Church of Rome. Eheu ! " On May 19th he noted a dinner-party at the Hopes', where the guests included three priests : Dr. Döllinger, a Jesuit and a priest from Munich. He was prepared for the event of Whitsunday, but his entry for that day has been blotted out. He told Croker briefly, on May 20th : " I am very far from well, and my daughter has romanized."

There was no break in the mutual affection between him and his children ; only sometimes a hint of sadness, sometimes of impatience when he found the atmosphere of their home over-Roman, as is the way with converts. " I saw Manning the other day in the street," he told Croker. " He looks much better in health, and very gay in spirits, and has been, for some time, staying with the Hopes who are living in a round of Catholic festivities so that I see little of them."

Writing to John Wilson, with whom at this time he

resumed a correspondence, he spoke of Hope's conversion as " my son-in-law's aberration " as " a painful one, chiefly on account of Charlotte, and the various risks of discomfort she has before her—not least, the inevitable clinging and creeping of priests. At present, she is a sound Anglican, and like all his other connections is quite sound. But the effects of constant society and sympathy—who can venture to say how these may be developed."

Manning he rightly thought to be " next, if not equal to Newman for importance as a pervert, his influence very great in society at large, as well as among the younger clergy. He is a very agreeable and polished gentleman—a fine, ascetical coxcomb and tuft-hunter, the image of a Jesuitical Cardinal of the sixteenth century . . . I expect him to be followed by a long train of ladies, including probably, the Duchess of Buccleuch and Lady Lothian."

Lockhart's opinion of Manning was to warm into friendship and liking ; they met, frequently, during J. G. L.'s last visit to Rome. He saw at the moment his less admirable side ; did not foresee the passion for social justice that makes Manning's memory beloved.

He was, however, much more concerned over the spread of agnosticism than over any advance of Popery. Miss Martineau startled him by her new book which no longer professed, as formerly, even a tepid Christianity, but denied " any deity but the law of matter . . . So flat an avowal of brute materialism had never appeared in English."

Miss Martineau took her revenge, after Lockhart's death, in asserting that Charlotte's conversion had broken their happy relationship.

His health was increasingly and depressingly bad. Gleig wrote of him, afterwards, that for a long time he was living on bread and butter and became thin to emaciation. He was aged by grief and anxiety ; and suffered from many maladies—rheumatic trouble, and an affection or inflammation of the mucous membrane among them. About this time, too, he had an attack of cholera which greatly weakened him ; and suffered from shock, after being knocked down by a cab. The thought of retirement may have been in his mind when, in January 1851, he wrote to

Croker about a new contributor who might give more help in future to *The Quarterly*. This was the Rev. Whitwell Elwin who held a living in Norfolk :

" I don't take him to be deeply read, nor to be a man of great original talents ; but he is apt and handy, and with practice is likely to be a popular writer—that is when he has got rid of some academical pomposity, and the sin of writers and preachers—that of explaining things that all but boys and clowns easily comprehend." Elwin was a Cambridge man, with " a Cantab's general science in which I am wholly deficient ", and was a sound Churchman " untinged either with Puseyism or Puritanism ".

The 1850's saw the slow advance of the Prince Consort in popular esteem, and the creation of his dream—the Crystal Palace Exhibition. Lockhart respected him—with an ironic twist in his expression of approval ; but he did not approve of royal book-borrowing. The volume in question, not named, but described to Croker as by " an acolyte of Whateley's ", and as " a very silly mass of blunders and confusions ", was borrowed by Sir Edwin Landseer for the Prince " who had heard about the book but didn't like to send for it "—quite in the manner of many borrowers of less exalted rank ; and who, after such manner, kept the book : " To pay the 7/- I had paid for my copy was below the consideration of either Sir E. L. or his patron ; rather funny to be thus victimized in 3 half-crowns."

He was in Scotland, as usual, in the late summer of '51, and then in France, visiting the châteaux of the Loire : " a magnificent country, new to me, and more interesting than any part of France I had before visited ". He found among the Tourangeaux a good deal of sympathy with the Legitimist Pretender to the Throne—Henri V ; but also a realistic acceptance of the probable rule of Louis Napoleon, as " a Prince with a certain sort of show . . . but still the servant of the people "—to be discarded at the will of the people. His exaltation as Emperor was still beyond the popular idea.

This tour was a good tonic ; but he was far from well : " nor, I think ever likely to be so again. One crack is no sooner mended than another opens—but so be it. Enjoy youth, health and affection and friendship while they last. To me Abbotsford, even with you in it," he told Charlotte, " must always be a mournful spot." He begged her not to keep any news from him if she had it ; even the worst, about Walter, " could be no worse than what he was ". That autumn and winter found him in wretched condition, with a form of blood poisoning for which arsenic was prescribed.

There was some happy gossip, however. John Murray III was building a villa at Wimbledon, and John IV entered this world in December. In January '52 Lockhart described to Charlotte his christening at 50 Albemarle Street : " A party of twenty-seven or eight dined with Maria in the remoter room behind the dining-room, but all gathered round the great table for the speeches and toasts which were superb. A paper-maker gave John IV with all the honours—a printer John III—a book-binder gave the ' immortal memory of the illustrious John II '." And so the continuance of " the dynasty " was assured, and in the house where his father had seen Scott and Byron meet, this very young John was made a Christian, under the sad, kind gaze of Scott's son-in-law and Murray's strongest link with the golden past.

In one letter—about Thomas Hamilton, once the Lockharts' tenant at Chiefswood, J. G. L. recalled sadly his youthful and broken friendship with Hamilton's distinguished brother, Sir William, the scholar and philosopher. Thomas, " a very handsome, fine, gay fellow, and much a favourite with all classes in Scotland " was the author of a " clever novel, *Cyril Thornton*, and of *A History of the Peninsular War*, and a book of travel in America ; he had died, twelve year's before, of palsy, and now that disease had taken hold of Sir William—as of John Wilson, his rival, long ago, for the Chair of Ethics in Edinburgh.

" I saw him " (Wilson) " a week ago in very poor plight, and never expect to see him again . . . Sir William thought Sir Walter had been influenced by men to excite Lord Melville's interference with the Edinburgh baillies in John Wilson's behalf, and the Bart, already cooled, could never forgive this."

From 1850 to 1852 the estrangement with Walter deepened. The poor prodigal would not say : " I will arise and go to my father." A gulf of pride lay between them.

" There is no dealing with such madness," Lockhart commented ; and, to Charlotte : " Holt . . . rather tends in your charitable direction. Paris is better, if he has really gone there, than Boulogne." Charlotte was unwell, and her father was anxious about her and her new hopes of a child. " May 1851 use us all better than 1850 has done. *Exit. Valete, non plaudite, iubeo* "—so he ended his last letter of the old year.

" As to Walter, his neglect of so many of my letters—one or two of them very serious ones—has utterly sickened and cooled me. He may write again without extracting, in his turn, a reply . . . It is very obvious that he has no feeling but for himself, and I can only hope what he is enduring now may tend to break down by degrees, the abominable hardness wrought by vice." Letters came for Walter, " in, I think, a female, certainly a foreign hand, with post-mark Aix la Chapelle ".

Charlotte was trying to take her mother's place, with much of her mother's tenderness and gentle wisdom in her ; but even she could not reach and bring back Walter. Had Sophia lived, she might have ended or prevented the estrangement ; but it is vain conjecture.

The steady discipline of work had its comfort ; and there was " laughter and the love of friends ", with plenty of the salt of gossip : about a wedding where " all the party looked as if it were a hanging " ; of the new Crystal Palace that : " It is like a ropery, and Albert's taste—the decoration is, I think, very bad and small— all twinkle, twinkle little star in blue, green and yellow." There was a popular song, much whistled by the butchers' boys : " I met her in the Crystal halls." Lockhart went one day, towards the end of the Exhibition—" but the squeeze and steam were such that I couldn't stay 5 minutes . . . I imagine 130,000 in one day, and with hardly an exception, all the lowest of the Bull family."

Croker was ill and Lockhart called to find him " to all

appearance as robust as an elephant, but grumbling and growling as a tiger "—which is an excellent description of the usual male convalescent.

There were difficulties at Albemarle Street. John Murray was " sick of Croker ", and Croker was " exceedingly jealous that he is supposed to be falling off in his mental vigour which I see no sign of . . . These annoyances are more, added to domestic afflictions, than I am well able to bear."

In 1851 a Life of Wordsworth, by his nephew Christopher, appeared : " I fear it is clumsily executed—but the opening chapters contain some very striking specimens of W's early letters. . . . *The Prelude* . . . I confess . . . much disappointed me. I found it, on the whole, heavy, and what there is of life, in far greater proportion strong, rhetorical declamation than poetry. But I fear I may have outlived any degree of capacity for feeling poetry that I ever had— albeit not much." This was in a letter to Wilson, part of the renewed, brief correspondence that was friendly, almost affectionate, and nostalgic for the past ; but which ended in disagreement, though not in personal acrimony, over Wilson's endeavour to thrust upon *The Quarterly* a virulent article on Wordsworth. Lockhart, in spite of finding *The Prelude* heavy going, kept the solid admiration for Wordsworth that he had in youth. For all his " arrogant chillness " Wordsworth had " a manliness . . . that separates him from R. S. [Robert Southey] . . . Or is it that the one was really a great poet, the other not—the one's conceit, in short, based on a really grand something . . . the other's erected on no similar foundation ? I cannot answer. What I know is that I liked W. W. and never liked R. S." But he remained tepid about the philosophy expressed in *The Prelude*. " It seems to be assumed that W. W. made some wonderful discovery—that Homer, Dante, etc., etc., lived and died without having had even a glimpse of . . . There is more exact observance of Nature implied in the epithets of the 2nd *Iliad* than declared in all W. W.'s tomes."

But he condemned Wilson's vituperation :
" Yours of yesterday beat all cock-fighting. But you

have sickened me about W. W. *in toto* . . . Could one make *The Q.R.* talk of W. W. as the fat ugly cur, for instance ? " and in a later note : " Since you are really serious I must return your sheets, and I do so now (tho' most sorrowfully). . . . I certainly could never venture to produce such an article in *The Q.R.* . . . You see, I send back everything. I have not mentioned, nor shall I mention a word about you having communicated with me on this topic, to anybody."

It was the end, or very nearly so, of an old song of friendship—though the two were to meet once more before death took them. About this time too came the last echo of an old enmity : when Lockhart reviewed Cockburn's *Life and Letters of Lord Jeffrey*. He commented to Croker that : " the locality of all his views with the Scotch of his style are to me among the alleviations of the book." He was startled by the indiscretions of the letters ; Jeffrey had had his *affaires de cœur*, chiefly with the wives of his friends : " About 20 years ago he was all but blown up in consequence of his liaison with one of these ladies, and I should have expected the husband at least to have shown more sense now. . . . I never read a biography in which religion was passed so completely *sub silentio*. Plenty of Presbyterian Kirk politics, but not from first to last the remotest allusion to either the beliefs of Christianity or its moral influence. I fancy the whole set [of Whigs and *Edinburgh Reviewers*] were really most thorough infidels, and S. [Sydney] Smith at the top of them in that respect as in all others."

Lockhart spent August of 1852 at Milton Lockhart, visiting the local gentry : the Seton Steuarts of Allanton, the kindred Lockharts of Cambusnethan, the Hamiltons of Dalzell ; and sent word of a marriage : " Jemmy Campbell of Dalserf aged 47 has been asked in marriage by his minister's sister, a strapping lass of 19, and he has consented." An " on-coming " wench ! Even more forward was the lady, cousin of the Hosiers of Mauldslie, the estate neighbouring Milton, " who invaded the house every other day at luncheon, and I really should not be surprised if the captain were to be entrapped—for never was such impudence and pertinacity in the siege of an old simpleton ".

During this holiday he wrote, occasionally to Elwin ; once enclosing something that had been declined by Elwin— possibly a cheque for some work done for *The Quarterly* which J. G. L. insisted on paying : " I would fain have encouragement not to be shy about asking your help again." He wrote of his last meeting with Wilson : " Very much better in all respects than I had left him in October or November. He is lame, and paralysis has left its mark on his mouth . . . but his mind was clear and strong as of old, and moreover his spirits and temper seemed to be in a satisfactory condition."

Had Lockhart lived, there might have been a long, and amusing intimate correspondence with his successor ; the letters he wrote to Elwin are not lacking in spice. In one there is a pleasant story about Wordsworth, who was never allergic to his own compositions :

" W. W. at Abbotsford alledged his weak eyes as a reason for not joining Sir W. S. and others in some ride, and remained at home with only Miss Wordsworth his daughter. On returning after 4 or 5 hours we found him in the same attitude we had left him, at the fireside in the library, the lady reading to him *The Excursion*."

Referring to a recent best-seller soon to become a classic, J. G. L. wrote—in October '52 : " If you should, like the rest of men, be taking much interest in *Uncle Tom's Cabin*, I do hope that very clever but very exaggerated and unskilful work might afford a capital opportunity for you."

There was still no letter from Walter ; but he appeared to have kept in touch with his sister and brother-in-law ; for on October 3rd James Hope wrote to him from Tunbridge Wells : " Charlotte had a daughter late last night and both are well. We are glad to see that your father is pleased about you and your plans for Italy." There may have been a brief revival of promise. Lockhart told Croker on the 4th of October : " I know it will give you much pleasure to hear that my girl had a girl on Saturday night, and that all seems to be going well with both."

This little daughter, baptised Mary Monica and known as Mamo, was of more importance than even her mother,

MILTON LOCKHART
From a photograph

bearing her after so many disappointments, or her grandfather realised. She alone, of Charlotte's babies, survived
her mother, and lived to make a link in the chain of succession at Abbotsford.

It was a great joy to Lockhart. " Your telegram came to
me fast asleep at midnight on Saturday night," he told
Hope, " and cost me a night's rest, but I didn't grudge
that . . . I will run down to see my children as soon as
you think I may safely see the one I conceived a certain
affection for some time ago."

About the baby's names he wrote : " I suppose your
selection of Monica has also reference to the history of Kent ?
At all events Mary Monica sounds charmingly." The
reference to Kent is a little puzzling. Was he, perhaps,
confusing St. Augustine of Canterbury with the earlier Saint
of Hippo who was the son of St. Monica ?

In September 1852 the Duke of Wellington died—an
almost legendary figure ; and Lockhart described some of
the funeral pomps. The procession would reach from the
Horse Guards to St. Paul's. Dean Milman had a heavy
load of preparation on his shoulders. Lockhart expected
to see the " envoi " from the windows of Albemarle Street ;
" but headache forbade, and the day has been the greatest
I can remember. I hope all may go over without loss of
life."

In December, he told Croker that he must go over to
France, in miserable anxiety about Walter. His first letter
of 1853, to Charlotte, told of his visit and return. William
had gone with him, and been kind and helpful " among
the many troubles that perplexed me out of life . . . We
at last contrived to see the young man and his attendant off
in the train for Lyons . . . He is certainly better in health,
and to the last spoke of his views and purpose in a satisfactory
way enough, but alas, the weakness of character is so
obvious that hope can find but slender footing . . . I envy
the hearing of M. M.'s prattle and rattle."

The hope was indeed fragile. Only a week later he was
summoned back to Paris by a doctor's telegram, and went
over at once, by night mail, with Holt. He was home again
in twelve days, by the 19th : all turmoil quenched in death.

Walter had come to the end of his vagrancy, and Lockhart once more mourned the loss of a son : but this time with bitterness in his grief, and not the tenderness with which he had mourned for Johnny. He had arrived in time to see his son and be recognised by him.

" It is a consolation that forgiveness and reconciliation preceded the close of that unhappy career. Even during his last delirium he never ceased to hold conversation with me as if present, and seemed to be constantly drawing comfort from the sense that we had exchanged estrangement for a renewal of natural feeling."

Walter died at Versailles, in a hotel. The people were kind ; he would seem to have stayed with them before, and to have returned to them " as a sort of friends when he found himself smitten at Fontainebleau ". Of his fatal illness there are no details told : a return, perhaps, of the fever that so nearly ended his days at Norwich.

It was a week of unspeakable grief for Lockhart ; with " the infinite difficulties which the French law imposes in the case of a foreigner dying in that country . . . Your poor brother sleeps close by the entrance of the Versailles cemetery, on the left hand at entering, and a modest stone will, ere another week passes, mark the spot." There was one final infliction of agony. The day of Walter's funeral— attended only by his father and Holt, was also that of the wife of the Mayor of Versailles, which was attended by the whole town in all the sombre amplitude of " *pompes funaibres* " [*sic*] of French custom. It was a day of driving rain. Walter's coffin had no sooner been laid in earth than the grave-diggers departed to assist at that other interment, which lasted for two hours. Holt had to return to the town to settle various matters of business ; Lockhart stayed alone, by his son's open grave, these two hours, with the rain beating upon him : with thoughts and memories he could not tell, even to Charlotte. But the little, beautiful son of so long ago, Sophia's darling Watt, must have been vivid in his mind and heart ; the brilliant boy of those holidays at Brighton and Rokeby and Milton ; the son who was laird of Abbotsford, who should have carried on the name of Scott, who could remember Sir Walter in the days when

294

Abbotsford was still a place of sunshine. It was all over now, the pride and joy, the anger and the estrangement.

> Be faithful to the dead,
> The dead cannot deceive

—or hurt us any more, by folly.

There must still be the sad business of disposing of Walter's possessions : some to be kept, others, clothes and the like, to be given to " persons having some claim on my feelings in reference to my poor boy ". Mrs. Hughes sent him a picture of Walter as a boy. " It breaks my heart to recall the date. It is of the sweet, innocent happy boy. Oh God ! how soon that day became clouded and how dark its early close. Well, I suppose there is another world—if not, sure this is a blunder."

Years before, he had quoted in an article, and, more recently in his diary, the Chinese saying that the three greatest miseries a man could suffer were : to lose, in youth, his father ; in middle age, his wife ; in old age, his son. He had been spared only the first. As years count, in modern estimate, he was not yet beyond middle age—58. But life had been laden for him with many cares, and his years were increased.

Charlotte was her brother's heiress, and became lady of Abbotsford. She and her husband added the name of Scott to that of Hope. Lockhart wrote to wish " that the name about to be assumed by you may henceforth be associated with nothing but prosperity and happiness. I can look to no other source of comfort, and am grateful that I can look to it with so much confidence " ; and again " I address you by your new name, hoping it may be attended henceforth with more prosperity than has been the case for a long while, and that it may be transmitted to your lineage."

His words to Charlotte, in telling her of those last days in Versailles, are among the most moving and revealing he ever wrote :

" My dear and now only child, bear up, and learn to endure evil which is the staple of this mortal life."

He had endured his full share. The darkest shadow had lifted now. There could never be happiness for him, but there was comfort in the new life at Abbotsford, in the tenderness to be found there. He had still some " laughter and the love of friends " ; much love, and a little laughter, for his own wit did not die. There was still loneliness, he was essentially a lonely man ; there was ill health with suffering of body ; but the brief way he had to follow before the end was as untroubled as love and kindness and his own courage could make it.

Chapter 21

ROME, AND HOME, AND PEACE
AT THE LAST

H E knew, by the beginning of 1853, that he could not, much longer, carry the burden of office. " It is now 28 years since I became Editor," he wrote to Croker, in April, " and in all that time there has occurred no sort of difference between Albemarle Street and myself. Indeed, now that I look back I feel that my course as a literary man has been remarkably smooth in one important respect "—his relations with his publishers. His intention to retire was a shock to Murray, who was " quite at sea about the selection of a successor ". There was a suggestion of only partial retirement ; his finances must be considered. Between editing *The Quarterly* and contributing reviews he had been accustomed to earn fully £1,500 ; his post in the Duchy of Lancaster brought in another £400. But he had enough money " to float me over a few years "; and he would be glad to be free.

" Even you, I think, cannot have more than a dim conception of the worry of the editorial correspondence. How many of my days have been spent in concocting roundabouts and white lies. Great indeed is my wonder how I got over these things in my early period before any authority could have been derived from experience. And yet I do think that among other changes of manner among us, there is now a degree of conceit and presumption in young men that did not often show itself a while ago in the letters of contributors. Whoever the next real editor may be, I can promise him anything but a cushion of roses."

There was a further reference to Elwin : " I believe when you meet him you will be very favourably impressed."

He spent the summer in Scotland ; and in October set forth, with his old friend Hay, for Rome. They sailed to Elba : a small island, poor, but clean in aspect, with Napoleon's palace : " not so big as Huntly Burn, and its garden abounding only in cannon and balls ". Arrived

297

in Rome, they were installed in an apartment in the Via Gregoriana ; Lockhart's courier served as houseman, with a boy to help, and a man coming in to cook, twice a day. " Hay very kind indeed, but very noisy, fussy, fidgetty." Rome was very quiet, before the winter season began. Fanny Kemble and her sister Adelaide Sartoris, the singer, were there, and with them one of the pleasantest of Lockhart's friendships was begun. He saw a doctor, who confirmed his own doctor's diagnosis that he was not suffering " from any distinct disease unless irritability of the mucous membrane, but rather from a general decadence of the vital powers, and I don't think his expectations of recovery are high ". He was tired ; some days prostrate, but on others able to enjoy walking or driving about Rome.

Charlotte sent gossip about a ball, and in return he reported a Beatification—of " one Bobola, I think a Polish Jesuit, murdered by the Russians 100 years ago ". He thought Pio IX looked " very comfortable, blessing away right and left between lines of French soldiers who seemed to pay little attention to the concern ".

It was the old Rome of the temporal power, with the Pope as sovereign, though not yet pronounced infallible : a Rome at once profoundly Italian and widely cosmopolitan. English visitors were beginning to arrive—in such numbers that there was almost an English city within Rome. Lockhart loved Rome—and sometimes hated it ; and his letters are a piquant mixture of his varying moods and emotions. Rome's faults were—and are—obvious ; her fascination was, and is irresistible. Above all she had life, and Lockhart even in his own failing vitality, adored life. He could sit in the stalls, now, and enjoy the spectacle.

Physically he began to feel some benefit ; he was stronger, and had a better appetite : " With eggs and fish I breakfast well, and with soup and fish dine tolerably ; meat not yet within my reach exactly, though once I did contrive to deal with part of a cold partridge." But he found Roman cooking rather bad ; one dinner, with a Colonel and Mrs. Caldwell, rich Anglo-(or Scottish)Indians, was splendid but tasteless, except for one merit, " the first good wine I have met with in Rome ".

Presently he was able to make an excursion to the site of Horace's Sabine farm. He had never seen " a more delicious bit of country. The ruins are nothing—at least a chaise box might convey them all off—but I have no doubt the spot is genuinely Horatian." They slept at Tivoli, returning to Rome after two days. Encouraged by this experience he hired a horse, and rode for two or three hours every day. The time was wintry only in cold—a bright, clear cold—with no bleakness of aspect, and he enjoyed the crisp air.

Adelaide Sartoris and Fanny Kemble took him driving in the Campagna. He found the former a most delightful companion—" her course of life having been one not imagined by me "—with its background of theatre and concert-hall, with music, rather than literature, the mainspring of her interests. She was a vivid creature whose charm and beauty have left something of a legend, and Lockhart yielded gladly to her spell : there was kindness in it, for he enjoyed her talk and reminiscences with " a marvellous though not at all harsh or uncharitable frankness ". He found her " worth 500 Fanny Kembles, even in talent "—but he had never greatly appreciated this, his second kind hostess and companion.

He met the Brownings too, and liked Robert, finding him refreshingly unlike a poet ; Mrs. Browning did not attract him. He was bored by her.

Thackeray took his daughters to Rome, that winter, and Anne Thackeray (Lady Ritchie) has left a clear picture of the society of the time, and a vivid one of Lockhart himself whom she saw, waiting in the carriage, for Mrs. Sartoris :

" He looked very ill, very noble, like a brooding solemn eagle, silent and mysterious. He was wrapped in a cloak and wore some soft travelling cap. I only saw his profile and the pale, clear-cut features . . . The incident, trifling as it was, impressed me. The sick man, the great Campagna waiting for him, the good and loving company, the glorious warmth of land and sky I shall never forget."

Among the artists in Rome was the future Lord Leighton, then young but by no means impoverished, enriching his knowledge of classical antiquity and no doubt preparing in his mind those opulent and respectable scenes he was to present to an approving public. Lady Shelley, whose husband was kin to the poet, and who was herself among the Duke of Wellington's close friends, spent that winter in Rome ; and found Lockhart one of the very few fellow-countrymen of any intellectual stimulus. English society in Rome she found formidably dull ; and on a later visit sadly missed Lockhart. Among the most noble visitors was the Duke of Northumberland, with whom Lockhart and Hay dined every week.

" Our life is gay. We dine out 4 or 5 times a week . . . may, if we please, go to drums every night." At an Assembly in the Palazzo Doria he saw " some splendid beauties and more red stockings than I perhaps ever shall again ". The Roman Cardinals wore black, with only their stockings and piping of their cassocks in scarlet ; but Wiseman persisted in flaunting the full " red and all red of Wolsey ". Lockhart had little love for the English prelate ; he thought him flamboyant and vulgar. But he was impressed by his preaching : " Capitally he performed—good contrast with the donkeys of our Anglican Chapel." The Anglican preachers, indeed, he found " bitter bad ". A true Scot, he liked a good sermon well delivered, for the Scot enjoys preaching much as the Frenchman enjoys the play. He told Charlotte that he was in bad odour with the English colony because of this predilection for Roman sermons. At Christmas and New Year he enjoyed, above all, pleasures and celebrations " the divine music of the Church services every evening " ; on New Year's Eve hearing Vespers at St. Sylvester's, and on New Year's Day going to S. Gesu, where the Pope was present and the choir sang gloriously.

" I must add that my Protestant bigotries were forced to bow perpetually before the profound feeling of the humbler audiences " ; and in St. Peter's he was impressed by the attendance of the Cardinal Penitentiary to hear and absolve penitents whose sin was beyond the absolution of any other priest : " victims of awful remorse whose regular appearance at altars and modest misery of gesture were most touching ".

He was diverted by a family of newly-rich converts, who

established themselves in splendour in the Sermoneta Palace, and proceeded to force themselves upon a reluctant society " in a most portentous style of impudence ". One lady who declined their invitations was reproached by Cardinal Wiseman, " making her comprehend her error as an old Catholic in not opening her arms to a new one "—especially to one so opulent. The dinners given by those pushing converts were singularly poor, because the hostess in ordering them from " the Roman Gunter " enjoined economy. The couple had chosen as their bedroom the former ball room, 60 feet in length. Wiseman was lodged in the Sermoneta Palace, which made it, Lockhart remarked, " *un drôle de ménage* ". One can hear behind his letters the buzz of gossip and mockery.

One can also imagine, though dimly and fearfully, the glower of his late grandmother, who thought Episcopalians little better than Papists, could she have beheld his enjoyment of Popish company. He liked many of the priests, and in that winter found Manning a kind and congenial friend, and a gifted orator : " I am greatly pleased with his voice and actions. The latter I think the most graceful I ever saw in a pulpit performer." (Preaching was, after all, a performance, like a play.) Manning introduced him to Dr. Grant, head of the Scots College, and was full of attentions to him, making his days more pleasant. Another new friend among the clergy was Father William Lockhart ; a kinsman, descended from the Lockharts of Lee ; and like J. G. L. an Oxford man. " Lockhart of Exeter " had been one of the most brilliant of his generation ; a Tractarian whose conversion to Rome in the early '40's was said to have brought about Newman's. After being received, he entered the Institute of Charity as a postulant. He took Roman Orders, and after some years in Rome returned to England where his Institute opened a house, in Holborn. " A fine, handsome, amiable young man " J. G. L. found him ; and said the same of Fr. Herbert Vaughan, " another handsome, elegant, good-natured young English gentleman, gone the way of Cardinal Newman "— and like Manning, a future Cardinal, following Manning at Westminster.

Lockhart was now lodging in the Piazza di Spagna, even then very much the English quarter of Rome ; too English, indeed, for his taste. It might " be very well matched by any 3 or 4 crescents of Leamington or Torquay ". In that " Anglo-Rome " he suggested that Bishop Philpotts of Exeter " would do well for Pont. Max."—and that " there would be no difficulty to fill the place of Monsignor Talbot who looks like a natural—all but, and they say preached quite in that character his part in the late series at St. Andrea ". To what English cleric as facsimile of the Monsignor this back-hander was delivered we cannot tell ; its pleasant malice must suffice us.

Did Lockhart ever remember, as he walked in this loveliest of Roman places, that in a house at the foot of the Spanish Steps, where the flower-sellers offer their blossoms and the artists' models posed for hire, Keats had lived his last months and coughed his life out in the last agony : the apothecary's apprentice who had enriched English poetry with faery gold that would not vanish, and the treasure of enchanted lands beyond magic seas ? Did he ever visit the Protestant Cemetery where the fragile body had been laid to rest—or think at all of a poet dead, or of some cruel words written long ago ? It was all so long ago ; he had, afterwards, felt some contrition ; he had no knowledge that he was striking a dying man.

In spite of much weariness and weakness of body, and discontent with food and other difficulties, Lockhart was renewing some measure of his youth, in mental activity. He renewed his study of Italian, he began learning Hebrew " with an eye to Arabic, that is, in case I spend a season in the East before settling down at Hampstead or Watford ". Rome amused him. There were major excitements too. The passions and feuds of the mediaeval and Renaissance city were far from quiescent. Rome was not altogether anglicised into a health-resort. The sensation of January '54 was a conspiracy led by some young Romans of the prosperous bourgeoisie, of whom one, Castellani, in panic betrayed his comrades. They were now imprisoned in St. Angelo " with prospect of trial next week, and guillotine of course ". Castellani himself was " only in a straight

waistcoat ", driven mad by remorse. But he remained
" the hero of feminine sympathy ", being " the handsomest
lad of this town . . . also its best singer ".

Some old friends and neighbours from Lanarkshire, the
Menteiths, a Catholic family, were in Rome ; their stay
a sad one, for they fell victim to fever. One little girl
died, and Mr. Menteith was gravely ill. " Wm. Lockhart
(the priest) sees them daily, and lets me know daily." He
cherished that link with home.

In February and March he felt unsettled, his health
declining, his mind restless. He longed for home, though
his plans as to a permanent home for himself were still
uncertain. Amusement was more and more overcome by
discomfort and weariness. " There is nothing wholesome
or refreshing to be had in this infernal place, for love or
money. Wherefore may perdition attend the population
from Pio IX to the beggar on the stairs." These sentiments he expressed again, more pungently, in rhyme :

> Beds black with bugs—
> Monks fat as slugs—
> Beggars groaning—
> Thieves intoning—
> Leering models, louzy artists—
> Strutting, drumming Buonapartists—
> Mutton young, and stinking mullet—
> Wine sharp enough for Rossi's gullet :
> —Fancying these, make speed to Rome,
> Curse beef and beer, Law, Worth and Home.
> For me, I'd jump at once to hell
> Before returning. J. G. L.

(Rossi was the victim of a recent assassination.)

Before leaving Rome, in March, he resigned his sinecure
in the Duchy of Lancaster, and was touched and pleased
by the Prince Consort's decision that he should receive a
pension equal to his salary. " This is exceedingly gracious,
and will in no inconsiderable degree lighten my difficulties,"
he wrote to Hope.

In April he was writing to Charlotte from " my own chair
in my own room once more ". He had brought back a
medal of Pius IX and " sundry rosaries " for Mary Monica.
Soon there came sad news for him in the death of his friend

of his youth, John Wilson. They had, almost inevitably, drifted apart, but there had been no estrangement ; and the friendship had been renewed, in sad kindliness, before Lockhart went abroad. Ten years earlier, before Wilson's illness, Lockhart had written to him in words that might serve as valediction—and as expression of his own autumnal mood :

" As for any very lively interest in this life, that is out of the question with me as with you, and from the same fatal date, though I struggled against it for a while, instead of at once estimating the case completely as I think you did. [Wilson's wife, like Sophia, died in 1837.] Let us both be thankful that we have children not unworthy of their mothers. I reproach myself when the sun is shining on their young and happy faces as well as on the violets and hyacinths and bursting leaves, that I should be unable to awaken more than a dim and ghost-like semi-sympathy with them, or in anything present or to come, but so it is."

Their last meeting was at Woodburn, near Dalkeith, where Wilson was staying with his brother. Wilson's daughter describes her father as disciplined by sorrow to " a peaceful calm ; not violent grief but a deep solemnity ", whereas Lockhart " seemed to live with a broken heart, while all about him had a faded, dejected air ". He told her : " I would fain return to Edinburgh, to be cheered by some of your young, happy faces, but you would have to nurse me and be kind to me, for I am a weary old man, fit for nothing but to shut myself up and be sulky."

The two old friends spent some hours together, talking of bygone days, and parted in kindness. Wilson stood at the door watching Lockhart drive away. " He never saw him again."

The spring in London was occupied with arrangements for retiring. Murray was very reluctant to lose him ; but he could no longer carry the burden of duty.

He came to Milton Lockhart, in August, to be most kindly welcomed by William, and cared for by cousin Kate Lockhart. It was a delightful season : " warm, very warm, but a gentle breeze is keeping the leaves in motion all about, and the sun sheathed, as Wordsworth hath it, with a grey layer of cloud. . . . I am glad to fancy you all enjoying yourselves, including Lady D. [Davy] and sweet M. [Mary Monica] in this heavenly summer season." He quoted a sentence from Leonardo da Vinci's *Note-books*, in Beyle's translation : "*Le chagrin profond produit un sentiment de langueur générale, la chute des forces musculaires, la perte de l'appétit, la petitesse du pouls, le reserrement de la peau, la paleur de la face, le froideur des extrémités, un regard presque farouche,*" perhaps the best diagnosis of his own case that could be made. But his native air and the kind nursing effected some improvement. Charlotte sent game, and he reported himself living on grouse soup and curds and cream, and butter-milk, with " a kebbock procured from a renowned dairy, hard by, for my special benefit ". He was able to ride again, though aware of increasing feebleness of limb. Brother Bob was about to be married, which made a pleasant stir in the family ; but J. G. L. felt that the wedding would be better without " so ghastly a visage " as his was now. His next move would be to Abbotsford.

Charlotte and her husband were now settled there as laird and lady. James Hope-Scott's biographer (Robert Ornsby) has described their life, and the background of Catholic Abbotsford, already becoming a centre for the new Catholics of Scotland and England, and for some of the old " cradle Catholics " too. Newman had spent some weeks there in the winter of '52–'53. Hope-Scott's wealth did a great deal for the place ; he added a wing to the house, including a chapel and a study (where some of the preliminary work on this *Life* was done).

Charlotte was truly the child of both her parents ; with her mother's gentleness and gaiety she had inherited much of her father's scholarly mind, much of his gravity and reserve. She loved books, and had the gift of languages, early developed in her childhood. But the quality perhaps most evident in her maturity was that of an almost Religious self-discipline. She lived a life as orderly as a nun's, following a rule drawn up for her by Bishop Grant, of Southwark, and later by Manning. Her day began at six in the morning with her devotions ; and the duties and pleasures of every hour were regulated : the duties first—

her housekeeping, her correspondence—then her reading (she read a great deal of Italian poetry, Dante and Tasso), her drives and visits in the neighbourhood. Like the Virtuous Woman whose praise is in the Scriptures, she looked well to the ways of her house ; indeed that Lesson, which is read, in Scotland, on the Feast of St. Margaret would seem apt for her as for the saintly Queen. Like her she was charitable ; generous in alms-giving ; " making her inner life, as far as possible, that of a Religious ".

But she was neither dull nor priggish. Lockhart's letters to her alone prove, if indirectly and implicitly, that she had humour, was responsive to his wit and mischief, enjoyed the savour of worldliness. Their minds were flint and tinder between them.

The Abbotsford to which Lockhart returned, in the autumn of '54, was described (for Robert Ornsby, by a guest of that time) as " the most perfect type of a really Christian household . . . A religious atmosphere pervaded the whole house, and not only the guests, but the servants, must, it seems to me, have felt its influence. But, apart from that, there was so much genial hospitality, and every one was made to feel so completely at his ease."

To that gentle household Lockhart came home in the late autumn, very weary, in need of rest. At first he was able to drive about, visiting the well-loved places where his happy years had been lived, long ago, taking leave of them in his heart. His small granddaughter brought him a little gladness, though he had not the vitality to play with her as Scott had played with Charlotte when she used to invade his study. He was established in the little break-fast-room next to the dining-room where Scott had been brought, on his last return, and where he had died, lying in the great bay-window that looked over the meadow towards the river ; hearing " the sound, of all others most delicious to his ear, the gentle ripple of the Tweed over its pebbles ".

It was Martinmas now, " when the nights are lang and mirk ", and the thoughts and prayers of the living dwell especially with the departed. Lockhart's night was upon him. The mists were rising from Tweed, making the dear

306

landscape shadowy, and in his mind thought was misted, gently, by memories. The house was full of ghosts, no less loved and kindly than the living who cherished him. He had his own pictures of memory, and the pictures made for him by Sophia : of Scott, riding in the woods with Johnny, telling him the tales of Scotland's kings and people ; of Sophia and Anne running down to " the burn " to bring a reluctant bairn in to dinner ; of Johnny, grown fragile, in his little carriage, leading his pony that Walter and Charlotte rode in turns ; of Walter, sturdy and exuberant, a beautiful boy, running wild in house and garden ; of Charlotte, small and resolute, invading Scott's sacred privacy and totally disarming him with her murmured : " Dear Grandpapa " as she climbed on his knee. There were earlier memories—of his first visit, his meeting with Sophia in her radiant youth, of that night when they danced in the new rooms, under the new gas-lamps, until the sun came up and dimmed that modish light ; of the visits between Chiefswood and Abbotsford, the walks and picnic suppers in the summer of his life.

While he had yet a little strength of utterance, he sent a letter to Croker, by Charlotte's hand : " If there had been anything comfortable in my own condition, or, as far as I understand it, anything in yours, I should not have been at all likely to drop the correspondence that has been for so many years one of the chief and most regular amusements of my life . . . My usual state is that of the most complete, childish helplessness in body, and almost equally so in mind. I am not, however, aware that my reasoning soundness is disturbed unless by occasional medicine which often confuses my memory. . . . Between the decay of my own physical powers, and the temptation of the Hope-Scotts' being established in Scotland, I saw no reason for refusing myself the pleasure of being under the same roof with my nearest and dearest relations, not excluding Charlotte's baby, who is a particular delight to me. Even a short letter is a considerable exertion. My daughter will let me summon her assistance as amanuensis, some day soon again. Meantime, I suppose, enough has been said to leave you with the impression that it is not possible for any of my inspectors to have a humbler notion of my prospects than I have long myself been content with. Charlotte joins me in kind regards to Mrs Croker, and I hope that when our hands fail altogether, that theirs may still continue to maintain the usual offices betwixt the families."

The end came less than a week after this letter, of 19th November. He collapsed suddenly ; Cousin Kate was summoned, and Fr. William Lockhart was staying in the house. Lockhart lay in the little room that also looked on Tweed : the sound of the river in his ears, and, nearer, and more solacing, the murmur of prayer as Cousin Kate read the Office for the Dying, and intercession was made for the Christian soul about to depart. He was as comforted and as little lonely as any one can be in the approaching solitude of death.

On the 25th of November, 1854, he died ; leaving the shadows and symbols for the light and truth that lie beyond them. He was buried at the feet of Sir Walter, in the precincts of Dryburgh Abbey : two loyal and loving men of heart, together in peace.

Epilogue

LOCKHART'S MEMORY

CHARLOTTE AND ABBOTSFORD

Lockhart was well and kindly remembered. There was, and is, that " floating dislike " noted by Saintsbury ; but those who had truly known him, for whom his heart was not held in fetterlock, made a memorial of good words for him. Gleig's Memoir of him in *The Quarterly Review* [1] has already been used and quoted ; did no other study of Lockhart exist, it would suffice for the essentials of his personality and of the events of his life, for within its limits of length it is wholly admirable.

Another tribute to him in *The Quarterly*, which may have been by his successor, Elwin, is an equally sympathetic character-study. Like every intimate account of him, from Scott's onwards, this stresses the contrast between his reserve and his gentleness. Too often his shyness, his very modesty were interpreted as pride :

" Those whose acquaintance he was expressly invited to make would find no access allowed them to his mind, and go disappointed away, knowing only that they had seen one of the most interesting, most mysterious, but most chilling of men ". For such, for the world at large, he did keep his heart in fetterlock. But beneath the silence lay a profound humility, not incompatible with his keen and often caustic power of criticism.

" There were occasions also when . . . the point at issue was one . . . of the subtler shades of right and wrong ; and then the scorn on the lip and the cloud on the brow were but the prelude to the strong, wiry sentence—withering in its sarcasm, and unanswerable in its sense, which scattered all sophistry to the winds before it."

Without this dominating moral sense, he would have been " the most brilliant but the most dangerous of men ". With it, this genius of integrity, even had he been " a dunce

[1] *Q.R.*, October 1864, Vol. 116.

in attainment, or a fool in wit, he must still have been recognised as an extraordinary man ".

The point made by Gleig and Christie in their Oxford days, that Lockhart was merciless towards anyone wounded in vanity, but tender towards a real sorrow, was again noted : " Many will believe what caustic he was to a false grief ; few could credit what balm to a real one ". And one unique quality was seized : his power to touch " the hidden chord of romance in all ". When he left any company, shy, reserved, apparently cold as he might have been, " there was not one who did not confess that a being had passed before them who stirred all the pulses of the imagination, and realised what is generally only ideal in the portrait of a man ".

When Mrs. Gordon's *Life* of her father, John Wilson, was reviewed in *The Scotsman*, Mrs. Norton wrote to the Editor, recalling her own impressions and memories of Lockhart, and quoting his poem : *When Youthful Faith has Fled*.

" Those who peruse those touching and melancholy lines may perhaps think, with Mrs. Gordon, that a drearier sense of loss remained in that proud and reserved nature than is common even under a like bereavement, and that such a loss weighed heavier on one who repelled instead of courted sympathy, than on those whose more expansive tenderness can meet pity half-way, and in whom the sealed fountains of ' the waters of Marah ' can gush forth in facile and lamenting tears."

Lockhart won from the few but choice minds who knew his inner mind, more than he ever sought : love and trust and understanding, even reverence for one who was tender and true, humble and faithful of heart.

For a sympathetic modern estimate we may read : *A Retrospect*, written by the late Charles Whibley for the Centenary number of *Blackwood's Magazine* in April 1917 :

" The ardour of his mind was repressed and restrained. Yet the fire within burned the more fiercely because he never permitted it to grow into a blaze. . . . Lockhart . . . was incredibly wise and mature for his years. . . . He was a true scholar. . . . Some of his earliest essays in *Blackwood's Magazine* dealt with the classics in the only true spirit of criticism, as living poems." The reverse of that medal was that he " regarded the classics of his own time with an eye of envenomed disdain. He was not a prophet of literature ; he looked back more gladly than he looked forward."

Few, if any, critics are without prejudice, or unperturbed by the temper of their own day ; that of Lockhart's was that of unrestrained bitterness against all political and other adversaries. The marvel is, not that he was at times so ferocious, but that he was so often a wise and generous critic.

He has achieved some immortality ; he is worthy of a larger place in tradition.

In lives of to-day his blood flows, through Charlotte and her one living child, the only grandchild he knew. Other two children were born to Charlotte and her husband : a son, Walter Michael, in June 1857 ; a daughter, Margaret Anne, in September 1858. Both babies were delicate, and from her last confinement Charlotte did not recover. She was, besides, suffering from tuberculosis. She died on the 26th of October, 1858, and was buried in the vault of St. Margaret's Convent, Edinburgh. Before the end of the year her babies were laid beside her : the little girl dying on 3rd December, the little son on 11th December.

Her husband wrote, in reply to Gladstone's letter of sympathy : " I cannot write to you of her . . . without reference to that Church whose doctrines and promises she had embraced with a faith which made them the objects of sense to her ; whose teaching now moulded her mind and heart." Her memory has added to the spiritual treasury of Abbotsford, begun by the genius of its first laird, a gentleness that is very near holiness.

James Hope Scott married again, in 1861, the Lady Victoria Fitzalan Howard, daughter of the Duke of Norfolk. Of that marriage there were six children ; two died in childhood ; one son, James Fitzalan Hope (later Lord Rankeillor), and three daughters lived to maturity.

Queen Victoria visited Abbotsford in 1867, on a tour of the Borders, from Floors Castle. She saw the enlargements made by Hope Scott : the new hall, the study and chapel, the courtyard laid out as a garden with the screen of Gothic stonework dividing it from the rest of the garden, the embankment thrown up between house and highway. Her Majesty was offered an elegant collation of cake and wine, fruit and ices, but chose to partake only of a cup of tea and a slice of Selkirk bannock.

In 1870 Cousin Anne Scott came again to the house of so many memories, and wrote to her brother Walter :

"Just a week ago we returned from a visit to Abbotsford where only Mr. Hope Scott and Mamo [Mary Monica] were—Lady Victoria in England. . . . Nothing could be kinder than they were, and the place looked lovely, all in perfect taste and order. The improvements really are great improvements." She had been visiting The Rhymer's Glen and driving round the neighbourhood, and " did not get to Abbotsford before nearly 1 p.m., and had been, carriage and all, three hours : on foot it would have taken much longer yet how often I have done it with Uncle Walter and Anne, and it seemed nothing of a long walk then."

The letter unconsciously emphasises the pitiful brevity of life granted to Scott's children and grandchildren. Cousin Anne was of Sophia's generation and Anne's, a woman still active and alert, but none who had known " Uncle Walter " and her cousins was there to welcome her.

In that year, which was that of her son's birth, Lady Victoria Hope died. James Hope Scott survived her for just over two years ; dying in 1873, he was buried beside Charlotte, in St. Margaret's Convent. He left a goodly heritage to his Scots fellow-Catholics in the chapels at Galashiels, Kelso and Selkirk.

Mary Monica, the only descendant of Sir Walter Scott and of Lockhart, married, in 1874, the Hon. Joseph Constable Maxwell, son of Baron Herries of Caerlaverock Castle, Dumfries, and of Everingham Park, Yorkshire ; one of the oldest Catholic and Jacobite families in Scotland, of the blood of the heroic Lord Nithsdale and his still more valiant Countess. He assumed the additional surname of Scott, so that the laird of Abbotsford, their eldest son, is now Sir Walter Maxwell Scott.[1] The baronetcy, which

[1] Sir Walter Maxwell Scott died 3rd April, 1954. R.I.P.

lapsed on the death of the second Sir Walter, was revived
in 1932, the centenary of Sir Walter Scott's death.   There
are, with his daughters and their cousins, nineteen living
descendants of Sir Walter, and of Lockhart and Sophia,
sprung from that marriage of true minds and loyal and
loving hearts which gave Scott a son of most filial devotion.

NOTE ON LOCKHART'S ANCESTRY

(From the MS. Family History by James Lockhart)

SCOTT himself told little Johnny Lockhart the story of his famous ancestor, which is part of the story of the heart of Robert the Bruce ; the heart carried by Douglas on crusade against the Saracens. Douglas never reached Palestine ; he fell in Spain, fighting the Moors. At the moment of death he " took from his neck the Bruce's heart, and speaking to it as he would have done to the King had he been alive, ' Pass first in fight,' he said, ' as thou wert wont to do, and Douglas will follow thee or die.' "

His body was found above the casket that held the heart. Then " there was one of the brave knights who was in the company of Douglas, and was appointed to take charge of Bruce's heart homewards again, who was called Sir Simon Lockhart of Lee. He took afterwards for his device . . . a man's heart with a padlock upon it, in memory of Bruce's heart which was padlocked in the silver case. For this reason, men changed Sir Simon's name from Lockhard to Lockheart, and all who are descended from Sir Simon are called Lockhart to this day. Did you ever hear of such a name, Master Hugh Littlejohn ? "

Along with the heart Sir Simon brought home the Talisman : a silver penny, part of the ransom of a Moorish prisoner, known thereafter as the Lee Penny, from Sir Simon's estate of Lee. It had, and has, miraculous healing powers ; its most famous achievement having been to stay the Plague, in 1645, from sweeping across Scotland. On this occasion the citizens of Newcastle, hearing of its beneficent power, implored the loan of it for their stricken city. The canny owner, Sir James Lockhart, demanded and received a fee of £1,000 ; and the Penny proved effective. It has been used within living memory ; when the late Sir Simon Lockhart of Lee produced it on behalf of a guest who had cut his hand badly. The Penny was dipped in water, the hand bandaged with lint soaked in the water, and by next morning the cut was completely healed.

The original name of the family, Locard, is very old. Locards are said to have come from Norway in the eleventh century, to aid Malcolm Canmore in his conquest of Strathclyde, and to have been granted lands. It is tempting and easy to change the name into Lockheart or Lockhart, with a pious pun, but the change may only be such as has changed Steward to Stewart; and the pronunciation, it must be noted, is not Lock-hart, with aspirated " h ", but Lockhart with emphasis on the first syllable, and the old Lanarkshire pronunciation gave a full, rounded " o " : like Loke-art.

The first Simon Locard of whom there is record gave his name to two country towns of Symington : one in Ayrshire, the other in Lanarkshire. Simon recurs constantly as a Christian name in the family, as do Stephen and Mungo : the latter celebrated in Dunbar's *Lament for the Makars :* " Sir Mungo Lockhart of the Lee ".

At some undiscovered moment in the family history there came a division between Lockhart of Lee and Lockhart of Cleghorn, also in Lanarkshire. From a younger son of Sir Stephen Lockhart of Cleghorn, Armour-Bearer to James the Third, descend the Lockharts of Wicketshaw or Waygate-shaw. A later cadet line was Lockhart of Birkhill. To come rapidly nearer J. G. L.'s time, a William Lockhart of Birkhill married Violet Inglis, niece and heiress of James, Lord Somerville of Corehouse, Lanark. Their elder son left three sons who died without issue ; their second son was the Rev. John Lockhart, father of J. G. L. Mr. James Lockhart traced their descent through the Somervilles and, on the distaff side, through the Grahams of Montrose, from King Robert the Third : Dr. Lockhart being sixteenth, his sons seventeenth in generation from their royal ancestor.

The Lockharts of Wicketshaw bear the crest of a Heart in Fetterlock, with the motto : *Corda Serata Pando.* Their coat of arms shows a boar's head with the motto : *Feroci Fortior.*

When William Lockhart, the Doctor's eldest son, bought the Lanarkshire estate that became known as Milton

Lockhart, he acquired therein part of the original lands of Wicketshaw. He died without issue ; was succeeded by his, and J. G. L,'s younger brother, Laurence, from whose two marriages the present representatives of the family descend.

BIBLIOGRAPHY
WORKS BY J. G. LOCKHART

Peter's Letters to His Kinsfolk (3 vols. ; and Abridged Edition published by Messrs. Nelson).
The Spanish Ballads.
Valerius; Reginald Dalton; Adam Blair; Matthew Wald.
Life of Robert Burns (in Everyman's Library).
Memoirs of Sir Walter Scott.
Contributions to *Blackwood's Magazine* and *The Quarterly Review.*

BOOKS ABOUT, OR REFERRING TO, J.G.L.

Life and Letters of John Gibson Lockhart, by Andrew Lang.
Letters of Sir Walter Scott, ed. Grierson, Davidson Cook, and Parker.
Journal of Sir Walter Scott.
Sir Walter Scott : A New Life, Supplementary to and Corrective of Lockhart's, by Sir Herbert Grierson.
Lang, Lockhart and Biography, by Sir Herbert Grierson (St. Andrews Lecture).
The Croker Papers, ed. Louis Jennings.
Memoirs of James Robert Hope Scott of Abbotsford, by Robert Ornsby.
A Publisher and His Friends, by Samuel Smiles.
At John Murray's, by George Paston.
Annals of a Publishing House, by Mrs. Oliphant.
Literary History of Scotland, by J. H. Millar.
Life of Francis Jeffrey, by Lord Cockburn.
Lord Cockburn's Journals.
Christopher North : A Memoir of John Wilson, by his daughter, Mrs. Gordon.
Christopher North, by Elsie Swann.
Rebellious Fraser's, by Miriam M. H. Thrall.
Romantic Criticism, by Louis Wain.
Lockhart's Literary Criticism, by M. Clive Hilyard.
John Gibson Lockhart : A Critical Study, by Gilbert Macbeth.
Harriet Martineau : Biographical Studies.
Memoirs of a Literary Veteran, by R. P. Gillies.
Essays in Literary Criticism, by George Saintsbury.
Life of John Keats, by Sir Sidney Colvin.
Edinburgh Under Sir Walter Scott, by W. T. Fyffe.
John Gibson Lockhart, by George Gordon. (Commemoration Address, Glasgow University, 1930.)
The Noctes Ambrosianae.

317

INDEX

Albert, H.R.H. Prince, Prince Consort : 220, 226, 281, 287, 289

Alexander, The Misses : 208, 215, 220, 269, 275–6, 279

Austen, Jane : 6, 69, 77, 79–80, 93, 99, 187

Baillie, Joanna : 42, 79, 103

Ballantyne, John and James : 114, 138, 209, 211–13

Barrett, Elizabeth (Mrs. Browning) : 249–50, 299

Blackwood's Magazine : 1, 26 et seq., 84–5

Blackwood, William : 24, 26 et seq., 35 et seq.

Browning, Robert : 299

Burns, Robert : 42, 54–5, 154–5

Byron, Lord : 20, 103, 109, 116–17, 185, 188

Cadell, Robert : 203–4, 211–12

Calderwood, Mrs. : 251–2

Carlyle, Thomas : 194–5, 207

Chaldee MS. : 35 et seq.

Chalmers, Dr. : 43–4

Christie, Jonathan : 2, 14–19, 21, 82–5, 206

Cockburn, Henry, Lord : 209–10, 291

Cockney School, the, 39–43

Coleridge, Samuel : 53, 192

Croker, John Wilson : 30, 105 et seq., 150, 154, 172 et seq., 174–5 (on Tennyson), 178, 206, 238 et seq. (on Oxford Movement), 256 et seq., 273–4 (on Macaulay), 276–7, 284, 289–90, 297, 307

Davy, Lady : 149, 204, 208, 261, 277–8, 305

Disraeli, Benjamin : 105, 118, 120

Disraeli, Isaac : 118

Edgeworth, Maria : 102–3, 109, 185, 187–8, 213, 223–4, 264

Edinburgh Review : 26 et seq., 41, 43, 291

Elwin, Rev. Whitwell : 287, 292, 297, 309

Exeter, Rt. Rev. Hugh Philpotts, Bishop of : 174, 280

Ferguson, Dr. : 138, 208, 256

Fraser's Magazine : 194–6

Galt, John : 194–5

Gifford, Lady : 154, 157

Gifford, William : 115, 119

Gleig, Rev. George : 14–15, 126–7, 136, 309

Gordon, Mrs. Mary : 33–4

Grierson, Sir Herbert : 166, 211

Hamilton, Thomas : 143, 158, 288

Hamilton, Sir Wm. : 14–15, 288

Hay, Mr. : 197–9, 216, 297 et seq.

Hazlitt, William : 41

Hogg, James (the Ettrick Shepherd): 29 et seq., 38, 167–70, 181, 196

Hook, Theodore : 122, 154, 195, 221

Hope, James (later Hope Scott) : 261, 265 et seq. (marriage to Charlotte Lockhart), 285 (conversion), 292, 311–12

Hunt, Leigh : 39–41, 188–9

Jane Eyre : 268–9

Jeffrey, Francis, Lord : 26, 41, 239, 291

Keats, John : 1, 20, 39, 41–3, 302

Keble, Rev. John : 234–5, 284